WESTERN CREED, WESTERN IDENTITY

Jude P. Dougherty

WESTERN CREED, WESTERN IDENTITY

Essays in Legal and Social Philosophy

***

The Catholic University of America Press
Washington, D.C.

Library of Congress Cataloging-in-Publication Data

Dougherty, Jude P., 1930–

Western creed, western identity: essays in legal and social philosophy /
Jude P. Dougherty.

p. cm.

Includes bibliographical references.

ISBN 0-8132-0975-7 (pbk. : alk. paper)

1. Christianity and law. 2. Religion and law. 3. Religion and sociology.

4. Catholic Church—Doctrines. I. Title.

BR115.L28 D68 2000

230'.2—dc21   99–049307

Contents

Contents

Foreword

As editor of the *Review of Metaphysics*, and during his long tenure as dean of the School of Philosophy at The Catholic University of America, Jude Dougherty devoted himself to publishing the works of others and creating conditions in which his colleagues could engage in research and teaching. These self-effacing efforts did not of course exhaust his contributions to the discipline he loves. His involvement in a wide range of philosophical associations and his international reputation added to the impression that, in the service of wisdom, he was rather a Martha than a Mary. This collection of essays makes it clear that Dougherty has been publishing all along. Bringing the essays of this volume within easy reach is a signal contribution.

What one is struck by in reading Dougherty is the firm way in which he places himself in the context when he writes. Thus the essays in Part I are written with a lively sense of the times. Have we indeed moved into the atheistic democracy that Santayana predicted sixty years ago? Dougherty addresses the conditions in which the contemporary philosopher works, and he also addresses trends inimical not only to his discipline but to human society itself. His discussions of religion—for Aquinas, the chief moral virtue—have at once a perennial flavor and a decidedly timely tang. This is perhaps even truer in the essays he gathers under the general rubric of the law in Part II. His discussion of punishment dovetails nicely with the critique of contemporary society implicit in the essays in Part I. In Part III Dougherty links religion and spirituality and gives us portraits of Edith Stein, Jacques Maritain, and John Paul II.

Even those who have prided themselves on being au courant with Dougherty's philosophical writing will find here essays that have escaped their attention. Others who may have allowed Dougherty's many services to the profession to eclipse his own writings are in for a bigger surprise. Jude Dougherty was never tempted by pedantry or the notion that the philosopher is someone devoted to the cultivating of his own garden in a kind of cognitive solipsism. There is something irrepressibly American in Dougherty's philosophical writing. He wants to make a point, but he wants to make a difference too.

Philosophy is the pursuit of wisdom, and its goal can seem forever to elude our grasp. It is not within the reach of the young, and many grow old still jogging toward the elusive prize. In Jude Dougherty one encounters a mind that can only be called wise. And if the mind, the man himself as well. This Martha became a Mary as well.

Ralph McInerny

Acknowledgments

With gratitude the author acknowledges permission to reprint articles first published in the journals indicated. To *The World & I* for "Western Creed, Western Identity,""Marx, Dewey, and Maritain: The Role of Religion in Society," "John Courtney Murray on the Truths We Hold," "Separating Church and State," "The Necessity of Punishment," and "Professional Responsibility"; to *The Monist* for "Christian Philosophy: Sociological Category or Oxymoron?"; to *The Modern Schoolman* for "Thomas on Natural Law: What Judge Thomas Did Not Say"; to *Crisis* for "Edith Stein: The Convert in Search of Illumination" and "The Interior Life"; to *Modern Age* for "What Was Religion?: The Demise of a Prodigious Power"; and to the *American Journal of Jurisprudence* for "Collective Responsibility."

Gratitude is also expressed to Philip G. Holthaus for his careful editing of the manuscript and a special word of appreciation is extended to Mary Rakow, without whose assistance this volume could not have been produced.

Introduction

The essays that constitute this volume were written in response to specific invitations, usually invitations to lecture on a topic of contemporary concern. They were written from a single vantage point, one that has come to be identified with Saint Thomas Aquinas, although the natural law outlook that they represent is older than Aquinas. To put it another way, they were written by someone steeped in a Catholic intellectual tradition that finds its roots in classical antiquity. Thus they represent not only a philosophical mind but a Catholic mind as well since many of the issues confronted are of particular interest to Catholics. While they are the reflections of a spectator formed in a particular tradition, they are not theological in character. They are meant to be observations and judgments that can be appreciated or perhaps even shared by others who may not identify with that tradition. The essay on Christian philosophy, for example, is designed to distinguish among theology, which has its roots in revelation; philosophy, which is an independent mode of inquiry; and the sociological fact that Christians, by virtue of their faith, take an interest in certain philosophical issues that their secular colleagues may not.

Part I of this volume examines the role of religion in society. It takes its lead from the Spanish-born Harvard University professor George Santayana, who, in 1937, in *Winds of Doctrine,* written with an American audience in mind, observed:

The present age is a critical one and interesting to live in. The civilization characteristic of Christendom has not disappeared, yet another civilization has begun to take its place. We still understand the value of religious faith. On the other hand, the shell of Christendom is broken. The unconquerable mind of the East, the pagan past, the industrial socialists' future confront it with equal authority. On the whole, life and mind is saturated with the slow upward flirtation of a new spirit—that of an emancipated, atheistic democracy.

In the early decades of this century that judgment may have required the perceptiveness of a Santayana. Today Santayana's assessment is almost universally accepted. Few are blind to the loss of a religious allegiance and its moral and cultural consequences.

Although morality and religion are not to be identified with each other, it is evident that religion carries with it a code of values. The question that is raised from several perspectives herein is: From what source may a society receive its moral compass if not from religion? The essay entitled "What Was Religion?" provides a historical perspective that is supplemented by a consideration of the views of Karl Marx and John Dewey, both of whom consider religion to be mistaken in referring things to God rather than to nature. Their materialistic perspective is contrasted with that of Jacques Maritain and John Courtney Murray. The latter addresses the situation as found in the United States as he discusses the relation of church and state in the context of Supreme Court rulings over a forty-year period.

Maritain suggests that one of the most valuable services that religion renders society is to focus attention on larger intellectual issues, not to mention the direction of individual wills to communal ends. Like Santayana, he believes that Western democracies are living off the capital of Christianity, and to the extent that its influence is diminished, to that extent those governments are vulnerable. The title essay of this volume addresses this judgment as it attempts to sort out the distinctive features of Western civilization.

Part II begins with a consideration of the nature of law and the relation between civil law and natural law. Contemporary legal issues bearing upon the assignment of responsibility or lack of it are addressed in an essay on collective responsibility and in another on the assignment of blame within the context of tort law. Responsibility and punishment are examined within the same framework. The broader issue of moral responsibility, especially professional responsibility, is treated in a separate enquiry.

Part III brings together a number of essays on the relation of faith to reason. One essay follows the intellectual journey of Edith Stein, from her days as a pupil of Husserl and a student of phenomenology to her discovery of Aquinas and finally to her death as a Carmelite; another, the thought of Jacques Maritain from the beginning of his career to his final works. John Paul II's *Fides et Ratio* as a defense of reason and the reasonableness of faith is presented in the light of contemporary discussion of the nature of belief. This part ends with an essay on the contemplative life and its implications for praxis.

RELIGION AND SOCIETY

* * *

WESTERN CREED, WESTERN IDENTITY

I

As the turn of the century approaches, calls for the renewal of America abound. There is a widespread belief that something is amiss, that the nation's policymakers have lost their way. This is driven home by the employment of a relatively new term, "procedural democracy," which has entered the vocabulary of political theorists, on both the left and the right, to designate a democratic government that remains neutral among competing conceptions of the good, endorsing none while accommodating all. A procedural democracy eschews value judgments on the assumption that it is not the business of government to espouse or advance one conception of the good over another. If we have not already taken it, such is the road to disaster, argues George Sher, whose *Beyond Neutrality* shows the impossibility, if not the absurdity, of value neutrality.[1] Respected political theorists have long argued that social policies cannot be neutral. Policies grounded in the principles supplied by John Stuart Mill are apt to be radically different in character from those grounded in an Aristotelian concept of human nature.[2]

---

1. Cf. George Sher, *Beyond Neutrality: Perfectionism and Politics* (New York: Cambridge University Press, 1997).
2. Morton A. Kaplan, "The Right to Be Left Alone Is the Right to Be No One," in *Morality and Religion in Liberal Democratic Societies*, ed. Gordon L. Anderson and Morton A. Kaplan (St. Paul, Minn.: PWPA/Paragon House, 1992), 290. There is evidence, Kaplan suggests, to hold that the conditions that Mill regards as essential for his form of liberalism actually foster the very control that liberals seek to avoid.

If not to procedural democracy, then where do we look for commonly acknowledged principles or conceptions of the good? American history should provide a clue, especially that history which focuses on the thought of the Founding Fathers and on the nation's charter documents. Certainly the instruments that brought the nation into being provide an account of the good sought in forming the Union. But even such reflection is precarious, writes Martin Marty. In his meditation on American public life, *The One and the Many*,[3] Marty reminds us that ours is not the nation it once was, composed of a European people united by a common culture. We are not one *people* but a plurality of *peoples*, each advancing its own objectives in the light of its own history. There are multiple histories—Marty calls them "stories"—and not one historical narrative with which all would be comfortable. The Jewish, black, Catholic, and Hispanic experiences produce different narratives, narratives not always flattering to other groups. Marty despairs of finding a common narrative acceptable to all parties and concludes that we must recognize conflicting narratives while at the same time maintaining an open and, where necessary, compassionate attitude toward the other. We need not insist on the supremacy of our own narrative, let alone inflict its practical implications on others.

Are we then without resources? The issue is critical because a certain unity of outlook is required to establish a rule of law. Justice demands common assent to certain principles before which the state cannot be neutral. Well, then, perhaps deep down we have an identifiable common philosophy. In a previous generation, John Dewey produced a series of lectures published as *A Common Faith*, in which he addressed the issue; Walter Lippmann wrote a book entitled *The Public Philosophy*. Mortimer Adler, Jacques Maritain, John C. Murray, Will Herberg, Sidney Hook, and others attempted to state the "American proposition." Few are so bold today. Are we led to despair with Marty that commonality cannot be articulated?

We still speak of "Western civilization," and it remains a reality

---

3. Martin Marty, *The One and the Many* (Cambridge, Mass.: Harvard University Press, 1997).

even though its spiritual foundation has been under siege within Western intellectual circles for more than two centuries. The skepticism with respect to the inherited, long present within the academy, has within the last half of this century reached the common man who is no longer in possession of the moral certainties that motivated his forebears. Should we leave it at that?

The English Lord Patrick Devlin, reflecting on the course of events over the present century, wrote that if the morality of a people crumbles, the laws based on that morality will themselves crumble.[4] Since midcentury we have witnessed, at least in this country, a rapid decline in both morality and the rule of law. In Devlin's judgment, "A recognized morality is as necessary to society as a recognized government."[5]

As more than one historian has suggested, if the twentieth century has taught us anything, it has forced us to recognize that ideas have consequences, that the barriers between civilization and the forces of destruction are easily breeched. Barbarism is not a picturesque myth or a half-forgotten memory of a long-past stage of history but an ugly underlying reality that may erupt with shattering force whenever the moral authority of a civilization loses its control.

Much is at stake. In socially turbulent times a clear diagnostic voice is one to be cherished. This has long been recognized to be the case. The first-century Roman historian Titus Livius (59 B.C.–A.D. 17), better known as Livy, recommended to a failing Rome:

I invite the reader's attention to the much more serious consideration of the kind of lives our ancestors lived, of who were the men and what the means, both in politics and war, by which Rome's power was first acquired and subsequently expanded. I would have him trace the processes of our moral decline, to watch first the sinking of the foundations of morality as the old teaching was allowed to lapse, then the final collapse of the whole edifice, and the dark dawning of our modern day when we can neither endure our vices nor face the remedies needed to cure them.[6]

4. Lord Patrick Devlin, *The Enforcement of Morals* (London: Oxford University Press, 1968), 11.

5. Ibid.

6. Titus Livius, Preface to his *History* (Cambridge, Mass.: Loeb Classical Library, Harvard University Press, 1924), 1.1.

This is ancient but timely advice.

Can one achieve a sense of identity without an understanding of ancestry, both immediate and distant? To pose the question in that manner is to already have the answer. To know who one is is to adopt a familial perspective. People in the midatlantic region of this country talk about Mr. Jefferson as if he were still among them. One exists within an inherited culture, and to understand that culture one needs a historical sense. One does not have to be a scholar, but one does require knowledge, shall we say, of the spiritual ends, the material conditions, and the social processes that have created the culture, whether those ends are defined according to religious or secular formulae. In the end, to achieve identity is to adopt not only, as Marty says, "a story," but a set of moral or social principles.

The way the past is viewed has a direct bearing on present action. Deep political commitment and open partisanship are often the result of historical understanding or misunderstanding. To vote in an election or upon a referendum may not be a simple political act; it is more likely to be an affirmation of faith in a particular social philosophy or a commitment to a particular theory of history. In some circumstances such decisions may even be judgments upon mutually exclusive forms of civilization. As Lord Devlin reminds us, sweeping and comprehensive changes in the framing and interpretation of law often rest on changing moral considerations.

History teaches us that social consciousness can not only produce unity but can be the gateway to civic conflict. Marx's doctrine of dialectical materialism has been used to support totalitarian regimes the world over. The myth of Aryan superiority has led to genocide; the myth of women's suppression has led to alienation of the sexes; and the doctrine of social progress has been used to support social programs with disastrous consequences. Images and metaphors can eat into reality and force the world to take on false shapes and colors, encouraging the politically engaged to bypass common sense and reasonable doubt.

Morton Kaplan, a University of Chicago social theorist, insists on the importance of the larger cultural context, that is, the social milieu that consciously or unconsciously frames our choices. Echoing John Donne's admonition that "no man is an island," Kaplan argues, as the title of a recent essay suggests, "The right to be left alone is the right to be no one."[7]

The right to be left alone with respect to social and moral matters may be a popular position,[8] but in Kaplan's view the doctrine of privacy is counterproductive because it fails to recognize how identifications and conceptions of the self arise within the social order. "External social constraints and internal inhibitions are complements to the enticements and opportunities that social structure, personality, and environment provide. They are required to diminish the likelihood of pathology and to preserve the integrity of the self that makes choices."[9] The freedom that any of us enjoys depends on cultural constraints. A social system that does not exclude some patterns of behavior even if they do not injure others is inconceivable. "If, for instance, every social rule—whether to bow to superiors, to dress for dinner, and so forth—was [sic] subject to personal calculation, society would be in danger of collapse."[10] The question to be confronted is: Do we today have a commonly accepted social system or set of moral norms to support a rule of law?

II

In a period of cultural decline to speak of national identity is problematic enough; to speak of Western identity is even more hazardous. And yet the West, meaning Europe and the lands colonized by European nations, historically considered is different from the East. De Rougement, in his book *The Meaning of Europe*, reminds us that it was Hippocrates who first described Europe as an entity.[11] We used to speak of "Christendom" and mean by this term all those lands touched by Western culture. Even today, in spite of the globalization of science,

---

7. Kaplan, "Right to Be Left Alone," 290.
8. Ibid.   9. Ibid., 292.
10. Ibid., 297.
11. Denis de Rougemont, *The Meaning of Europe*, trans. Alan Braley (New York: Stein & Day, 1965), 29.

technology, and trade, there remains a difference between European and Oriental cultures and among Latin, Islamic, and Confucian modes of thought. True, advances in telecommunications have united the world at a superficial level, particularly through access to global television, but as often as not those global reports display the vast differences that steadfastly remain in place. One has to acknowledge that in spite of the availability of worldwide channels of communication, in spite of the multinational corporations, and in spite of global trade, cultural differences prevail. Although the world's major cultures are identified primarily with geographic regions, it is notable that at the same time they transcend continental boundaries. North and South America perpetuate Western culture in a way in which Indonesia does not. Similarly, the Islamic mind is not confined to North Africa and the Middle East, and Chinese and other cultural enclaves are to be found throughout the globe. While those differences are amenable to description by the sociologist, other modes of assessment are important.

When the sociologist talks about "culture," he usually means a common way of life grounded in a community of thought and a community of work stemming from a particular adjustment of man to his natural surroundings and economic needs. Both sources, spiritual and material, need to be acknowledged. In the introduction to his *Critique of Political Economy*, Marx placed a heavy emphasis on material resources:

The mode of production in material life determines the social, political, and spiritual processes of life. It is not the consciousness of men that determines their existence, but their existence that determines their consciousness.[12]

Christopher Dawson in his critique of Marx offers a different assessment:

The great cultural changes and the historic revolutions that decide the fate of nations or the character of an age are the cumulative result of a number of spiritual decisions—the faith and insight, or the refusal and blindness, of in-

---

12. Karl Marx, *Das Kapital: A Critique of Political Economy* (Chicago: C. H. Kerr & Co., 1906).

dividuals. No one can put his finger on the ultimate spiritual act which tilts the balance and makes the external order of society assume a new form.[13]

No one can deny that important aspects of culture have a material basis in the economic life of the people, but the roots of any culture are certainly deeper. In China, we have the example of Confucian ethics serving as the moral foundation of Chinese culture for more than two thousand years, with the result that it is impossible to understand any aspect of Chinese history without an understanding of Confucianism. In his many studies of Western and Asian cultures, Dawson often reminds the reader that the great civilizations of the world have not created the great religions of the world but rather it is the great religions of the world that have created the great cultures. Werner Jaeger, in his monumental study *Paideia: The Ideals of Greek Culture*, offers an entirely different but interesting notion of culture. Jaeger distinguishes between culture as "a simple anthropological concept," as used by Marx and Dawson, and culture as a "concept of value, a consciously pursued ideal."[14] In its "vague analogical sense, it is permissible to talk of Chinese, Indian, Babylonian, Jewish or Egyptian culture, although none of these nations has a word or an ideal which corresponds to real culture."[15] It was the Greeks who created the ideal of culture. "The culture of the present," writes Jaeger, "cannot impart any value to the original Greek form of culture, but rather needs illumination and transformation by that ideal, in order to establish its true meaning and direction."[16] "Human nature," "objectivity," "universality," "timeless," and "ideal" are terms inherited from antiquity. We cannot slip into the posture of regarding classical antiquity simply as a piece of history, "for education has from the very beginning been closely connected with the study of the ancient world.

---

13. Christopher Dawson, *The Historic Reality of Christian Culture* (New York: Harper & Row, 1960), 18.
14. Werner Jaeger, *Paideia: The Ideals of Greek Culture*, trans. Gilbert Highet (New York: Oxford University Press, 1939), xvii.
15. Ibid.
16. Ibid., xviii.

The ages which succeeded it always regarded classical antiquity as an inexhaustible treasure of knowledge and culture—first as a collection of valuable external facts and arts, and later as a world of ideals to be imitated."[17]

III

The intent of these reflections is not to belabor the distinction between East and West or to distinguish among Judaism, Christianity, and Islam; nor is it to compare Oriental thought with that of the West. Its focus is on Western identity before the advent of modernity, allowing history to provide a standard for assessment.

Western culture is woven out of strands provided by Athens, Rome, and Jerusalem. Although the world was already very old when Greek science and philosophy began, the originality of Greek philosophy goes uncontested. In spite of a certain debt to the Egyptians and Babylonians in mathematics and astronomy, Greek philosophy emerged untutored by any other civilization.

For the Greeks, philosophy was the pursuit of wisdom, both theoretical and practical. It rested on the assumptions that nature is intelligible and that the human mind is powerful enough to ferret out the secrets of nature. Science is to be pursued for its own sake, and yet it yields a useful technology as man learns to cooperate with the powers of nature.

The Greek philosopher looked upon the world through an atmosphere singularly free from the mist of allegory and myth in contrast to the thought patterns of the East, which were heavily dependent on religion. Popular Greek religion, crude and without speculative content, had little or no hold on the mind of the philosopher.

Greek philosophy in its origin and in its Hellenistic development was continuous with a commonsense approach to reality. Common sense tells us that there are things apart from the mind and that they are what they are, independent of any human opinion or desire. It tells us that by painstaking observation and experiment we can ac-

17. Ibid., xvii.

quire some knowledge of them. And furthermore common sense tells us that such systematic knowledge is the safest and most reliable guide to human action.

These basic insights led the Greeks to differentiate between the study of nature and the study of 'being' in its widest sense, later called metaphysics. Metaphysics has as its object not only material being but the immaterial order as well. Metaphysics reasons to the existence of a *prime mover* (in the order of efficient causality) and to a *summum bonum* (in the order of final causality).[18]

Plato taught that nature is intelligible as the result of *nous* (intellect), a divinelike artificer. There is a reality, he maintained, behind the appearance of things that is more real than that which outwardly appears to be real. Behind the constant flux of becoming there is permanence and universality. The existence of such universals as Goodness, Truth, and Beauty is the key that unlocks the door to understanding and wisdom. Plato understood these universals to be archetypes or Ideas which the beings of sense experience reflected in varying degrees. Augustine, who owed much to the Neoplatonism of his day, put them in the mind of God as creative ideas. Against the contention of the Sophists that morality is simply social convention and that "might makes right," both Plato and Aristotle argued that there are certain universal principles of goodness and justice that man by virtue of his reason can discover. Man is by nature a moral and social being who cannot live apart from his fellows. To be moral is to be fully human. The primary purpose of the state is to enable men to attain the good life.

For Aristotle, living beings come to be by a process that has a natural end, or *telos*. Each organism comes to be not at random, but in an orderly manner, starting from some relatively undifferentiated but nevertheless specific seed produced by parents of the same species and developing, unfolding, and informing itself from within in successive stages that tend toward and ultimately reach a limit, itself the

18. Joseph Owens, *The Doctrine of Being in the Aristotelian Metaphysics*, 3d ed., rev. (Toronto: Pontifical Institute of Mediaeval Studies, 1978).

fully formed organism. There is a natural end to the process of development that defines the previous motions throughout the various stages to its proper end.

It is not without reason that Aristotle is frequently called the "Father of Western Science." The twin concepts of *nous* and *cosmos* produced the confidence that with effort the human intellect is able to discern patterns in nature with indications for control. The buoyant realism of Aristotle may in retrospect be contrasted with the second-century skepticism of Sextus Empiricus, which had a deadening effect on purposive aspiration, and which by placing greater dependence on animal appetite led eventually to purposeless drift and cultural decay.

The Academy of Plato and the Lyceum of Aristotle were to last nine hundred years and six hundred years, respectively. Although Emperor Justinian dissolved the Platonic Academy in A.D. 529, Greek philosophy remained an important constituent of Western intellectual life and culture, influencing Islam and in turn being enriched by that contact. From Greek philosophy, the whole of European philosophy has descended.

With the disintegration of the Greek city-states and the coming of the Alexandrian and later the Roman Empires, a number of schools arose, some in conflict with the inherited tradition, some perpetuating its basic insights. Of the many schools that arose in this period, one in particular, Stoicism, exerted an influence that was to have profound consequences for Western civilization. It was through Stoicism that much of Greek philosophy was transmitted to Western Europe in the early centuries before Christ. Stoicism flourished for about five hundred years, from the time of its founder, Zeno (340–265 B.C.), to the death of the Roman emperor Marcus Aurelius (A.D. 121–180).

For the Stoic, the universe is governed by natural laws of reason that are immanent in nature. The wise man lives according to nature, allowing his reason to guide his conduct and restrain his emotions. By cooperating with natural necessity, he achieves a harmonious relationship with the universe. The highest virtue and supreme good consists in obedience to the universal law of reason. Self-control through reason is the highest good. Man is free when he freely wills that which reason decrees. Man is linked to man by a common necessity to obey the universal law of reason. Recognized is the universal brotherhood of man.

True law, Cicero taught, is right reason consonant with nature, available to all, constant, and eternal. It summons to duty by its commands and hinders fraud by its prohibitions (*De Republica* 3.2).[19] Reason forbids enactments by the people or by the Senate contrary to the laws of nature. There is but one law, immutable and eternal, which shall embrace all peoples for all time. There cannot be one law in Rome and another in Athens.

This conception of law and the acknowledgment of its divine author were to dominate Western political thought until the period of Enlightenment. Not until then did men seriously challenge the idea of the existence of a law of reason that is eternal, absolute, universal, and immutable. In the Stoic conception, natural law is common to God and man. It antedates the state and all civil law, which is but the expression of this natural law of reason. The state is nothing more or less than a partnership in law, an assemblage of men associated in consent to law.

Roman political thought envisaged man as prior to the state. It is in Roman political philosophy that we find the origins of the modern doctrine that government rests upon the consent of the people. This contrasts with Greek thought, which had difficulty conceiving of man apart from the state.

It may be argued that these two ideas—the idea of a universal law and the idea of the state's being founded upon consent—taken together laid the foundation for the concept of "individual rights" so prized in recent decades. These ideas were passed through the Middle Ages by the great canonists of the period and are ultimately reflected in English common law and American constitutional law.

This is not to ignore the importance of the *Digest of Roman Law*, compiled and published in the sixth century by a commission appointed

19. Cicero, *On the Good Life: [Selected Writings of] Cicero*, trans. Michael Grant (London: Penguin Books, 1971).

by the Emperor Justinian.[20] Three other important works were published about the same time: *The Institutes*, a handbook of law; the
Codex, a codification of the laws then in effect; and the *Novellae*, an
appendix to the *Codex* containing the decrees of Justinian. These
were the texts that were to influence legal theory and the codification
of law throughout Europe until modern times.

IV

One cannot discuss the West without discussing Christianity. Prepared by the Greeks to conceive of God as the embodiment of cosmic
Reason and by the Jews to conceive of God as the embodiment of
perfect Righteousness, Western man was prepared to recognize in
Jesus the incarnation of perfect Wisdom and perfect Justice. Christianity taught that man is the creature of God, that he is essentially a
spiritual being with a transcendent nature and destiny. Beyond the
Kingdom of Man there is the Kingdom of God. The concept of natural law as developed by the Stoics was identified explicitly with divine
law. The brotherhood of man became the brotherhood of man
under the Fatherhood of God.

Christianity provided an uncompromising affirmation of a personal God, a provident God, directing the universe with loving,
watchful care, a God who has revealed Himself to mankind through
the Hebrew prophets and in the person of Christ.

In its Judaic phase, Christianity may well have considered itself
the particular religion of one people. But it soon understood itself as
called to address every man and every class of men. Christianity inherited the traditions of the Roman Empire. Through its missionary
efforts Mediterranean culture was carried to the barbarian north,
which until the advent of Christianity had no written literature, no
cities, no stone architecture. It was only through Christianity that the
elements of a higher culture were transmitted to the North, with the
result that Western Europe acquired unity and form.

---

20. Justinian, *The Digest of Roman Law: Theft, Rapine, Damage, and Insult*, trans.
C. F. Kolbert (New York: Penguin Books, 1979).

Out of these elements—a Hebrew sense of justice, the love of the Gospels, Greek faith in the human intellect, and Hellenistic asceticism—the Fathers of the early Church molded an organic whole we know as Christianity. Historian John H. Randall Jr., writing from a purely secular point of view, acknowledged:

This body of beliefs the barbarians found ready-made for them, a thing of life and beauty which they were drawn to reverence, but which for centuries they were unable to understand. When the slow growth of social life brought them to the place where they could readily assimilate it, they found in it a vehicle admirably adapted to express their own aspirations and energies. By the thirteenth century this Christian scheme of things had really taken root in the soil of the Western mind.[21]

Randall adds, "and it is this great medieval synthesis that makes such an appeal to those weary of the cross currents and confusions of today."[22]

Christianity, Randall reminds us, had its origins in the semioriental world of the great Hellenistic cities where it offered new life and new hope to classes and individuals spiritually estranged from the soulless materialistic culture of the Roman Empire. The mother tongue of the Church was Greek, and its theological development was mainly due to Asiatic Greek councils and Asiatic Greek theologians.[23]

It was the acceptance of the teachings of Christ that gave Western peoples their spiritual values, their moral standards, and their conception of a divine law from which all human laws ultimately derive their validity and their sanction. Dawson remarks, "It is hardly too much to say that it is Christian culture that has created Western man and the Western way of life. But at the same time we must admit that Western man has not been faithful to the Christian tradition."[24] Europe, in spite of a common heritage, has been fraught with centuries of devastating conflict.

21. John H. Randall, *The Making of the Modern Mind* (New York: Houghton Mifflin, 1940), 49.

22. Ibid.

23. Cf. Irena Backus, ed., *The Reception of the Church Fathers in the West: From the Carolingians to the Maurists*, 2 vols. (Leiden: E. J. Brill, 1997).

24. Dawson, *Christian Culture*, 17.

Trying to understand Anglo–German antagonism in the late nineteenth and early twentieth century, Paul Knaplund has written, "How these great nations became rivals and finally enemies has challenged and will perhaps for all time challenge the curiosity of students of history."[25]

De Rougemont, in *The Meaning of Europe*, is reluctant, in the manner of Belloc or Novales, to equate Christianity with Europe, but he raises a historically interesting question: "Why was Europe the only, or the first, part of the world to adopt this religion which came from the Near East and not from Europe itself?"[26] The standard Christian answer is that Christ came in the fullness of time when the intellect of the West was prepared to receive the truths of divine revelation. De Rougemont makes the further point that to identify Christianity with Europe is to do an injustice to the universal claims of Christianity, to its claims to be the vehicle of time-transcending truth of which Europe in de Rougemont's judgment "is not a fitting embodiment and in which she has no copyright."[27]

V

These Chagall-like impressions of Western identity will have to do for the present or, should I say, in lieu of a ten-volume exhaustively documented study. They are impressions, but I trust they are faithful enough to the historical record. They leave room for the development of other impressions. As Martin Marty argues, we need our stories to achieve our identity.[28] The above is but one story, a broken one. Clearly within what we are calling Western civilization there was a major break with antiquity during the period of the Enlightenment when the inherited sacral and political orders, represented by miter and crown,

---

25. P. Knaplund, ed., *Letters from the Berlin Embassy: Selections from the Private Correspondence of British Representatives at Berlin and Foreign Secretary Lord Granville, 1871–1874, 1880–1885*, Annual Report of the American Historical Association for the Year 1942 (Washington, D.C.: American Historical Association, 1944), 5.

26. De Rougemont, *Meaning of Europe*, 16.

27. Ibid.

28. Marty, *One and the Many*, 102.

were repudiated in favor of what we today call "modernity." The conflict was not resolved in the eighteenth century. The battle for the soul of the West continues. Is man a purely material organism with no end beyond the grave, or is he a material/spiritual entity with a transcendent end? Is there an eternal order to which he is finally accountable?

Modernity's answer is but one answer. There indeed are many narratives to be given. The study of antiquity, the Middle Ages, and Renaissance Europe reminds us that for centuries the West lived off a different set of principles from those fostered in the period of the Enlightenment. While modernity has its appeal, to understand the West, one needs a longer historical perspective. To understand the modern mind is to study its genesis, to study it within the larger intellectual and social milieu that gave it birth. Most of all, to understand modernity is to place it in relief against that which it repudiated and sought to supersede. John Herman Randall Jr., in his lasting study *The Making of the Modern Mind*, spends the first 250 pages laying the historical foundation for his discussion of the seventeenth and eighteenth centuries, the immediate context of the Enlightenment. Randall even uses as a subtitle to his work the phrase "A Survey of the Intellectual Background of the Present Age." Christopher Dawson, a social historian with credentials in philosophy and theology, was convinced that the distinctive feature of the West has been its attempt to separate itself from the religious roots that had provided moral unity to European peoples. Whether one agrees or not with Randall and Dawson, the quest for Western identity is inseparable from a history that begins with the Greeks. One may interpret that history from various perspectives, but the historical map is accessible to all who choose to join the exploration. Livy's recommendation previously cited is to be taken seriously. What were the lives our ancestors lived?

TWO

CHRISTIAN PHILOSOPHY

A Sociological Category or an Oxymoron?

The theses to be entertained here can be set forth simply. To address the question "Is there Christian philosophy?" it is necessary, first, to acknowledge that there is no such thing as "Christianity." As a sociological category "Christianity" may have some content. People the world over profess to be "Christian," but when we look to the content of belief, we find so little in common among professed Christians that the designation becomes almost meaningless. Professed Christians subscribe to a multiplicity of faiths with varying degrees of sophistication; they adhere to tenets, many of which are contradictory, many irrational, many unexamined. Orthodox Christianity is difficult to define even within the Roman Catholic community where a premium is placed on universality, unity, and the apostolic mandate. That is my first observation: the lack of unity in Christianity that might give meaning to the term "Christian philosophy."

The second is that both logically and chronologically, philosophy is prior to Christianity. The type of philosophy one espouses, implicitly or explicitly, either opens one to faith or closes it as an intellectual option. Furthermore, the type of philosophy one espouses determines the kind of Christianity one embraces. Classical Greek and Roman intelligence gave rise to, and forever will lead to, the institution shaped by the Fathers and Doctors of the early and medieval Church. If one starts with modern philosophical nominalism or epistemology, one will not end up in the belief system that shaped Aquinas and to which the Parisian master contributed. The differences between Plato and Aristotle, for example, or between realism and nominalism, are carried through history as Christians attempt to understand their faith. Ancient skepticisms and Pyrrhonism have their modern counterparts that make belief as impossible today as those outlooks made it impossible in antiquity.

The third thesis, which is likely to meet with no dissent from the orthodox but will nevertheless be challenged within the group that may be called "sociologically described Christians," is the belief that Christianity is based on divinely revealed truths inaccessible to human reason. Such truths consist of propositions such as "Christ is God," "Christ redeemed mankind by his sacrificial act on the cross," "Eternal beatitude consists in union with God in a life hereafter," and "God has revealed Himself as triune: Father, Son, and Holy Spirit." All will admit that Christ taught truths accessible to human reason, but not all will subscribe to the literal truth of assertions that go beyond those provided by reason itself. In sum, if one distinguishes among types of Christianity, one soon realizes that for the orthodox there may be one type of relation between faith and philosophy and for the nonorthodox another. If, in the spirit of the *Redaktionesge-schicte* movement, the whole of Christianity can be reduced to metaphor or to moral teaching, there is no problem concerning the relation of philosophy to revelation. Supposed revelation is nothing but a poetic manner of stating truths accessible to purely human intelligence. Averroes took this approach when he identified three modes or levels of teaching, each proportioned to or determined by the audience sought.

Distinguishing among religion, theology, and philosophy, Averroes held that these are but three modes of discourse corresponding to the three classes of men. *Religion* is truth made accessible to the common man who must be induced to live virtuously by eloquent preaching, that is, by appeals made to the imagination rather than to the intellect. *Theology* is the attempted rational justification of common belief, but it is only *philosophy* that provides the nucleus of truth contained in the fancies of the men of faith. The three approaches to the same truth ultimately agree with one another. The beliefs of the common people and the teachings of the theologians are simply philosophical truths adapted to inferior minds.

Yet Averroes did not consider religion to be merely a rough approximation of philosophic truth. For him, it was much more. It had a definite social function that could not be fulfilled by anything else, not even by philosophy. The Koran he believed to be a miraculous book and one "divinely inspired" because he found it more effective than philosophy in raising people to the level of morality. Thus Moses, Jesus, and Mohammed can be considered true prophets and messengers of God to mankind, but their religions were only popular approaches to the truth found in its purity in philosophy.

This position was to be partially reiterated in Hegel's all-embracing system in which Christian faith was treated as a moment in the unfolding of Absolute Spirit. For Hegel, religious language expresses in a symbolic manner the universality of truth that philosophy alone brings to rational explicitness.

It is appropriate to recall that Marx as a believing Jew learned from a Protestant biblical exegete how to interpret the Book of Isaiah in a purely secular fashion. Engels, too, lost his pietist faith under the tutelage of similarly disposed biblical scholars. If the so-called Sacred Scriptures are but poetic ways of teaching certain truths about human nature, morality, and the social order, then philosophy is the proper science of those things, although other modes of discourse may have indispensable educative roles to play.

For the orthodox believer, such as Augustine, philosophy retains its proper methodology, yielding important truths about nature and human nature, but it begs to be completed by divine revelation. Augustine can assert that he believes in order to understand, that is, to *fully* understand. For Augustine, the understanding provided by faith is greater than that available to natural reason; a contemplative union with God in whom all is manifested is seen as the goal of human life. Aquinas is well known for his doctrine that the natural prepares the way for the supernatural, that the two complement each other, with revelation adding to the store of natural truths about God and man.

These two intellectual giants used the categories of Greece and Rome to understand the faith they received from Jerusalem, and they developed theologies that remain alive today.

Thomas Aquinas, in constructing his theology, employed the philosophy of Aristotle to such an extent that not only his strictly philosophical works but his theological treatises are studied for the philosophy they contain. Most who use Aquinas recognize the distinction and keep the two modes of discourse separate.

This distinction is universally recognized in the ordering of higher studies within the Catholic educational complex. One will never find a Department of Philosophy and Religion in a Catholic institution, although the two disciplines have been and continue to be placed under one organizational schema in state and many private institutions. The name "American Catholic Philosophical Association" has through the years given pause to many a novice, but each generation of scholars seems to find through experience that it is a sociological category and not the designation of a particular *ism*, membership in the organization consisting mostly of Catholics or of those who teach in Catholic-sponsored institutions.

I implied earlier that there is a major difference between Protestant and Catholic attitudes toward philosophy. Of course, it is no more possible to define Protestantism than it is to define Christianity. If we distinguish between "high" and "low" churches or between "evangelical" and other denominations and concentrate on those that have clearly separated themselves from Catholicism, we find little resort to philosophy per se. Yet in many quarters a previous suspicion of philosophy has been replaced by its cultivation. Fundamentalist seminaries, in this half of the century, have added philosophers to their staffs and have even created departments of philosophy where none existed a generation ago.

Protestant attitudes toward philosophy are in part determined by the biblical theology embraced by the Reformers. Luther's doctrine of the Fall certainly colored his attitude toward speculative philosophy. Accepting the biblical account of the Fall of Adam, Luther was convinced that intellect was so darkened as a result of the Fall that it could not conclude to the existence of God unaided. Consequently, Luther had little regard for philosophy. A sworn enemy of Scholasticism, he once remarked that God had sent Aristotle as a punishment for the sins of mankind. Calvin, too, was suspicious of the intellect's ability to achieve unaided a knowledge of God, although he was convinced that at least God's existence was ascertainable apart from revelation.

Kant with his *Critique of Pure Reason* became for many the Aquinas of Protestantism. His boast that he had destroyed reason to make way for faith was compatible with a fundamentalism that emphasized the gratuitous character of faith. Whereas Catholic apologetics insists on a rational preamble, that is, upon the reasonableness of belief, the tradition represented by Luther, by Calvin, and later by Kierkegaard called for a leap into the dark.

The Enlightenment reaction to both the fideism of mainstream Protestantism and a weakened Scholastic legacy established a rationalism that still holds sway. For nineteenth- and twentieth-century English-speaking philosophers, such as John Stuart Mill and John Dewey, the problem is one of justifying the moral legacy of Christianity by providing a proper rationale for many of the values formally justified on a religious basis.

History suggests that the problem of Christian philosophy is largely a problem of the relation of faith to reason. It is a problem for the Christian who wishes to keep the sources of his knowledge distinct, that is, what he has learned from revelation and its development in sacred theology, on the one hand, separate from the natural sources of his knowledge, on the other. It is an issue for the nonbeliever who tends to regard the philosopher who is open to the testimony of faith as a "theologian in disguise," and thus a tainted witness. There is no doubt, as Etienne Gilson has shown, that Western philosophy has been influenced by religion and that the believer often has distinctive interests in the practice of philosophy. Clearly, philosophy used in the analysis and development of doctrine is theology. No one questions the use of philosophy by the theologian who is disposed to use it. The fundamental questions are: Can philosophy remain unalloyed in the presence of biblical revelation? And need it do so? The answer to the second question, as I have suggested above, depends on the type of Christianity embraced.

The answer to the first question is that philosophy must remain unalloyed if it is to be true philosophy. It must justify to its hearer every conclusion it reaches by the evidence it produces and the inferences it makes. This explains the peculiar affinity of the believer to classical philosophy; he finds in Greek and Roman thought the rational preamble without which he would find it difficult to believe.

Contributions to philosophy by Christians can hardly be denied, even when that philosophy is developed within a theological context. The Christian is not compelled to defend, even against the most strident agnostic, the work of Augustine, Anselm, Albert, Aquinas, Scotus, Suarez, Maritain, or Lonergan. Aquinas's commentaries on Aristotle, even today, despite centuries of similar work, remain a valuable guide to the work of the Stagirite. The plurality of philosophical approaches among believers is noticeable. There is no *one* philosophy among those whose faith may be in substantial agreement. The term "Scholastic philosophy," for example, embraces a heterogenous collection of systems from Albert and Aquinas, through Bonaventure and Scotus, to Ockham and Suarez. There is no single method, no single doctrine; one may say, paraphrasing Gilson, "only intellect in the service of Christ."

Philosophy is obviously employed by those who seek to understand the "mysteries" of their faith and to probe the implications of what they take to be revealed truth. Most who profess the Catholic faith guard the integrity of their philosophy because it alone provides a common language, a common set of distinctions, that enables the believer to enter into dialogue with those who do not share his faith. Sidney Hook could challenge the believer with the assertion: "We have as much evidence for the existence of God as we have for the existence of leprechauns and fairies." Ernest Nagel could proclaim reason "sovereign" against those who invoked Scripture. John Dewey could explain to the believer, in the fashion of a Schleiermacher or a Ritschl, the true secular meaning of the doctrines to which the believer subscribes.

But with each, the believer, philosophically equipped, remains in a position to argue the evidence pro and con.

In the last analysis the battleground is metaphysics. Without the principles of intelligibility, causality, substance, finality, potency, and act, intellect is left, so to speak, dead in the water. There can be no movement from contingent being to self-existent being, the cause of the existence of things. Without an acknowledgment that intellect can achieve a notion of 'being,' there can be no inference to Being Itself. Without intellect as a collaborator supporting the proposition that God exists and that things insofar as we can know them are as revelation presents them, those propositions that reason does not teach will necessarily have to be accepted on blind faith.

The Catholic mind cherishes philosophy as the rational preamble to its faith, but the philosophy cherished is of a select strain. It is largely the philosophy of Aristotle and the Stoics as developed and commented upon through the ages; it is not the empiricism of Hume or the critical philosophy of Kant or the materialism of Marx. It is a philosophy confident of the intelligibility of nature, of the power of intellect to ferret out the secrets of nature, and of the intellect's ability to render at least partially intelligible that which is not self-intelligible. To ask about Christian philosophy inevitably forces one to raise the question: "What think you of the Greeks and their detractors?"

The position defended here is not unlike that taken a generation ago by Jacques Maritain, one of several twentieth-century giants who debated the issue. In his *An Essay on Christian Philosophy*, Maritain distinguishes between philosophy considered in the abstract and philosophy considered in its concrete state of existence.[1] Philosophy as abstracted from its concrete conditions of existence

---

1. Trans. E. H. Flannery (New York: Philosophical Library, 1955). Two major explorations of the Maritain and Gilson positions deserve special mention: Joseph Owens, *Towards a Christian Philosophy* (Washington, D.C.: The Catholic University of America Press, 1990), and John Wippel, "Thomas Aquinas and the Problem of Christian Philosophy," in *Metaphysical Themes in Thomas Aquinas* (Washington, D.C.: The Catholic University of America Press, 1984).

is a purely natural and rational discipline: it cannot be "Christian." But as found in those who philosophize, it will be characterized one way or another. The Christian is apt to be influenced by his faith even as he philosophizes. On that point one may question Maritain. If the influence is regarded as subliminal, so to speak, there is no way to ascertain whether it is operative or not. If the guidance is open, as in the case of the biblical account of God revealing Himself to Moses as Yahweh, interpreted as "He who is," we can acknowledge with Gilson that "[a]ny Christian convert who was at all familiar with Greek philosophy was then bound to realize the metaphysical import of the new belief."[2] "I am who am," restated in metaphysical terms, becomes "self-existent being," or "I am He whose essence it is to exist." And from the biblical account of Creation, it is easy to add "the cause of the existence of things." Thus revelation has suggested to the philosopher a key distinction, namely, that between essence and existence, between *what is* and the act *whereby it is*. This distinction is either philosophically defensible or it is not. Similar distinctions from the natural sciences, particularly from quantum mechanics, are absorbed by philosophy and defended philosophically without troubling effect. The distinction, for example, between iconic and mathematical models of natural structures is not one to be ignored and can readily be incorporated into philosophy without leading one to doubt the difference between epistemology and physics.

Etienne Gilson took a position somewhat different from Maritain's but one that I believe is compatible. Gilson, invoking the literal meaning of the word *philosophy*, takes it to be the pursuit of wisdom. It is Gilson's position that in the Christian era, as opposed to that of the Greco-Roman period, the pursuit of wisdom cannot avoid cognizance of Christian revelation. As Gilson put it, if you asked any early Christian, "Have you a philosophy?," he would have answered, "I do have a philosophy indeed! Its name is Christianity."[3] In presenting

2. Etienne Gilson, "God and Christian Philosophy," in *A Gilson Reader* (New York: Doubleday Image Books, 1957), 193.
3. Ibid., 178.

itself as the quintessence of wisdom, Christianity presented itself as far superior to anything available to unaided reason. Gilson, after surveying the history of Western thought, after chronicling the course of philosophy during the many centuries of its association with Christian faith, that is, from the time of the early apologists and the Fathers of the Church to the Scholastic Doctors, draws the conclusion: "Christian philosophy cannot be reduced to the content of any single philosophy; it is neither a system nor even a doctrine. Rather it is a way of philosophizing; namely, the attitude of those who (in the words of Pope Leo XIII) 'to the study of philosophy unite obedience to the Christian faith.'"[4]

"Obedience to the Christian faith," even for Gilson, has to be a metaphor since adherence to any faith outlook is a voluntary and not a commanded act. All that "obedience" can mean in this context is that one cannot affirm and deny at the same time and in the same respect a particular Christian outlook and its contradictory.

That one acts on the basis of a belief system needs little elaboration. Sidney Hook, as an agnostic and materialist, spent his whole life fighting religious education, which, like Dewey, he thought was not only intellectually misleading but distracted one from addressing the affairs of this world—there being no other world. Gilson obviously did not have in mind the relation between an intellectual stance and its implications. His thesis is rather that in a peculiar way revelation is a safeguard for reason. In the Christian era, the fortunes of philosophy are bound up with the fortunes of revealed religion.

In *The Spirit of Medieval Philosophy*, Gilson writes that the "content of Christian philosophy is that body of rational truths, discovered, explored or simply safeguarded, thanks to the help that reason receives from revelation."[5] If the term "Christian philosophy" is to have any meaning "it must be frankly admitted that nothing less than an intrinsic relation between revelation and reason will suffice to give it meaning."[6]

---

4. Ibid., 198.
5. Trans. A. H. C. Downes (New York: Charles Scribner's Sons, 1940), 35.
6. Ibid.

In spite of his use of the word "intrinsic," Gilson's thesis may be designated a sociological perspective. Its justification or denial will have to be advanced by methods other than strictly philosophical ones. It is the observation that a historian can make and one that an equally informed or better informed historian may deny. Its affirmation or denial does not touch the issue "Is there a Christian philosophy?" To affirm the thesis "There is only philosophy, which is neither Christian nor non-Christian" is not to refute Gilson. The issue as stated in this way is different from the one he frequently addressed as a historian.

I return to my thesis. "Christian philosophy" is a label that may be given to what philosophers do when they deliberately relate their professional work to their religious or ecclesiastical commitments. It doesn't characterize the philosophy related—it refers only to a relation, a relation observable to a historian or perhaps to a trained sociologist.

THREE

WHAT WAS RELIGION?

The Demise of a Prodigious Power

I

The recent shift in North America from a predominantly Protestant to a secular or humanistic culture has created for the religious mind a new set of problems. The religious mind is no longer faced with the task of defining its vision of the contemporary meaning of Christianity or Judaism against other religious outlooks; each is now called to defend itself in the face of major secular attack, hostile to religious belief and practice.

It may take considerable learning and analysis to recognize the full extent of the secular threat to religion, but little reflection is required to recognize its negative social effects, that is, a general disintegration of religious commitment, manifesting itself in a startling increase in promiscuity, in divorce and abortion, in the widespread acceptance of pornography and homosexuality, and in a growing tolerance of deviant behavior ranging from civil and religious impiety to the use of drugs.

The loss of a certain loyalty to family values immediately reflects the displacement of a biblical morality. Of a more subtle character is the loss of sustaining values in the classroom, where the underpinnings of a Western, largely Christian, perspective, namely, classical learning, ancient and modern languages, history, philosophy, and theology—all disciplines that provide the materials through which revealed religion is received and developed—have been neglected or abandoned. Furthermore, in the interpretation of the religious mission, the secular mind has all but convinced the religious mind that the latter's role is primarily that of tending to the needs of the disadvantaged in the narrow sense of physical and economic needs. As a result of the neglect of its intellectual heritage in favor of a social activism, mainstream Christianity has failed to teach with sufficient clarity and unity of voice to be a sure guide to believers.

As many have observed, a community cannot long exist without a core of common convictions. Some of the social tensions evident in North America are but a reflection of a deeper conflict between religious and secular outlooks. If the secular is not to totally eclipse the religious and become the standard for the measure of thought and conduct, representatives of religious outlook will have to consciously confront the challenge. The reflections that follow are an attempt to understand the causes that have led to the present impotence of the religious mind and its prospects for the future.

II

A skepticism with respect to Christian convictions has been forming among the Occidental intelligentsia for at least two centuries. In the last century Nietzsche had already observed that Western culture no longer possessed the spiritual resources that had formerly justified its existence and without which he believed it could not survive.[1]

What is more disturbing is that this loss of religious sense has made itself felt on the level of the common man. In more ways than one, the last quarter of the twentieth century is the misguided product of the French Enlightenment.[2] Views entertained in eighteenth-

1. The nineteenth-century German philosopher Frederick Nietzsche was an influential critic of the culture and ethos of his time, particularly Christianity. *Beyond Good and Evil* (1886) and the *Genealogy of Morals* (1887) are sweeping critiques of Western culture.

2. For a historical and interpretive account of the French Enlightment at variance with the one offered here, see John H. Randall Jr., *The Making of the Modern Mind* (New York: Houghton Mifflin, 1940). Randall writes from a purely naturalistic perspective and shares the views of many of his subjects.

and nineteenth-century drawing rooms and in the academy of those days have in our own lifetime entered the marketplace. Diderot set the tone in the preface to his famous *Encyclopedie* when he wrote: "Every thing must be examined, every thing must be shaken up, without exception and without circumspection." Voltaire urged the eradication of Christianity from the world of higher culture. But he was willing to allow it to remain in the stables and in the scullery, mainly as a moral force, lest a servant class emancipated from the traditional sources of morality might pilfer. Like Diderot, he was convinced that the critical spirit could do its constructive work only after it had liberated man from the shackles of traditional belief. There are times, he says, when one must destroy before one can build. Voltaire readily admitted his intolerance, declaring that his was an intolerance directed against intolerance.

Jeremy Bentham thought the state should actively work to stamp out religion. His disciple John Stuart Mill repudiated Christianity but not the religion of humanity, which he thought to be, from the point of view of the state, a useful thing. Auguste Comte was more benevolent in his attitude toward Christian practice than either Voltaire or Mill. In spite of his denial of all metaphysical validity to religious belief, he was willing to accept as a civic good the moral and ritual traditions of at least Catholic Christianity. Emil Durkheim, carrying the Enlightenment spirit through the last quarter of the nineteenth century and into the first decades of the twentieth, was not so positive. For him, a major task of the state is to free individuals from partial societies such as the family, religious organizations, and labor and professional groups. Modern individualism, Durkheim thought, depends on preventing the absorption of individuals into secondary or mediating groups.

Feuerbach, whose materialism was to have a significant influence on both Marx and Freud, assigned to reason the role of destroying the illusion of religion, "an illusion, however, which is by no means insignificant, but whose effect on mankind, rather, is utterly pernicious." Freud took up the theme, and in his *Future of an Illusion* he describes the struggle of the scientific spirit against the "enemy" religion.[3] "Criticism," he writes, "has gnawed away at the probative power of religious documents; natural science has shown the errors they contain; comparative research has been struck by the fatal resemblance of the religious conceptions we revere to the mental products of primitive peoples and times." The religious mind itself has recognized this and in retreat has made itself over in an effort to become more acceptable. In a letter to Princess Marie Bonaparte, Freud complained that intellectuals had slackened their pursuit, but understandably "that comes from the most varied drinks being offered in the name of 'religion,' with a minimum percentage of alcohol—really nonalcoholic; but they still get drunk on it." Showing little respect for social-gospel or for accommodationist religion, Freud wrote, "The old drinkers were after all a respectable body."[4]

On this side of the Atlantic, many of these ideas were to find twentieth-century expression in the writings of John Dewey, a philosopher who played an influential role in the development of American educational philosophy and social policy. In his theory of education Dewey provided no place for religion or for religious institutions, no matter what roles they may have played in the past. Religion, he thought, is an unreliable source for knowledge and, in spite of contentions to the contrary, even for motivation. He admitted that many of the values held dear by the religious are worthy of consideration and should not be abandoned but argued that a proper rationale ought to be sought for those deemed commendable. Through his critique of religion, Dewey sought not merely to eliminate the church from political influence but to eliminate it as an effective agent even in private life. Religion, he taught, was socially dangerous insofar as it gives practical credence to a divine law and attempts to mold

3. Freud's attack on religion, particularly Christianity, is to be found throughout his writings but principally in *The Future of an Illusion: Basic Writings of Sigmund Freud*, ed. A. H. Brill (New York: Modern Library, 1938). For a critical study of Freud, see Rudolph Allers, *The Successful Error* (New York: Sheed & Ward, 1940). The contrast between Freudian and Christian concepts of man is to be found in Reinhold Niebuhr, *The Nature and Destiny of Man*, vol. 1 (New York: 1943).

4. Sigmund Freud to Marie Bonaparte, 19 March 1928, as quoted by Peter Gay, in *A Godless Jew* (New Haven, Conn.: Yale University Press, 1987), 12.

personal or social conduct in conformity with norms that look beyond and therefore neglect temporal society.[5]

At the very time many ideas characteristic of the French Enlightenment were finding adherents in the academic mainstream on this
side of the Atlantic, the schools themselves were changing hands. At
the turn of the century the land-grant colleges were coming into
being. Lacking religious sponsorship or identity, they tended to reflect the current secular spirit of the intellectual mainstream. At the
same time, the older Protestant-founded colleges were losing their
denominational identity. Whereas in the last quarter of the nineteenth century nearly every major chair of philosophy in the United
States was held by an idealist whose philosophy was thought to support Christianity, the situation was soon reversed.

By 1916, nearly every chair was held by a naturalist, whose philosophy is defined by the twin beliefs that nature is self-intelligible, man
having his origin, growth, and decay in nature, and that science as
ideally practiced by the mathematical physicist is the only reliable
method of inquiry. In the words of one of its proponents, man has as
much evidence for the existence of God as he does for the existence
of leprechauns and fairies. Any explanation of the transition from
idealism to naturalism would have to take note of the widespread
confidence placed in certain social theories emanating from the Continent, in the discoveries of Darwin, in the views of Freud, and in the
kind of biblical scholarship that tended to cast doubt on the uniqueness of Christianity. Though these ideas did not have immediate social or cultural effects, the academy was severed from its Christian
parentage and, in Enlightenment fashion, came to construe itself as a
critic of established institutions rather than as the bearer of a tradition or culture. Science was equated by Dewey and his disciples with
"critical intelligence." Ernest Nagel, whose work in the philosophy of
science influenced generations of students, once published a book

---

5. Of the many works of John Dewey three may be taken as setting forth his philosophy in outline: *Experience and Nature* (Chicago: Open Court, 1925), *Theory of Valuation* (Chicago: University of Chicago Press, 1939), and *Reconstruction in Philosophy*
(New York: New American Library, 1939).

entitled *Sovereign Reason.*[6] Empirical methods were to be turned on everything heretofore considered sacrosanct. It took another generation or two before such a critique was to reach the textbooks utilized in the primary and secondary schools. An examination of those textbooks would disclose not a neutrality but an activist secular perspective, one that in recent years has come to reflect every passing social and political cause.

Until the close of World War II, the common schools were largely Protestant. From the beginning of the Republic, their Protestant character was taken for granted. It was because of Catholic dissatisfaction with Protestant public schools that the parochial school system came into being. That dissatisfaction, plus the massive European immigration of the second half of the nineteenth century, brought into being a dual educational system. But in the post–World War II period, the Protestant character of the public school began to be challenged. The secular philosophy of the academy began to make itself felt through a series of decisions by the U.S. Supreme Court. In ruling on religious matters, the Court habitually appealed to the anti-establishment clause of the First Amendment, but after 1947 it began to read into that amendment outlooks that the Founding Fathers did not press and that were contradictory to the views of most of them. This is not the place to develop the thesis, but it can be demonstrated that in the course of little more than forty years, decisions of the Court have, in effect, secularized public education. Whereas the schools previously fostered basic Protestant Christian values through their traditions of common prayer, Bible reading, use of textbooks such as the McGuffy reader, and the celebration of religious feasts, those values are no longer explicitly fostered. To be sure, the Court did not prohibit teaching about religion or the reading of Sacred Scripture as a form of literature, but there is little doubt that reflections of Protestant Christianity in the curriculum had not only been challenged, but removed as a positive influence. Protestantism was replaced in the schools by a secular humanism, which, while not a

6. Glencoe, Ill.: Free Press, 1954.

religion, is clearly an ideology, consisting of a metaphysics, an episte-mology, and an ethic, with antireligious implications for society and for the individual.

Significant, too, is the Court's refusal to recognize the school as an extension of the parental right to educate the child in accordance with parental beliefs. Under existing rulings, parents possess options with respect to schools only on the condition that they forfeit their claims to a tax-supported school and are financially able to pay the cost of private education. At the same time that parental control has diminished, secular federal control has increased. Through its many agencies, the social objectives of the federal government are fre-quently translated into programs designed to alter the attitudes of schoolchildren. One can say that as religious influence has declined, state influence, as dogmatically secular influence, has increased.

In the judgment of Christopher Dawson, the secular state school is an instrument of the Enlightenment.[7] Insofar as the state preempts education, the schools have become the seats of a new ideology: the ideology of secularism. Others have argued that a secular state re-quires a secular state school, assuring us that the secularization of the state does not mean the secularization of society. But this opinion, as Walter Berns has pointed out, was not shared by Rousseau; Washing-ton and even Jefferson had their doubts, and Madison proclaimed the need for a diversity of religious loyalties. Experience can be no guide here because we have no experience of living under wholly secular auspices.[8] It is only in our day that we have approximated the secular state. It is unfortunate that, although many of the Court's decisions have been countermajoritarian, in recent years public opinion has in-evitably begun to follow the Court and the elites that the Court fol-lows. America, unfortunately, has become a conformist society, mak-ing it hard for an individual or a social group to maintain separate

7. For selections from the work of Christopher Dawson, see *Christianity and Euro-pean Culture*, ed. Gerald J. Russello (Washington, D.C.: The Catholic University of America Press, 1998).

8. Walter Berns, *The First Amendment and the Future of American Democracy* (New York: Basic Books, 1976), 18.

standards of value or independent ways of life. The state's near monopoly on education and the uniformity encouraged by the media have produced decisive changes in American society.

This scenario would suggest that if religious literacy is to be achieved, it will be achieved without help from, and sometimes against, the interference of the state. If it were once true, as de Tocqueville reported, that all Americans regard religion as indispensable to the maintenance of republican institutions, that claim cannot be made today.

If the religious mind is to recover a former intellectual leadership, it will first have to understand and then counter the excesses of the Enlightenment spirit now permeating Western culture. It will do that only by standing back from the flow of contemporary events to take an objective measure of its past and its accomplishments and, with the wisdom uncovered, assess the present.

III

One useful analysis in thinking about the importance of traditions and their transmission is that of Alasdair MacIntyre. In his books *Whose Justice, Which Rationality?* and *Three Rival Versions of Moral Enquiry,*[9] MacIntyre argues that "philosophical theories give organized expression to concepts and theories already embodied in forms of practice and types of community. As such they make available for rational criticism and for further rational development those socially embodied theories and concepts of which they provide an understanding."[10] MacIntyre speaks of the "illusion of the autonomy of philosophical thought." The truth of the matter, he argues, is that theories of justice and practical rationality are but aspects of a traditional allegiance, a tradition that entails specific modes of social relationships, each with its own justification and

9. Alasdair MacIntyre, *After Virtue* (Notre Dame, Ind.: University of Notre Dame Press, 1981), *Whose Justice, Which Rationality* (Notre Dame, Ind.: University of Notre Dame Press, 1988), *Three Rival Versions of Moral Enquiry* (Notre Dame, Ind.: University of Notre Dame Press, 1990).

10. MacIntyre, *Whose Justice.*

interpretation. Ideas not only have consequences but require proper nourishment. One can be, suggests MacIntyre, an Aristotelian or a Humean, but one cannot be both. In practice one cannot be either without appropriate social organization, or without a congenial *polis*. The conditions of the administration of Aristotelian justice are different from the conditions of administration of Humean justice. MacIntyre would say that both traditions exist as actual forms of practical life and command the allegiance of many, although few adherents may be aware of the sources of the conceptions of justice and practical rationality that they embrace. What each person is confronted with is at once a set of rival intellectual positions, a set of rival traditions embodied more or less imperfectly in contemporary forms of social discourse. Each has its own specific modes of speech, argument, and debate; each makes an intellectual claim upon the individual's allegiance.[11]

In his recent book MacIntyre identifies three major rival traditions: nineteenth-century rationalism, the subjectivism of Nietzsche, and the Aristotelian-Thomistic. There is, in MacIntyre's judgment, reason to maintain one's frame of discourse. Genuine intellectual encounter does not and cannot take place in some generalized abstract way. The wider the audience to whom we aspire to speak, the less we shall speak to anyone in particular. MacIntyre admits that most contemporary life is led somewhere betwixt and between conflicting traditions, but unless those conflicting traditions are sharply delineated, we are not apt to discern what is at stake. MacIntyre's "Hume" can be taken as a symbol of the Enlightenment as readily as Diderot or Voltaire. In contemporary philosophy of science, for example, the polarity is graphic; the major alternative outlooks are a Humean-inspired empiricism, on the one hand, and an Aristotelian realism, on the other.

To appropriate any tradition, certain attitudes of mind are required. A respect for the past entails the conviction that the ancients have

11. MacIntyre argues this thesis in *After Virtue, Whose Justice,* and *Three Rivals.*

something to say across the ages about an essentially timeless human nature. The value of the past was not denied by the Encyclopediasts. In their respect for classical learning they were not to be outdone, but it was a selective recognition. The fathers of the Enlightenment consciously attempted to subvert the foundation of Christian historiography by treating man's past as a wholly secular, not as a sacred, record. The primacy of Greece meant the primacy of philosophy, and the primacy of philosophy reduced to nonsense the claim that religion was man's central concern.

In the decades that witnessed the erection of the secularly oriented land-grant universities, those private institutions that had been founded under religious auspices effectively became secular, abolishing the requirement of religious affiliation for the members of their faculties. Their previous concern for religion had ensured a certain uniformity of belief and a unity in the way the curriculum was organized, presented, and developed through enquiry. That the religiously affiliated university embodied a particular tradition of rational enquiry can be seen in the structures and programs of those confessional New England seminaries that subsequently became colleges and later prominent universities. It can also be seen, as MacIntyre observes, in the Scottish universities of the seventeenth and eighteenth centuries, which articulated one kind of Protestant tradition of enquiry, and in the Dutch universities of the same period. It can be witnessed in the Louvain of the late nineteenth and early twentieth centuries and in many Catholic universities in North America in the middle decades of this century.

When universities without religious tests were founded or religious tests were abolished in universities that formerly employed them, what happened, MacIntyre suggests, was not the encouragement of a plurality of religious views within the university; instead, under the new system university teachers were appointed without any consideration of belief and allegiance. A conception of scholarly competence, independent of standpoint, was adopted in the making of appointments. A corresponding conception of objectivity in the classroom required that teachers present what they taught as if there were indeed shared standards of rationality accepted by all teachers and accessible to all students. Universities became institutions committed to upholding a fictitious objectivity. Parts were thought to be interchangeable. A professor of philosophy could move from a secular into a religious university without changing pace; the reverse was not always possible. Little harm was done in the sciences, but in the humanities the loss of context provided by traditions of enquiry deprived teaching of any standard by which some texts might be regarded as more important than others. Without much attention given to the process, the secularization of major Catholic universities occurred in the 1960s and 1970s in a fashion reminiscent of the secularization of Protestant institutions at the turn of the century. Respected and sympathetic observers have called this process inevitable.

In certain contexts, one is almost embarrassed to point out that there is a deep incompatibility between Christianity and the dominant modes of contemporary teaching, discussion, and debate. Given this state of affairs, if any religious tradition is to survive, its proponents must recognize that they are engaged in a debate with competing and conflicting worldviews, what MacIntyre would term "rationalities." Even with such recognition, they may remain impotent. There is evidence that religious bodies have lost without hope of recovery many of the major educational institutions that were brought into being with their support. If the value of religion to society is to be rationally asserted, the secular mind itself may have to take the initiative.

IV

This leads us to the fundamental question: Does one have to free society of religion to be free in important respects? The Greeks and Romans thought not. In ancient times the state sought the unity of religion as a matter of self-preservation. In the *Timaeus*, Plato attached the death penalty to the repeated offense of atheism. The Roman persecution of the Christians was understandable, given the cultural role that religion played in their society and the value the Romans placed upon concerted belief and action. Although we would today look upon some Roman practices as superstitious, the basic outlook that motivated a referral of all things to the gods showed considerable insight into human nature, if not into the divine nature. The augur who read the signs and auspices to determine whether military or civic action ought to take place represented considerations beyond the momentarily expedient.

In early Christian times many ancient practices were absorbed as pagan feasts and rituals and even temples were transformed in the service of the biblical God. The religious mode of marking the seasons of the year and of celebrating the important passages of life became an art form that could bring elegance and joy to human life. In due course Christianity was to produce some of the greatest artifacts the world has known, from painting and architecture to music, poetry, and drama. Its inherited confidence in speculative intellect, its respect for nature's order, and its practical bent eventually gave rise to the natural science that the ancient world was posed to create but which for internal failings it was never able to effect. As the early Church Fathers were quick to perceive, Christianity contains within itself both a speculative and a practical wisdom. It provides a way of looking at things, but more so, guidelines for behavior. With its sacraments it exists to pick up the inevitable failure and to set man back on the path. The secular mind finds much of this offensive. Misreading the lessons of history, it sets in opposition science and religion, confuses morality with religion, and in some versions cut off from both classical learning and Christianity seems vulnerable to every passing fad.

Barring a global catastrophe that would bring the race to its knees, it is difficult to see how Christianity or traditional Judaism are apt to fare better in the twenty-first century than they did in the twentieth. In the case of Christianity, it is true that one cannot identify Christianity with the West, but the Western media and Western universities have set the tone for much of the world. Evangelical Christianity will retain and perhaps expand its hold, bringing the solace of Sacred Scripture into the lives of many, but, given its fideistic nature, it is not likely to have much influence over the intellectual sources of the common culture. The media and the university are apt to remain in secular hands, promoting a secular culture, making it difficult for the religious mind to maintain itself at a high intellectual level or to exercise mass influence. There is no intrinsic reason why this should be so. We may never return to the day when an abbot of St. Denis could at once be an architect and a regent of France, giving birth to the new gothic style soon to sweep the whole of Europe, but something equally important could happen.

One could wish that the secular mind, if for no other reason than self-interest, imbued with nothing more than the perspective of a August Comte, would assess from its perspective the value of religion. But before doing so, it should in all honesty first acknowledge its own peculiar status. Modern atheism and ignorance of God are not the products of a grassroots movement that has made its will felt; rather, it is something propagated from the top down. A few years ago, a study conducted by Stanley Rothman and S. Robert Lichter under the auspices of the Research Institute at Columbia University provided an interesting profile of the leadership of the most influential media outlets. As a result of interviews with 240 established journalists and broadcasters (the emphasis is on "established," not aspirants to influence), Rothman and Lichter concluded that there is a wide chasm between the media elite and Middle America.[12] A significant characteristic of the media is its predominantly secular outlook; only half of those interviewed acknowledged a religious affiliation. Although 23 percent were raised in a Jewish household, only 14 percent claim to be of the Jewish faith. One in five identifies himself as a Protestant, one in eight as a Catholic. Only 8 percent attend a church or a synagogue weekly; 86 percent never or rarely attend services. On moral and social issues, 90 percent believe that a woman has a right to an abortion; 75 percent believe that homosexuality is not immoral; and 85 percent uphold the right of homosexuals to teach in public schools. Less than 50 percent believe that adultery is wrong, and only 15 percent strongly

---

12. S. R. Lichter, L. Lichter, and S. Rothman, *Prime Time: How T.V. Portrays American Culture* (Washington, D.C.: Regnery, 1994).

agree that extramarital affairs are immoral. Most believe that the business community has too much influence in the nation; most believe that the media itself should have more influence than it has, although it perceives itself as already having a great deal of influence. Yet, in spite of the media's endorsement of the permissive society and its challenge to authority and to the roots of common loyalties, the outlook of the media elites has not prevailed. The overwhelming majority of the people retain a belief in God, even if that belief is imperfectly or only vaguely formulated.

One conclusion seems inevitable. For the religious mind to maintain itself in all of its richness, it will require the support of scholarship of the highest order. Christopher Dawson once remarked that the secular leviathan is vulnerable only at its brain. The scholarship required is of that sort that usually takes place only within a research university. But now we enter a vicious circle. While universities have responded with alacrity to minority and feminist concerns, they steadfastly stand resistant to claims from the religious sector. A mind formed by the philosophy of the Enlightenment is manifestly illiberal when it comes to the recognition of alternative modes of thought; it is not inclined to give ground easily.

Given its influence on the elite media and on the Supreme Court, the academy can speak with an unnaturally amplified voice. Under its influence, the Court as supreme arbiter of the nation's intellectual conflicts has reversed the wellsprings of the received culture. The Court has not shied away from this role. Broad cultural debates unresolvable in any other forum inevitably reach the Court as constitutional issues. Cases are not only framed but argued and judged by persons trained in the major universities. Often the issues presented for litigation are manufactured for the occasion as interest groups seek to remove yet one more vestige of a Christian heritage. The Court, in an activist mood, is likely to rule in the light of the same zeitgeist that created the issue. The Constitution itself, the historical circumstances of its framing, and the traditions of the people count for nothing before such a Court, as it instantiates the programs of the reforming secularly committed social theorist. That is the circle: the academy influences the Court and the Court advances the objectives of the secularist academy.

But the circle can be broken at more than one place. The university is not completely immune to criticism, and the Court itself is responsive to the political process. No trend is irreversible. If in the United States the educational franchise were returned to the believer, so that no penalty were attached to religion's free exercise, then parental choice, with its ripple effect, would soon reverse the secular control of education. The religious mind could then compete on equal terms with the secular mind. It would still have to test its vision and its morality against natural canons, but with the resources provided by its rich traditions and by modern techniques it could not fail to provide a viable alternative to the present secular outlook. Much is at stake. Unless a moral and cultural voice somehow gains the attention of a Western audience, the West itself, having forsaken the speculative and practical wisdom provided by classical and biblical learning, will lose also the discipline required for self-maintenance. Although in principle philosophy may be capable of providing the needed intellectual and moral precepts, philosophy is notoriously weak when it comes to marshaling resources or directing the lives of the many. Contemporary philosophy itself seems to be in a skeptical and self-flagellating period, uncertain of its role even as an academic discipline. In the East, and perhaps for Oriental peoples wherever they settle, Buddhism and Confucianism may carry the intellectual and cultural traditions that effectively shape and give stability to life, but outside of biblical religion no comparable spiritual vehicle exists in the West.

On the positive side we may take note of certain shifts in attitude. The supposed opposition between science and religion has long been put to rest, at least where scholarship prevails. Freudian interpretations of belief, as is widely recognized, fail for lack of empirical support. A fusion of temporal and spiritual authority offensive to the secular mind is rarely found even in those nations that retain established churches. And given the social consequences of the disintegration of personal morality, responsible scholars, even among those schooled in the prevailing naturalism, are beginning to recognize a role for organized religion in the maintenance of civic virtue.

These slight trends provide little cause for optimism. Without political leverage the religious mind is not apt to achieve parity within the academy. Those in leadership positions who recognize the contribution that the nation's religious past has made to the common good cannot remain passive as the inherited culture is further subverted.

FOUR

MARX, DEWEY, AND MARITAIN

The Role of Religion in Society

Almost before our eyes, in the brief span of the few decades since World War II, this nation, like much of the West, has become intellectually secularized, with consequences for the social order. It is a well-established principle that if a society's laws are based on a particular worldview and that worldview collapses, the laws themselves will crumble.[1]

We have seen this happen gradually in the United States as the universities, many of which were founded by religious organizations, became secular and contributed to the secularization of the nation. How that happened is too long a story to tell here, but its outline is well known. Largely through court decisions and aided by the major media, our intellectual elites have been able to instantiate a set of laws and gain acceptance for a lifestyle that anyone with memories of a prewar period would regard as alien. From a Christian perspective on life, and from laws that protected that perspective, this nation has come to embrace a secular mentality and laws that foster an almost unrestrained hedonism.

Once with Sunday closing laws we publicly proclaimed the Sabbath; with laws against the sale of contraceptives, we affirmed the procreative end of marriage; with laws against pornography, we taught the meaningfulness of the sexual act; with laws against abortion, we

---

1. Patrick Devlin makes this point in *The Enforcement of Morals* (London: Oxford University Press, 1965), 1–25.

taught the sacredness of human life; and with stiff penalties for criminal activity from homicide to drug peddling, we taught other uncontested values. Lord Patrick Devlin has been proved correct by the course of events, as the presuppositions behind these laws were challenged by important segments of society and the laws gave way. The ethics of our current intellectual elites prevail, with tragic consequences for the people. It now takes two working people to support a household whose permanence is not ensured as the divorce rate approaches 50 percent and the reproductive rate is well below population-replacement level.

What went wrong? The answer is bound to be complex, and there are many ways to view the period. By exploring two fundamental ideas of Western civilization, democracy and religion, from three major alternative viewpoints that are all still eminently influential yet representative of the divergence between this and the previous period—those of Karl Marx, John Dewey, and Jacques Maritain—we will advance toward an answer. The selection of Marx needs no explanation, given his historical and contemporary global influence. Dewey represents the perspective of secular humanism that he not only helped define but promoted from its intellectual roots to an activist social program. Maritain represents a historically and religiously informed mind, and, in the tradition of his fellow countryman de Tocqueville, finds a close connection between the practice of religion and the viability of a democracy. This is not meant to be a mere textual exercise, for if one focuses on the global situation and finds there a contest between two superpowers, the deciding factor is not apt to be the presence or absence of a market economy. One has to probe beneath economics. From that perspective one can see that what our dominant intellectuals believe is not remarkably different from Marx's beliefs. Among the three, Dewey and Marx are closer to each other intellectually than are Dewey and Maritain.

It is not by accident that the Soviet Union distrusts and suppresses all but subservient forms of religion. No matter how removed from its initial Marxist charter, it is still bound to an ideology that is suspicious of all intermediary institutions. Since the beginning of Bolshevik control, religion has not merely represented an alternative ideology, it has been an obstacle to the progress of state control. "Believers" within the jurisdiction of the Soviet Union know what to expect of their government; this is less true in the West. In most Western countries the prevailing relationship between the ecclesial and the secular orders is thought to have been worked out long ago to the mutual benefit of both. But I am convinced that this belief is false. There is, in fact, a wide chasm between the agnosticism of the intellectuals who determine policy and the religious beliefs of the populace. And the former seem steadily to increase their influence on the laws that prevail in most Western nations.

In a previous century we might have considered our generation as an ebb tide in the rise and fall of cultures, certain that matters would right themselves in the course of time. But with a formidable military foe to the East bent on subduing the West, the situation is different today. The West must take stock of its resources, material and spiritual. The basic question is: Can a Western form of materialism, a liberal secularism, withstand the ideological assault of the East with which it does not differ in important respects? An examination of conscience is long overdue. We must attend to the wellsprings of our culture and to the role that religion has played in shaping that culture.

MARX'S CRITIQUE OF RELIGION

With respect to his views on religion, Marx was a product of the then current literature, greatly influenced by Hegel, but also by the theologians and biblical scholars David Strauss and Bruno Bauer.[2]

2. David Strauss (1808–1874) in his first major work, *Das Leben Jesu, kritisch bearbeitet*, 2 vols. (1835–1836; translated into English by George Eliot as *The Life of Jesus, Critically Examined*, 1846), denied the historical value of the Christian Gospels and rejected their supernatural claims, describing them as historical myths, unintentionally created, embodying the primitive hopes of the early Christian community. Shortly before the end of his life he published *Der alte und neue Glaube* (1872; translated into English as *The Old Earth and The New*, 1873), in which he ventured to replace Christianity with a Darwinian-influenced "scientific materialism." Bauer (1809–1882) similarly concluded that the Gospels were a record not of history but of human fantasies. Marx, when a student in Berlin, enrolled in one of Bauer's courses on the Prophet Isaiah.

From Hegel he accepted the notion that religion was a comprehensive account of human existence, somewhat more refined and precise than the ambiguous conception allowable to the poet but lacking the rigor and precision that only philosophy can provide. This perception of the quasi-poetic nature of religion was reinforced by Strauss and Bauer, who showed Marx how to understand biblical literature. In the 1830s and 1840s when this idea was relatively new, Strauss and Bauer convinced Marx that the Sacred Scriptures were simply a work of the human imagination. The message of the Scriptures is wholly metaphorical; it is merely an imaginative expression of men's moral ideas. Strauss and Bauer agreed with Hegel that God is only an imaginative way of looking at the Absolute. Accordingly, they were convinced that we must move beyond the traditional notion of God and recognize that religion is merely one way of portraying the relationship between man and his moral ideas—an imperfect way, Feuerbach would say, since religion puts moral ideas into a separate and distant realm. The task, says Feuerbach, is to recover the purely human meaning of religion. We have to bring religion back to its proper proportions as an expression of human moral aspirations.[3]

Marx was in strong agreement with Feuerbach's ideas. He declared: "For Germany, the criticism of religion is in the main complete, and criticism of religion is the premise of all criticism."[4] From now on the criticism of religion would be translated into criticism of politics and the social order. Marx meant that he accepted the current secular understanding of religion and did not wish to redo the work of Hegel, Strauss, Bauer, and Feuerbach. He thought it important, however, to add one note. Feuerbach had been extremely vague about the reason men tend to project their ideas into the objective order or tend to personify them in God. Marx, taking his cue from Feuerbach,

3. Ludwig Feuerbach, *Das Wesen des Christentums* (1854; translated into English as *The Essence of Christianity*).
4. Karl Marx, "Contribution to the Critique of Hegel's Philosophy of Law: Introduction," in Karl Marx and Friedrich Engels, *Collected Works* (New York: International Publishers, 1976), 3.175.

concluded that because of intolerable social conditions engendered by the capitalist economy, people were forced to project their moral ideal into an afterworld.

This addition gives a more precise meaning to Marx's concept of religion. In his essay on Hegel Marx calls religion the theoretical counterpart of private property. He uses the phrase "the perverted consciousness of a perverted world."[5] In the practical order we have the inhuman capitalist system that has resulted in the creation of the relief of religion in the theoretical order, or within our own reflection. Thus we have Marx's famous dictum "[Religion] is the opiate of the people." The best way to break the habit of religious reference is not to attack it head-on but to attack the practical conditions that engender the religious ideal. The true abolition of religion will occur automatically as a by-product of changing economics and social structures. Eventually, religion will wither away as capitalism withers away. Marx wrote:

> To be radical is to grasp things by the root. But for man the root is man himself. . . . The criticism of religion ends with the doctrine that man is the supreme being for man. It ends therefore with the categorical imperative to overthrow all those conditions in which man is an abased, enslaved, abandoned, contemptible being.[6]

If man and his world are self-created, then man cannot and should not expect to be liberated from his sufferings by some superhuman force—good or evil—but must set about freeing himself. In other words, belief in self-creation implies that one must also accept the idea of self-emancipation. The proletariat, in liberating the whole of mankind, can liberate itself as a class. This is the foundation of Marx's socialism. The struggle for fulfillment demands a militant humanism, with a goal nothing less than the formation of a classless society. The goal is projected not merely for German society but for mankind in general. Struggle is unavoidable. Marx is not hesitant to enlist hatred of the enemy in the name of love of neighbor: this is a

5. Ibid., 3.175.
6. Ibid., 3.182.

contradiction only if one does not see beyond the surface. For Marx, the humanist must approach the problem of love not abstractly but in a concrete way. He enjoins actions to frustrate and render harmless all those who, for the sake of their private interests, bar men's way to happiness. For in a society demarcated by class, they are enemies of mankind, whether their behavior is conscious or unconscious. Anyone who understands this truth must also realize that the enemies of brotherly love—enemies of the cause of humanity—must be fought actively, and this fight is inseparably connected with feelings of hate. Love of mankind, far from excluding hatred of those who act objectively in the name of the oppressed, in fact presupposes it.

JOHN DEWEY'S THOUGHT

John Dewey, another student of Hegel and Feuerbach, taught for half a century in three major universities and played a critical role in the training of public-school teachers. The longest part of Dewey's teaching career was spent at Columbia University, which at one time trained 95 percent of all superintendents of the U.S. public schools. Dewey transmitted his views to educators who wrote the manuals that were used in teachers' colleges throughout the country. The evangelical character of his philosophy, with its emphasis on utility, change, progress, and the future rather than the past, caught on and became the standard American credo.

The core of Dewey's philosophy can be found in a small book he produced near the end of his teaching career, *A Common Faith*. Dewey opens the book with the observation that throughout history men have been divided into two camps over the question of religion.[7] The focal point of this division is, in his view, "the supernatural."[8] Religionists maintain that no belief can be genuinely called religious that is not connected with the supernatural. Among believers there is a range of positions, from those of the Greek and Roman churches who hold that their dogmatic and sacramental systems are the only

7. John Dewey, *A Common Faith* (New Haven, Conn.: Yale University Press, 1934).
8. Ibid., 1.

sure means of access to the supernatural to the nondoctrinal theist or
mild deist. Also in this spectrum are many Protestant persuasions
that consider Scripture and conscience to be adequate avenues to religious truth. Those who are opposed to religion believe that the advance of anthropological and psychological studies has adequately
revealed the all-too-human sources of what has customarily been ascribed to the supernatural. The extremists in this group believe that
with the elimination of the supernatural not only historical religions
but everything of a religious nature must be dismissed.

Having appraised the situation, Dewey sets out to examine the
root cause of the division among men over the issue of religion. He
attempts to determine the reasons for the identification of the religious with the supernatural and the ensuing consequences. In so
doing, he offers another conception of the nature of the religious experience, one that separates it from the supernatural and its deriva-
tions. Removing these, in his view, will enable genuinely religious
human experience to develop freely on its own account. To this end,
in the first of the three chapters comprising *A Common Faith*, Dewey
introduces a distinction between the noun *religion* and the adjective
religious.[9] This distinction provides a hermeneutical tool for salvaging
that which is valid in "religious" experiences and freeing it from the
encumbrances resulting from efforts of various historical religions to
explain those experiences.[10] There is, in Dewey's estimation, a validity
to what is globally designated as religious experience. Yet such can be
had apart from historical religions, which have in fact hampered the
full import of such experiences.[11] If this valid core can be brought to
light, then men will stop thinking that they need religions to have religious experience.

Dewey acknowledges that religion plays a part in the lives of most
men. When fully embraced, it can modify one's attitude to life in a
significant and enduring way. In the face of adversity, religion can inspire a sense of peace and security; in a period of change, it can help

9. Ibid.   10. Ibid., 2.
11. Ibid., 3.

one to adjust and adapt. Unifying the diverse elements of experience, it can produce a vision that entails a voluntary submission to reality, not in stoic acceptance of what cannot be changed but through an interior redirection of will and attitude.[12]

While Dewey does not deny that a religious attitude has these and many other benefits, he does deny that these effects are peculiar to religion. Religions claim to bring about a change in attitude, yet institutions use these attitudes to create established churches, thereby changing moral faith into speculative faith and dogma. Moral faith entails the conviction that some spiritual end should be supreme over one's conduct; speculative faith, by contrast, attributes existence to that end, objectifying it and making it a truth for the intellect. Moral faith subordinates itself to an end that asserts a rightful claim over one's desires and purposes. It is practical, not intellectual. And while it goes beyond evidence, it has only the authority of a freely admitted ideal, not that of a fact. Institutional religions take this attitude, give objective reality to what was a moral ideal, and present it as the final reality at the heart of everything that exists. Religion has no difficulty in doing this, for desire has a powerful influence on intellectual beliefs. Men tend to believe what they ardently desire to be the case. At any rate, it is always easier to believe that the ideal is already a fact than to strive to make it so.[13]

Dewey regards the ideal of moral faith as fundamentally more religious than its reification in formal religions, for the ideal points to possibilities, and all human endeavor is better motivated by faith in what is possible than by adherence to what is already actual. Furthermore, such an ideal can be denotive of activity on the natural level. It is consonant with nature and does not divorce us from it. He states: "Faith in the continued disclosing of truth through directed cooperative human endeavor is more religious in quality than is any faith in a completed revelation." Thus, nature and man's experience in it become both the source and the object of the ideal that directs life. Any

12. Ibid., 16–17.
13. Ibid., 22.

activity pursued on behalf of an ideal end is religious in nature. The essentially irreligious attitude is that which attributes human achievement and purpose to man in isolation from nature and his fellow men. To regard the religious act in this way is to avoid the antagonism between religion and modern science:

> The positive lesson is that religious qualities and values, if they are real at all, are not bound up with any single item of intellectual assent, not even that of the existence of the God of theism; and that under existing conditions, the religious function in experience can be emancipated only through surrender of the whole notion of special truths that are religious by their own nature, together with the idea of peculiar avenues of access to such truths. For were we to admit that there is but one method for ascertaining fact and truth— that conveyed by the word "scientific" in its most general and generous sense—no discovery in any branch of knowledge and inquiry could then disturb the faith that is religious.[14]

It is worth noting that Dewey takes leave of William James's pragmatic approach to religious belief. James had been willing to grant some validity and meaning to a belief that produced satisfactory results in the life of the believer. Dewey is more cautious. He asks whether James employs the pragmatic method to discover value in the consequences of some religious formula that has its logical content already fixed or uses his pragmatic method to criticize, revise, and, ultimately, constitute the meaning of the formula.[15] Dewey is afraid lest some may understand pragmatism in the first sense and be disposed to attribute existential value to fixed dogmas that science has rendered untenable. If pragmatism is of any value in the religious sphere, its contribution is to replace faith in the supernatural order found in traditional religion with faith in the religious possibilities found in ordinary experience. There can be faith in intelligence, a devotion to the process by which truth is discovered, which would include a commitment both to science and to the worth and dignity of man. In this way, morality and religion will become an integral part

14. Ibid., 32–33.
15. See also Dewey's *Essays in Experimental Logic* (Chicago: University of Chicago Press, 1916), 313.

of everyday living, emerging out of nature and renovating the nature out of which it has arisen.

> The ideal ends to which we attach our faith are not shadowy and wavering. They assume concrete form in our understanding of our relations to one another and the values contained in these relations. We who now live are parts of a humanity that has reacted with nature. The things in civilization we most prize are not of ourselves. They exist by grace of the doings and sufferings of the continuous human community in which we are a link.[16]

Although Dewey's naturalism rules out a God who is responsible for the creation and governance of the universe, he nevertheless attempts to understand the concept "God," its origin and function. In this effort his work is not unlike that of Feuerbach, though it is not certain that Dewey ever read *The Essence of Christianity*. Putting the question to himself, "Are the ideals which move us genuinely ideal, or are they ideal only in contrast with our present estate?," he replies that the answer determines the meaning of the word "God." For Dewey, the word "God" denotes the unity of all the ideal ends arousing us to desire and action.[17]

According to Dewey, the origin of the traditional notion of God is easy enough to explain. There has always been in human nature a tendency to attribute prior existence to the objects of desire. Qualities are discovered in nature; goods are grouped in experience. Physical and psychological tendencies and activities are observed. These become entwined and united in human emotion and activity. It is not at all surprising that they should be thought to have a unified existence in their perfect state apart from the conditions under which we find them in experience.

To reseparate the various qualities may, indeed, be a difficult task, but the benefits to be derived from such an effort are many. In the first place, such a separation will free the religious attitude from tenets that are daily becoming more dubious. Witness the doubt that discoveries in geology and astronomy have cast on the doctrine of Creation, the

---

16. Dewey, *Faith*, 87.
17. Ibid., 42.

findings in modern biology that have rendered ancient conceptions of soul and body obsolete, and the explanations in psychology for what were once understood to be supernatural phenomena.

There is another inherent difficulty with the search for a personal God. Such an inquiry necessarily diverts man's attention and energy away from ideal values and the conditions by which they may be promoted. To the extent that we argue about the existence of God, we choose to spend valuable time on something from which no good can come in preference to devoting that time to more fruitful enterprises. History has shown that men have never fully used their power to advance the good life as long as they have waited upon some extrinsic power to remedy the situation for them. Such an attitude necessarily neglects the value intrinsic to the natural order. It leaves the world alone and seeks a solution for difficulty elsewhere. It substitutes personal prayer for cooperative effort.

If, on the other hand, we do not identify the ideal as a reified personal being, then this ideal may be thought of as being grounded in natural conditions. The ideal emerges as man's imagination idealizes existence with respect to the possibilities offered by thought and action.

There are values, goods, actually realized upon a natural basis—the goods of human association, of art and knowledge. The idealizing imagination seizes upon the most precious things found in the climacteric moments of experience and projects them. We need no external criterion and guarantee for their goodness. They are had, they exist as good, and out of them we frame our ideal ends.[18]

It is also true that these ideals do in a sense exist. They direct our actions and exist in the conditions that prompt their fulfillment. With a new ideal end, a new vision emerges and familiar objects are seen in new relations as they serve that end. As these values and ideals are dwelt upon and tested by practice, they are purified and strengthened. The values become more definitive and coherent and so have greater effect upon present conditions.

18. Ibid., 36.

Values and situations modify each other. We have neither ideals that are completely embodied in existence nor ideals that are merely rootless fancies. This active relation between the ideal and the actual is what Dewey calls "God." By so conceiving God, he seeks to make man a citizen of earth and to restore him to the fatherland in which he has his roots and his destiny.

This concept of God encompasses all the possibilities that nature exhibits. These possibilities beckon each and every man. They point to the possibility of a fuller and more perfect reality as a result of action aimed at bettering the natural situation. They are perceived by the imagination, clarified by the method of science, and tested and modified by experience. Thus reshaped and purified, they in turn shape and purify the activity that they inspire.

Criticizing the traditional idea of God, Dewey cannot see how a God who exists apart from the universe can in any way be a God for man. To direct man to believe in such a God is to dehumanize and denaturalize him. Dewey thought that even the Absolute Mind of Hegel, immanent in nature, denied the reality of the finite and the natural.

In chapter 3, the final chapter of *A Common Faith*, Dewey addresses what he calls "The Human Abode of the Religious Function." There he observes that the core of religion has generally been found in rites and ceremonies. But given the secular character of our present society, few persons can understand, without the use of imagination, what it means socially for a religion to permeate all the customs and activities of group life. Since the Renaissance there has been a shift in the social center of gravity from the sacred to the secular. Today the conditions under which people meet and act together are thoroughly secular. Interests and values are neither derived from nor related to the church. Religion is a matter of personal choice and not a matter of social order.

This is not to be regretted, however. When religion was grounded in the supernatural, a sharp line between the religious and the secular prevailed. In Dewey's view, religion necessitates no such division, for when the religious function is emancipated from religion the distinction between the sacred and the secular fades. Protestantism has rightly emphasized the fact that the relation of man to God is primarily an individual matter, a matter of personal choice and responsibility. Beliefs and rites that make the relation between man and God a collective and institutional affair erect barriers between the human soul and the divine spirit. When primacy is given to the direct relation of the conscience and will to God, religion is placed on its only real and solid foundation. Social change is better accomplished through the common effort of men and women than through any institutional effort. Contrary to a popular misperception, Dewey argues that the secularization of society has not been accompanied by increasing degeneration. Rather it is the forces that are independent of organized religion that have worked to enhance human relations and have resulted in intellectual and aesthetic development. In fact, the churches have lagged behind in most social movements.

Dewey is convinced that a depreciation of natural social values results from a comparison with a supernatural source. His objection to supernaturalism is that it stands in the way of an effective realization of the sweep and depth of the implications of natural human relations. "It stands in the way of using the means that are in our power to make radical changes in these relations."[19]

Though Dewey discounts religion as the "only finally dependable source of motivation," he would nevertheless have the churches show a more active interest in social affairs. But they would have to do so on equal footing with other institutions. This participation would require their surrender of any claims to an exclusive and authoritative position. "Secular interests and activities have grown up outside of organized religions and are independent of their authority. The hold of these interests upon the thoughts and desires of men has cowed the social importance of organized religions into a corner and the area of this corner is decreasing."[20]

19. Ibid., 80.
20. Ibid., 83.

Dewey suggests that thoughtful persons should work to emancipate the religious quality of experience from the accretions that have grown up about it that limit its credibility and influence. Philosophers should develop and make explicit those principles and values inherent in civilization to which the race is heir, values that are inherent in the continuous human community of which the present generation is but a link. In these are contained all the elements for a religious faith that is not confined to sect, class, or race. "Such a faith has always been implicitly the common faith of mankind. It remains to make it explicit and militant."[21]

Democracy as understood by Dewey does not refer to a system of balloting. Nor is it a government with checks and balances intended to prevent the majority from running roughshod over the rights of a minority.[22] Rather it is a method for dissolving majorities and minorities; it is a way of conceptually resolving differences. The majority must give up its claim to truth, correctness, or rightness in the face of serious challenge. Numerical strength does not provide a warrant. Unrestrained legislation that favors one point of view is not justified by the fact that an overwhelming majority shares that viewpoint as long as a minority exists with different opinions.

Democracy calls for compromise, conceptually and practically. Between affirmation and negation lies the "truth." The truth is not simply expedient, nor is it to be anchored in a historically given constitution. A constitution is itself not strictly an immutable document; it must be interpreted in the light of contemporary circumstances. Appeals to a Christian past, to a Christian heritage, to a Christian rationale for our present law are not to be admitted. Problems have to be resolved in the present context. Our forebears have no hold on us. Like Marx, Dewey provides a purely naturalistic account of religion limited to a progressivist view of human nature and history.

---

21. Ibid., 87.
22. Jacques Maritain, *Democracy and Education* (New York: Macmillan, 1961), 88ff.

JACQUES MARITAIN

The views of Jacques Maritain developed out of his study of Aristotle and Thomas Aquinas. In common with the Greeks, he emphasizes moral virtue as a condition for the achievement of the commonwealth. As a philosopher, he subscribes to a natural-law outlook; as a Christian, he believes in divine revelation. In *Man and the State*, a small work that includes his Walgreen Lectures at the University of Chicago, Maritain makes an important distinction among "nation," "body politic," and "state."[23]

As Maritain defines it, a *nation* is something ethicosocial. It is a natural structure, a community, and has its basis in regional, ethnic, linguistic, class, and/or religious affinities.[24] It is not identical to a society. A *society* is deliberately brought into being as its members organize to achieve common ends. Maritain writes:

An ethnic community, generally speaking, can be defined as a community of patterns of feeling rooted in the physical soil of the origin of the group as well as in the moral soil of history; it becomes a *nation* when this factual situation enters the sphere of self awareness . . . when the ethnic group *becomes conscious* of the fact that it constitutes a community of patterns of feeling . . . and possesses its own unity and individuality, its own will to endure its existence.[25]

On the basis of Maritain's language, it is obvious that the Ukrainian people are a nation, but it is not so obvious that the United States is a nation.

Both the body politic and the state are societies, yet although the terms "body politic" and "state" are often used synonymously, they should be distinguished. They are related as a whole is to its parts. The body politic is the whole. The primary condition for the existence of the body politic is a common sense of justice, though friendship may be said to be its life-giving element. A civic outlook requires a sense of devotion and mutual love as well as a sense of justice and law. These attitudes of mind and will develop as part of a

---

23. Jacques Maritain, *Man and the State* (Chicago: University of Chicago Press, 1951).
24. Ibid., 2ff.
25. Ibid., 5.

heritage that is preserved by mediating or secondary institutions. Nothing matters more to the life and preservation of the body politic than the accumulated energy and historical continuity of the national community that it has caused to exist. Common inherited experience and moral and intellectual instinct are its basis. The political life as well as the very existence and prosperity of the body politic depend on the vitality of family, economic, cultural, educational, and religious life.[26]

The state in Maritain's analysis is the part of the body politic that is concerned with the common welfare, the public order, and the administration of public affairs. It is the part that specializes in the interest of the whole. It is not comprised of men but is rather a set of institutions combined into a unified machine. The goals of the state are implemented by experts or specialists in public order and welfare. It constitutes an impersonal, lasting superstructure. When functioning properly, the state is rational and bound by law. As an instrument of the body politic, the state is an agency entitled to use power and coercion. Although the state is the superior part of society, it does not transcend its members entirely; it exists for the sake of man. The state is neither a whole nor a person, nor does it hold rights. The common good of the political society is the final aim of the state and comes before the state's goal of the maintenance of the public order. The state overreaches its mandate when it ascribes to itself a goal simply of self-preservation and growth.

When the state identifies itself with the whole of political society and takes upon itself the performance of tasks that normally pertain to society or its organs, we have what Maritain calls the "paternalistic state." From the political point of view, the state is at its best when it is most restrained in seeking the common good. When it takes upon itself the organizing, controlling, or managing of the economic, commercial, industrial, or cultural forms, it has transcended its skill and competence. If the state attempts to become a boss or a manager in business or industry, or a patron of the arts, or

26. Ibid., 11.

a leading spirit in the affairs of culture, science, and philosophy, it betrays its nature.[27]

The state receives its authority from a community of people. The people have a natural right to self-government. They exercise this right when they establish a constitution, written or unwritten. The people are the multitude of persons who unite under just laws by mutual friendship for their common good. But the people not only constitute a body politic; each has a spiritual soul and a supratemporal destiny. The people are above the state; the state exists for the people.

Maritain takes pains to emphasize the primacy of the spiritual. From the religious point of view, the common good of the body politic implies an intrinsic, though indirect, ordination to something that transcends it. The state is under the command of no superior authority, but the order of eternal life is superior to the order of temporal life. The two orders need not create a conflict. From a secular perspective, the church is an institution concerned with the spiritual life of the believer. "From the point of view of the political common good, the activities of citizens as members of the church have an impact on that common good."[28] Thus the church in one sense serves the body politic, but in another and important sense transcends it.

The church and the body politic cannot live and develop in sheer isolation from and in ignorance of each other. The same person is simultaneously a member of the body politic and a member of a church. An absolute division is both impossible and absurd. There must be cooperation, but what form should the cooperation take? It is evident that we no longer live in a sacral age. If classical antiquity or medieval Christianity were characterized by a unity of faith and if that unity of faith were required for a political unity, such does not now seem to be the case. Religious plurality is a fact, and the modern situation seems to demonstrate that religious unity is not a prerequisite for political unity. Nor can the church wield authority over the state, calling presidents, prime ministers, dictators, or nations to

27. Ibid., 21.
28. Ibid., 152.

account. Indeed, the opposite is frequently the case, with the church demanding freedom within the political order to develop her own institutions.

Maritain leaves unresolved the problem of the moral unity of a people. While he cannot opt for the "common faith" described by John Dewey, a naturalistic credo that goes beyond the merely political, he is tempted by the "civic faith" delineated by his friend John Courtney Murray in *We Hold These Truths*.[29] But how are the wellsprings of conscience and civic faith to be maintained? Before his death Maritain was to witness the breakdown of inherited morality discussed in the opening pages of this essay. A common Christian outlook on matters such as civic decorum, contraception, divorce, abortion, homosexuality, pornography, and capital punishment gave way. The morality commonly affirmed in the nineteenth century came to be widely denied. The denial has since been translated into law, if not by legislation, then by the courts as they have interpreted the law.

Maritain recognizes that if religious institutions are to possess any authority, it will be through their moral influence as their teachings touch man's conscience. Still this spiritual influence may be checked by an opposite course of action, chosen by other citizens. But Maritain believes that a free exchange of ideas, despite possible setbacks, is a surer way of attaining influence in the long run. The church is less likely to lose her independence. If the state were to be enlisted to implement ecclesiastical goals, it is likely that it would serve its own purposes first. History teaches us that the secular arm, always eager to exercise control, takes the initiative. Maritain proposes that the church should be free to educate and that she should be positioned to compete as an equal in the marketplace of ideas. He is conscious, however, that such may not be the case, even in his primary paradigm, the United States.

In the twentieth century governments have taken upon themselves more and more of the role of an immense and tutelary power,

29. John Courtney Murray, *We Hold These Truths* (New York: Sheed & Ward, 1960).

catering to all needs. In an age of limited government, before government began to play a role in ordering a vast range of social and economic activities, the doctrine of "strict separation" or of "a benevolent neutrality" that prohibited the government from giving aid of any kind to religion may have made some sense. But in an age of positive government, equating neutrality with a strict "no aid" position may be less tenable. The Framers of the Constitution expected religion to play a part in the established social order and also assumed that the state would play a minimal role in forming that order. In our own time, the question of how to treat religious groups and interests has become a fundamentally different one.

The issue is not clearly resolved. Maritain affirms, on the one hand, that "freedom of inquiry, even at the risk of error, is the normal condition for men to access truth, so that freedom to search for God in their own way, for those who have been brought up in ignorance or semi-ignorance of Him, is the normal condition in which to listen to the message of the Gospel."[30] Yet he is convinced that "willingly or unwillingly states will be obliged to make a choice for or against the Gospel. They will be shaped either by the totalitarian spirit or by the Christian spirit."[31]

The West, symbolically at least, continues in many ways to reflect its Christian heritage. Thus, the public acknowledgment of God's existence, Maritain believes, is good and should be maintained. It is to be expected that a public expression of common faith will assume the form of that Christian confession to which history and the traditions of a people are most vitally linked. The citizens who are unbelievers will have only to realize that the body politic as a whole is just as free with regard to the private expression of their nonreligious conviction.

If Maritain has a fault, it lies in his idealism, in his optimism that good will and common sense will prevail and that public assessments of the value of religion will result in conclusions similar to those reached by him. He believes that these conclusions have been reached

---

30. Maritain, *Man and the State*, 161–62.
31. Ibid., 159

by reflective men in every period of the history of the West. Maritain may also be accused of an excessively optimistic view of the United States. He seemed to ignore the fact that manifestations of religion vary and are not all beneficent. If assessors of the value of religion are not of one mind as they measure its contributions to the social order, the fault may lie in part with the division and feebleness of religious witness and institutions themselves. Religion seems more to follow than to lead, to sanction what is rather than to encourage progress. But even if this sobering view is more correct than Maritain's, the question needs to be posed: What should the state's attitude toward religion be? If social observers are right in decrying the loss of a common religious vision, then an assessment of this social fact ought to be made a public concern. For it cannot be assumed that religion's loss of cultural influence is a social good.

Maritain's contribution to the debate shows religion's indispensable function in society and the state's concomitant obligation to provide an impartial and unencumbered aid to ensure enlightened internal development within religious bodies, development that makes a superior cultural contribution possible. Maritain's genius lies in his interpretation of a tradition that has its roots in the Gospels yet has developed through twenty centuries in the West. It is a tradition that recognizes the two interrelated orders of church and state and the common social good that must prevail when inevitable tensions arise. While political contexts vary, man is by nature a citizen of two cities. Maritain in effect says that the best government recognizes this fact and impedes growth in neither domain.

CONCLUSION

Although Dewey, Marx, and Maritain do not represent the full spectrum of theological and social views, they do represent very different intellectual directions. Obviously, religion is more than a community of worshipers paying a commonly acknowledged debt to an unseen God. Religion carries within it its own intellectual tradition. The very awareness of God's existence presupposes some kind of consideration, be it metaphysical in the classical Greek sense or hermeneutical in the Hebraic manner. Included within those traditions are attitudes toward ritual and sacred art, from vestment, statuary, and architecture to painting and music. Since revelation is given over time, religion entails a historical sense and a relationship to the past. As Dewey correctly saw, religion robs the present of its uniqueness, for both speculative and practical wisdom suggest that human nature has not changed since antiquity and that it will face familiar challenges in the future. No one who is acquainted with the Hebrew Scriptures can believe in the unlimited perfectibility of man or society. And it will not do to give a Voltairean romantic interpretation to the sacred texts and rites of a people, regarding them all as poetic expressions of something that can be stated more accurately by philosophy. The religious mind holds that "God is" and that certain things flow from that belief. A flat denial that such a belief can be true (no one purports to offer proof) is more than an intellectual sleight of hand. In the political realm, this denies the believer the full rights of citizenship as it refuses to take his views seriously.

While the ultimate debate may center on the existence of God, the immediate contest concerns the role of religion in society. Those who hold that the religious mind is mistaken are not likely to place much confidence in its role as a bearer of the culture. Marx and Dewey believed that the past would be overcome as men moved into a future shaped by technological progress. Both Dewey and Marx might have felt justified in excluding religion from education, but the cost of this position in modern society has been heavy. Not only are the great majority of people illiterate regarding religion but, conversely, religion is deprived of the aid of the best minds.

The people, cut off from the tradition that has produced their culture, grope for a source of enlightenment. Who would claim that the worldview once presented by Christianity has been adequately replaced by the secular mind that challenged it? Dewey's common faith has not replaced Christianity in any important respect and no longer inspires popular confidence. The question is: Can European or Western civilization endure apart from its historic roots? Need the nonbeliever in order to feel secure insist that the heritage acknowledged by the great majority remain a dim and impotent intellectual force, or is accommodation possible? Can the secular mind acknowledge the cultural and moral importance of the Western religious tradition and allow it to proceed unencumbered, or must it claim for itself exclusive control of the wellsprings of culture? These questions need to be addressed.

FIVE

JOHN COURTNEY MURRAY ON
THE TRUTHS WE HOLD

In its cover story of December 12, 1960, *Time* magazine used John Courtney Murray to symbolize the coming of age of American Catholicism.[1] John F. Kennedy had just been elected president of the United States and would become the first Catholic to hold that office. Significantly, Murray was pictured against the backdrop of a sixteenth-century manuscript of Robert Bellarmine's *Disputationes de Controversiis Christianae Fidei.* A diagonal yellow banner announced the title of the cover essay: "U.S. Catholics and the State." Murray, a theology professor at the Jesuit seminary Woodstock College, was then a major academic participant in a debate concerning the nature of American democracy and its presuppositions. It was the time of a vigorous and self-confident Catholicism. Issues were sharply defined as Murray challenged both secular liberal and Protestant social and political thought.

Many things have changed since Murray wrote. In the political order Vietnam was yet to come; in the religious order the culmination of the Second Vatican Council was six years off. Murray never lived to witness the fall of Saigon or to experience a Church recreated in the "spirit" of Vatican II. He was sixty-three years old in 1967 when he was stricken with a fatal heart attack while riding in a taxi in his native New York City. The subsequent collapse of the American will to prosecute to its successful conclusion a war in Southeast Asia would not have surprised him; but the dissolution of

---

1. *Time,* 12 December 1960, p. 65.

his beloved Catholic Church into a friendly, mindless, liturgically impoverished religious body would have come as a shock. Murray had more confidence in the Catholic Church than he did in the United States, principally, because, in his view, the Church possessed a tradition much wider and deeper than any that America had elaborated, and, with a history many times as long, it commanded the intellectual resources indispensable to the formulation of a public philosophy. He was under no illusion that the United States could, in fact, develop a public philosophy, but he was convinced that the country needed one. He was confident that the materials required were available in the natural law tradition carried within the Catholic intellectual community. He was pleased to observe that the Catholic Church in America was not divided into Left and Right as was the case in France. With confidence he could represent an essentially unified Church, articulating what he took to be a common outlook with respect to the fundament of law. That fundament in its ideal formulation is what he called the "public philosophy," and insofar as it was broadly accepted, he was willing to call it the "public consensus."

No doubt the experience of the World War II years had led many public figures to reflect on the difference between the American republic and the totalitarian regimes that it had just defeated and others that were seen as emerging. The debate was many sided, and its participants represented a wide range of disciplines from philosophy and theology to sociology and economics. Prominent among those engaged in this debate were Mortimer Adler, Will Herberg, Sidney Hook, Walter Lippmann, Jacques Maritain, and Gustav Weigel.[2]

---

2. Mortimer Adler, *Philosophy, Law, and Jurisprudence* (Chicago: Encyclopaedia Britannica, 1961), and *Scholasticism and Politics* (New York: Macmillan, 1940); Will Herberg, *Judaism and Modern Man* (New York: Atheneum, 1970), and *Protestant—Catholic—Jew* (Garden City, N.Y.: Doubleday, 1955); Sidney Hook, *Political Power and Personal Freedom* (New York: Criterion Books, 1959), *Reason, Social Myths, and Democracy* (New York: John Day, 1940), and *Education for Modern Man* (New York: Dial Press, 1946); Walter Lippmann, *Essays in the Public Philosophy* (Boston: Little Brown, 1955); Jacques Maritain, *Christianity and Democracy* (London: Geoffrey Bles, 1946), and *Man and the State* (Chicago: University of Chicago Press, 1951); Gustav Weigel, *Faith and Understanding in America* ((New York: Macmillan, 1959).

There was a sense that things were changing and that it was necessary to elucidate, to use Lincoln's term, "the American proposition." In retrospect, it is clear that the nation was moving from a Christian past to a secular future, a drift that was even then dimly perceived. Many thought that America was entering a state of ideological disarray, having lost the certitudes that formerly were provided by metaphysics and religious faith. Throughout the 1950s the sociologist Will Herberg could say, "To be American is to be religious, and to be religious is to be religious in one of three ways, as a Protestant, as a Catholic or as a Jew." Sidney Hook would dissent. America is not simply a pluralist society in the sense of religiously plural. For Hook, to be an American is to be religious or irreligious.

Murray, an attractive and articulate speaker, was a frequent lecturer throughout the country. In 1960 he collected a number of his speeches and published them as *We Hold These Truths*.[3] In his book, Murray described for a Catholic audience the truths they held as Americans, as Catholics, and as Catholic-Americans. But in a sense Murray was after bigger fish. He wished to find those truths that *all* Americans presumably shared by virtue of citizenship. The basic problem, he was convinced, was not one of the relation of church to state, but of the intellectual unity required for a nation to act. The nature of the "public philosophy" is the issue that would bring Hook, Lippmann, and Murray into the same forum. All three were to ask: Is there a constitutional consensus whereby the people acquire an identity, a sense of purpose as a collective, sufficient to serve as the basis for action? "Can we or can we not," Murray wrote, "achieve a successful conduct of our national affairs, foreign and domestic, in the absence of a consensus that will set our purposes; furnish a standard of judgment on policies; and establish the proper conditions for political dialogue?"[4] For Murray, the civic consensus is constructed neither of psychological rationalizations nor of economic interest nor of purely pragmatic working hypotheses. "It is an ensemble of substantive truths, a structure of basic knowl-

3. John Courtney Murray, *We Hold These Truths* (New York: Sheed & Ward, 1960).
4. *Time*, 12 December 1960.

edge, an order of elementary affirmations that reflect realities inherent in the order of existence."[5] But he recognized that any systematic formulation of these truths is apt to meet resistance.

If there was once an American consensus, if the Founding Fathers knew what they meant by "liberty," by "law," and by "God," that consensus does not exist today. "The ethic which launched Western constitutionalism and endured long enough as a popular heritage to give essential form to the American system of government has now ceased to sustain the structure and direct the action of this constitutional commonwealth."[6] Murray was convinced that the grounds for such a consensus still exist, at least ideally, in the natural law philosophy of Aristotle, the Stoics, and Aquinas. It is that tradition, reflected in the writings of Richard Hooker, John Locke, and others, that provided the principles on which the nation was founded. It is a philosophical tradition that surmounts religious difference, an intellectual tradition that is confident that the order of nature can be discerned and that what is good for man can be established.

For Murray, political life aims at a common good that is superior to a mere collection of individual goods. The fruit of common effort must, of course, flow back to the individual. But he was disturbed by the following question: In the absence of a common way of looking at things, can there be an ascertainable common good? Murray's answer contrasts sharply with that entertained by John Dewey and Sidney Hook, both of whom subscribed to an essentially Hobbesian account of the social order. From the point of view of Hobbes, society is not one entity but a collection of action groups each pressing for advantage. According to Hobbes, the source of government is the consent of those governed taken one by one. The individual is the sole source of the right or of the good, and as an autonomous agent is subject neither to given norms nor to a naturally determined end. Hobbes makes no attempt to subordinate the individual act of self-aggrandizement to the public good. Self-interest, he holds, is not only

5. Murray, *These Truths*, 9.
6. Ibid.

the dominant motive in politics, but enlightened self-interest is the proper remedy for social ills. Men, he believes, are constituted differently in biography, temperament, and intelligence, and consequently identify the good for themselves in radically different ways. Self-interest is not to be taken as evidence of moral defect but as evidence of disparate personality. In the absence of a common good, separate from and superior to the private goods of individual men, the function of government becomes that of conflict management. Given the fact that litigious subjects are likely to press for special privileges and exemptions for themselves, bargaining and negotiating are natural features of public life. The sovereign is not the representative of the common will; he is the common object of separate wills. In the exercise of his authority, the sovereign is restrained by the diverse purposes of his subjects. The sovereign assists his subjects in the pursuit of happiness not by defining the goals that the members of society ought collectively to pursue, but by removing obstacles to happiness, privately defined. Public order thus has its sources in negotiations between individually situated political actors.

In North America this Hobbesian analysis of society is nowhere more evident than in the area of sexual morality. Sexual union has been made a purely personal affair with society's interest downplayed. Abortion, divorce, homosexuality, and pornography are sanctioned as if their presence had no social repercussions. It is also evident in various rights movements where an invocation of the common good is thought to be a betrayal of a social agenda. In both theory and practice, those who defend special interests do not acknowledge any need to attend to the perceptions or reactions of others who do not share their view. Rights are to be pushed no matter what the consequences. This, in spite of the fact that many communities are presently suffering from the effects of a one-sided pressing of rights, a pressing that in the making identified success with the achievement of a particular gain, even if that gain meant the loss of the setting wherein that gain might have become meaningful. To offer one notorious example, in Washington, D.C., in the 1950s a federal judge struck down a "track system" in the public schools of the District of Columbia

(D.C.) because its stated purpose, to discriminate between the gifted and the not-so-gifted, also seemed to discriminate against blacks. The result was the flight of white families to other school districts and a D.C. public school system in which 97 percent of the students enrolled were from black families. The gifted black students who remained in the system were themselves put at a disadvantage by the judge's ruling, which prevented instruction on the basis of talent. A judicial emphasis on equality of treatment failed to recognize that the common good demands appropriate education for the gifted. After decades of inferior education, the D.C. school system is only now beginning to reverse its losses. It is doubtful that Hobbes himself would have looked with favor on the extremes to which his doctrine has been carried.

To return to my theme: In the absence of a common way of looking at things, can the notion of the common good play a role in thinking about the ends of government? Lord Patrick Devlin, the English jurist, reflecting on the social order in his own country, not unlike Murray, saw the need for a public philosophy that would provide secular, as opposed to the fading Christian, underpinnings for his nation's laws and culture.[7] Devlin, also like Murray, realized that any single candidate for the title "public philosophy" is unlikely to gain universal acceptance. But one may ask if it is necessary that a philosophy prevail in order to exercise a beneficial influence in the social setting. Is it not sufficient that it keeps alive and defends a vantage point? May not calls to attend to the common good have their effect on policy even if the philosophy underlying the concept is imperfectly understood or flatly rejected? Murray's answer is that a working consensus need not embrace all sectors of the society and that it need not embrace equally those that do share it. The existence of intellectual conflict, suggests Murray, is not evidence that there cannot be agreement on very important matters. The acceptance of principles such as the rule of law, the separation of powers, the freedom of belief, the

7. Lord Patrick Delvin, *The Enforcement of Morals* (London: Oxford University Press, 1965).

freedom of association, and the representation of beliefs and inter-ests does not depend on metaphysical agreement, although these principles obviously need a defense. Sidney Hook, normally an oppo-nent, would concur. The danger, of course, is that in the absence of a set of commonly acknowledged principles special-interest groups may prevail. Irving Babbit saw this when he wrote in *Democracy and Leadership*, "No movement illustrates more clearly than the suppos-edly Democratic movement the way in which the will of highly orga-nized and resolute minorities may prevail over the will of the inert and unorganized mass."[8]

Interestingly, when Murray attempts to articulate the truths we hold as a people, the list is surprisingly long. On his account, we can readily identify the broad purposes of the nation, or, if you will, the aims of government. With respect to means, standards of judgment may vary and there will be policy differences, but we can speak about these things because there is a basis of communication, a universe of discourse. "We hold in common a concept of the nature of law and its relationship to reason and to will, to social fact and to political pur-pose. We understand the complex relationship between law and free-dom."[9] As a people we have in common an idea of justice, we believe in the principle of consent, we distinguish between law and morality, and we understand the relationship between law and freedom. We also recognize criteria of good law, that is, norms of jurisprudence. As a people we "grasp the notion of law as a force for orderly change as well as social stability."[10] Most law is rooted in the shared idea of the personal dignity or sacredness of man, *res sacra homo*. This sacred-ness guarantees him certain immunities and endows him with certain empowerments, and this is universally recognized.

Neither ideally nor in the United States need consensus prevent dissent. In the United States the dissenter is not placed beyond the pale of social or civil rights. Those who refuse to subscribe often

8. Irving Babbitt, *Democracy and Leadership* (New York: Houghton Mifflin, 1924), 290–91.
9. Murray, *These Truths*, 81.
10. Ibid.

come from the ranks of the literati and have the media at their dispo-sal. They are not only the academicians and the professional students of philosophy, politics, economics, and history but also the politi-cians, writers, journalists, and clergy. Murray calls them "clerks." Ox-ford professor John Gray calls them "intellectuals" and is wary of them because of their nonconformist tendencies.[11] They lack the same stake in society that those responsible either for economic pro-duction or for governance possess. They are apt to be disruptive in any scenario.

We need to readdress Murray's big question: "Can we or can we not achieve a successful conduct of our affairs, foreign and domestic, in the absence of a consensus that will set our purpose, furnish a stan-dard of judgment on policies, and establish the proper condition for political dialogue?" Murray's answer was "No." In Murray's judgment, the United States of his time was doing badly. He uses the words "in-secure" and "political bankruptcy." Writing thirty years later, John Sil-ber begins the introduction to his volume *Straight Shooting* with the observation: "Our society is in trouble and we all know it. We know that something is terribly wrong—the way we might know in our own bodies that we are seriously ill."[12] Silber is forced to address many of the issues previously explored by Murray and comes to many of the same conclusions. Only now the nation is further downstream and its problems are more serious, showing how prescient was Murray's analysis. The cause of our weakness, Murray thought, is not simply the Soviet threat. If the communist empire and communist ideology were to disintegrate overnight, our problem would not be solved. We would be worse off in many ways. Anticommunism is not a public philosophy. This is never more evident, he thought, than in discussions concerning the structure, content, and orientation of military policies. We have not articulated, for example, the political and moral ends for which we are prepared to use force. In 1960

11. John Gray, "Society and Intellectuals: The Persistence of Estrangement and Wishful Thinking," in *The Many Faces of Socialism* (New Brunswick, N.J.: Transaction Books, 1987).

12. John Silber, *Straight Shooting* (New York: Harper & Row, 1989), xi.

Murray could cite Henry Kissinger's 1957 book *Nuclear Weapons and Foreign Policy,* and its chapter "The Need of Doctrine," in support of his own outlook: "It is not true that America can intelligently construct and morally put to use a defense establishment in the absence of a public philosophy concerning the use of force as a moral and political act."[13] Until we can articulate an American consensus with regard to our truths, our purposes, and our values, unless we can agree on fundamentals, "public policy will continue to be projected out of a vacuum in the governmental mind into a vacuum in the popular mind."[14] The only bright spot is that in the absence of intellectual agreement, our instinctive wisdom permits us to cope and survive.

Murray is careful to note that consensus does not mean majority opinion:

Public opinion is a shorthand phrase expressing the fact that a large body of the community has reached or may reach specific conclusions in some particular situation. Those conclusions are spontaneously, perhaps emotionally reached usually from some unstated but, very real premises. The "public consensus" is the body of these general unstated premises which come to be accepted. It furnishes the basis for public opinion.[15]

The consensus is a doctrine or a judgment that commands public agreement on the merits of the arguments for it. "The consensus is not in any sense an ideology; its close relation to concrete experience rescues it from that fate."[16] The public consensus is a moral conception. "Only the theory of natural law is able to give an account of the public moral experience that is the public consensus. The consensus itself is simply the tradition of reason as emergent in developing form in the special circumstances of American political-economic life."[17]

Murray is aware that the doctrine of natural law is associated with Catholicism. He is quick to point out that the doctrine has no Catholic presuppositions. Its presuppositions are threefold: "that man is intelligent; that reality is intelligible; and that reality as grasped by intelligence imposes on the will an obligation that it be obeyed in its

13. Murray, *These Truths,* 91.   14. Ibid., 95.35
15. Ibid., 102–3.   16. Ibid., 106.
17. Ibid., 109.

demands for action or abstention."[18] The assumption is that rational human nature works competently in most men, although intellectual judgment alone is not enough. Not only knowledge but rectitude of judgment is required.

"Natural law theory does not pretend to do more than it can, which is to give a philosophical account of the moral experience of humanity and to lay down a charter of essential humanism."[19] It does not show the individual the way to sainthood, but only to temporal fulfillment. "It does not promise to transform society into the city of God on earth, but only to prescribe, for the purposes of law and social custom, the minimum of morality which must be observed by the member of society, if the social environment is to be human and habitable."[20] To inquire what natural law is means to inquire, on the one hand, what the human mind is and what it can know and, on the other hand, what human society is and to what ends it should work. Its hallmark is its empirical character and its fidelity to evidence derived from common experience and from the sciences. Natural law is best considered as a meta-ethic. As a meta-ethic it amounts to this advice: Proceed with confidence that intelligence can determine in a general way what is good for the human race. Put another way, natural law encourages the observer to look for regularities in nature, human and nonhuman. Regularity indicates structure, and a knowledge of structure will in turn yield functional explanation, which has a major role in the determination of moral norms. Systematic reflection on human nature will reveal certain constants that are the same everywhere and remain the same from generation to generation. But there are variables, too, that differ with culture, economic situation, and even topography. But Murray was engaged in formulating a public philosophy not on a global scale but for the nation.

An interesting study of contrasting views on the nature of the public philosophy and its justification is provided by an examination

18. Ibid.   19. Ibid., 297.
20. Ibid.

of the views of Murray and Sidney Hook. For Murray, democracy is an effective mode of government. The democratic charter is not to be made an object of faith. The Constitution and the articles of its First Amendment, "Congress shall make no law respecting an establishment of religion nor prohibiting the free exercise thereof . . . ," are articles of peace, not part of a secular credo that renounces a role for religion in civic affairs. "If history makes one thing clear it is that these clauses were the twin children of social necessity, the necessity of creating a social environment, protected by law, in which men of differing faiths might live together in peace."[21] The American solution to the relationship between church and state was purely political. Among the various churches vying for allegiance none was to be preferred for the nation as a whole; although in the beginning of the American Republic nine states had established churches, eventually this federal principle was to be applied to the states as well. The result was political unity and stability without uniformity of religious belief and practice. The Gallic "One law, one faith, one king," had been replaced by "political unity in the midst of religious plurality." But it does not follow from this that political unity can long endure in the absence of a moral consensus. "Nor has experience yet shown how, if at all, this moral consensus can survive amid all the ruptures of religious division, whose tendency is inherently disintegrative of all consensus and community."[22]

In 1960 Murray could write: "In America we have been rescued from the disaster of ideological parties."[23] Where such parties exist, the struggle for office becomes a struggle for power, for the means by which the opposing ideology may be destroyed. In contrast to certain Latin American countries, the American experience of political unity has been striking, and to this unity the First Amendment has made a unique contribution. Murray is convinced that the Catholic Church has profited from the American arrangement. In Latin countries the Church has alternately experienced privilege and persecution. Where

---

21. Ibid., 57.   22. Ibid., 73.
23. Ibid.

it is thought that the business of government is the fostering of the commonwealth as ascertained by the Church, the fortunes of the Church wax and wane with the transfer of political power. "In contrast, American government has not undertaken to represent transcendental truth in any of the versions of it current in American society."[24] It has not allied itself with one faith over another, but it has represented a core of commonly shared moral values. In a religiously plural society, government must be neutral; it cannot set itself up as a judge of religious truth. But pluralism is the root of certain problems. How much pluralism and what kinds of pluralism can a pluralist society stand? Thus arises the debate concerning the need for a public philosophy.

As noted, Murray's public philosophy is one grounded in the natural law which he believes is accessible to all, believer and nonbeliever, Protestant and Catholic, although he recognizes that the Catholic Church in a unique way is the bearer of the natural law outlook. The principal function of the public philosophy is the articulation of a set of standards external to the civic order against which the actions of the state can be measured. The standard is right reason shaped by a time-transcending metaphysics and anthropology.

Orestes Brownson, writing in 1856, was similarly confronted with the problem of holding the state accountable, but he came to a conclusion that Murray rejected. In an essay entitled "The Church and the Republic," Brownson argued that the church is necessary to the state.[25] Surveying American political and social life, Brownson found two powerful and dangerous tendencies: on the one hand, an excessive power of the state leading to social despotism, and, on the other, an excessive individualism leading to anarchy. Brownson thought that the Catholic Church provided a necessary corrective to both tendencies. As an institution, carrying a moral tradition, it could call the state to account; it could also mitigate, in a way in which Protestantism could not, a destructive individualism by fostering a respect for

24. Ibid., 74.
25. *Quarterly Review*, reprinted in *Works*, 12.409.

authority and tradition. But the church had to exist as an institution with the power not only to teach but to provide moral sanctions. In the interest of the common good, it could not avoid political engagement. Brownson's was the classic notion of political engagement, with antecedents in Greece and Rome, which Murray happily found absent on the American scene. Brownson, himself, was reacting to the Jacobian separation of the church from the civic order and the denial to it of any influence. Murray stands somewhere between Brownson and Sidney Hook, who can be taken as a representative of the Enlightenment program.

For Hook, there can be only one society, one law, one power, and one faith, namely, a civic faith that is the unifying bond of the community. Hook would banish from the political sphere the divisive force of religion. He has no quarrel with religion taken as a "purely private matter." What alarms him is religion in an institutional form, visible, corporate, and organized, a community of thought that presumes to sit superior to and in judgment on the community of democratic thought. Religion possessed of social structures by means of which it can voice its judgments and perhaps cause them to prevail is foreign to Hook's concept of civic life. Civil society is the highest societal form of human life. Civil law is the highest form of law and is not subject to judgment by pure ethical canons. Thus Hook, while recognizing its legality, would decry the existence of the parochial school system as "educationally and democratically unsound" because it separates out a large segment of our youth and imbues them with quite a different outlook.[26] For Hook, there is no eternal order of truth and justice; there are no universal verities that command assent; there is no universal moral law that requires obedience. The ultimate values espoused by society do not flow from the recognition of some antecedently derived notion of the common good. Rather, ultimate value is to be identified with the democratic process itself. The democratic faith is belief in the efficacy of the process.

Both Hook and Murray would agree that democracy is a form of

26. As quoted by the *New York Times*, 10 October 1963.

political judgment and as such is to be measured by the extent to which it achieves more security, freedom, and cooperative diversity than any of its alternatives. But Hook also speaks of democracy as a way of life, a set of procedures for critical discussion and discovery, which are preeminently exhibited in the work of the scientific community. Even so, democracy as a social philosophy is to be considered a hypothesis. Considered as a hypothesis, Hook believes, it is justified by experience. For Hook, the essence of democracy consists in the equal treatment of persons of unequal talent and endowment. "This method of treating human beings is more successful than any other in evoking a maximum of creative, voluntary effort from all members of the community."[27] It enlarges the scope of our experience by forcing us to understand the needs, drives, and aspirations of others without abandoning our own viewpoint. In nurturing the capacities of each, it adds to the existing stores of truth and beauty. "Regard for the potentialities of all individuals makes for less cruelty of man toward man, especially where cruelty is the result of blindness to, or ignorance of, other's needs."[28] Essential to the democratic process are the methods of public discussion, criticism, and argument. Though these are postulates themselves, they are the postulates of democracy. To undertake their justification is to begin "a new inquiry into a new problem."[29]

Murray's natural law philosophy and Hook's pragmatic naturalism lead to many of the same conclusions, and both men recognized this. Their differences illustrate the metaphysical and epistemological difference between an Aristotelian-Thomistic natural law outlook and a Dewey-type instrumentalism. For Murray, there exists a body of truths about human nature and about what is required for human fulfillment that can be passed from generation to generation. Thus the ancients, no less intelligent or observant than we, can speak to us

27. Sidney Hook, "The Justification of Democracy," in *Political and Personal Freedom* (New York: Criterion Books, 1959); reprinted in *The American Pragmatists* (New York: Meridian Books, 1960), 396.
28. Ibid., 397.
29. Ibid., 398.

across the ages about an essentially unchanging human nature, and it behooves us to return to those authors whose works have been appreciated and commented on for centuries. That body of truths rests on a set of metaphysical assumptions—for example, that there is such a thing as human nature and that certain ends can be identified as proper to it and others as not proper to it. Thus one can say that a life of the mind is preferable to a "simple sense life," that the laws of the state should promote those structures and activities that contribute to self-fulfillment, that self-fulfillment cannot take place apart from community, that the state, for example, is obligated to defend the family and the rights of private property and ensure access to a basic education for all of its citizens. Those commonly accepted truths serve as principles in the prudential order. The prudential judgment itself does not share in the certitude characteristic of the universal or time-transcending principle. The prudential judgment is made in context; its value is determined not solely by principle but by the empirical data available. Concrete options may even foster a reexamination of abstract principles. The further removed from the basic truths regarding human nature and society, the more precarious the judgment. Thus Murray, recognizing the importance of the family for personal growth and for the stability of the social order, could never sanction contraception, abortion, divorce, or voluntary euthanasia for the hopelessly afflicted, as Hook would. Of a different order is the judgment, for example, to place an aging parent in a nursing facility when care could be rendered by the family. "Respect for one's parents" taken as a principle does not dictate a specific conclusion. Circumstances direct prudential decision making.

The pragmatist's preference for solving each problem in the context in which it arises does not abrogate for him an appeal to principle. He, too, will invoke principle, but he is not willing to weave those principles into a consistent whole or to anchor them in a particular conception of human nature or conception of human fulfillment. Thus contradictory principles may be appealed to in different contexts without inconsistency. If a principle itself is challenged, it too is defended in the context at hand without recourse to a set of constants.

For this reason the pragmatist is often considered to be slippery in argument. The metaphysics to which he is committed often goes unstated and is placed beyond direct confrontation.

The history of philosophy in the United States can provide many examples of pragmatism. Lovejoy in his famous work identified thirteen. That form which has dominated the American scene, however, has been the instrumentalist or pragmatic naturalism of the Dewey-Hook variety. Murray finds this outlook nothing less than "barbarous." He was, of course, not the first to find it wanting. Writing a generation before Murray, Irving Babbit, in his *Democracy and Leadership* (1924), came to the conclusion that the influence of Dewey and his kind on education "amounts in the aggregate to a national calamity."[30] The ill effects of "progressive education" were apparent to Murray in the 1950s and are even more so now.

The pragmatic naturalism of the Dewey-Hook variety reduces science to technology, to problem solving of the sort in which answers are not so much to be expected as are reliable predictions. Though it eschews metaphysics, it is nevertheless a materialism that rules out the existence of God and therefore the need for religion in the lives of the people. The beauty attendant to the temple, the ritual, and the feast is held to be built on chimerical foundations. Man is regarded as through and through physicochemical, having his origin, growth, and decay in nature. This has implications for ethics since there is no transcendent end for human life. The most one can aspire to is to make this a better place for future generations—hence the pragmatist's emphasis on training for service and power. Dewey's educational philosophy, with its assumption of "progress," its insistence on personal experience, and its orientation to an idealized future, tends to denigrate the inherited and even the study of history. Classical languages are not required to gain access to an irrelevant antiquity. Indeed, for Dewey, one of the primary aims of education is that of challenging the inherited. Education does not consist in an

---

30. Irving Babbitt, *Democracy and Leadership* (1924; reprint, Indianapolis, Ind.: Liberty Classics, 1979), 339.

appropriation of the literature that has nourished the West since classical Greece but is rather a training for change.

Thus Murray could speak of the "new barbarism" that threatened the life of reason embodied in law and custom. The perennial work of the barbarian is "to undermine rational standards of judgment, to corrupt inherited wisdom by which the people have always lived, and to do this not by spreading new beliefs but by creating a climate of doubt and bewilderment in which clarity about the larger aims of life is dimmed and the self confidence of the people destroyed."[31] In his day Murray was not optimistic that the West could recover its patrimony in the near future. He would have even less grounds for optimism today. Many outside his Church look to it to supply the intellectual and moral void that is increasingly apparent. Yet that Church as a visible organization in North America appears as muddled and as confused as the larger society that it seems more to reflect than to challenge. But the legacy is there and can be tapped for the direction it provides. The key, of course, is the learning that gives one access to Athens and Rome and medieval Paris and Padua. A respect for the time-transcending wisdom of the ancients follows acquaintanceship. The Greeks can teach us much about human nature, about the nature of science, and about the requirements for virtue. The Romans can instruct us on the subject of law and on the nature of religion and its importance to civic life. Their medieval commentators can weave both into a synthesis that contains a third element, namely, revealed religion.

Revolution and Reformation not withstanding, there is a great literature that remains to be explored by the open mind, but Murray would not be content simply with its recovery. A heritage is to be appropriated, built upon, and utilized. That is exactly what Murray did in his own life.

31. Ibid., 13.

SEPARATING CHURCH AND STATE

The first ten amendments to the U.S. Constitution are commonly known as the "Bill of Rights." Like other declarations of rights before it, it is a document that both describes the fundamental liberties of a people and forbids the government to violate them. The first eight amendments to the Constitution list rights and freedoms possessed by every citizen. Amendments IX and X forbid Congress to adopt laws that would violate these rights.

The First Amendment reads, in part, "Congress shall make no law respecting an establishment of religion, or prohibiting the free exercise thereof." The first of the religion clauses has come to be known as the "establishment clause," the second as "the free-exercise clause." The meaning of these clauses, then and now, is the subject of this enquiry. I propose therefore to organize my material under four headings: (1) the role of religion in society, as understood by the Framers of the Constitution; (2) the meaning of the religion clauses, as given in the Bill of Rights; (3) the relationship between church and state, as determined by the U.S. Supreme Court over the past fifty years (that is, since the landmark 1947 *Everson* case); and (4) the implications of what I take to be a loss of respect for the intellectual and cultural role of religion in our society.

We can hardly imagine a United States without the freedoms guaranteed by the First Amendment. Yet we are vaguely aware that when our nation came into being established religions existed not only in Europe but within the colonies themselves. The colonists were for the most part an English-speaking people who emigrated from a land where the Anglican Church was the established religion. That church retained its ascendancy in the New World. At the outbreak of the American Revolution in 1775, there were established churches in nine of the thirteen colonies. The Anglican Church had been established in Virginia in 1609, in New York starting in 1693. Establishment of the Anglican Church occurred in Maryland in 1702, in South Carolina in 1706, in North Carolina in 1711, and in Georgia in 1758. The Congregational Church was established in Massachusetts, Connecticut, and New Hampshire. True, there were dissenters: Methodists and Presbyterians were not of one doctrinal mind with their Anglican brethren and repudiated certain features of the Anglican episcopal structure. There were also various forms of Pietism, which were influential in some colonies.[1]

The Framers of the Constitution, taking into consideration dissent within the Church of England itself and cognizant of religious conflict on the Continent, decreed that there would be no established church for the nation as a whole. The principle of federalism dictated that each state was to be free to establish as it saw fit. The Framers had no intention of disestablishing churches in New England or in the South. Congress was to keep its hands off all local establishment policies. The religion clauses of the First Amendment were designed to establish a separation of church and national state and to prevent the Congress from interfering with individual religious conviction.

In the age of the Founding Fathers, religion permeated the whole society, from school to Congress. Its presence and presumed beneficent influence were not challenged until after World War II. Only since that war has the U.S. Supreme Court developed what one constitutional scholar has called a "gloss on the First Amendment."

Given the Court's propensity to use historical material to support its decisions in religion cases, we have reason to look to the past to determine original intent.

In the debates that led to the adoption of the Constitution, and

1. For a thorough study of this topic, see Robert L. Cord, *Separation of Church and State: Historical Fact and Current* (New York: Lambeth Press, 1982). See also Walter Berns, *The First Amendment and the Future of American Democracy* (New York: Basic Books, 1976).

subsequently of the Bill of Rights, James Madison's role was significant. In the opening debates of the First Congress, Madison included among his several proposals an amendment forbidding the establishment of a national religion. The House Select Committee agreed to the following formulation of Madison's proposal: "No religion shall be established by law, nor shall the equal rights of conscience be infringed." Benjamin Huntington of Connecticut feared that such a formula might be interpreted to forbid state laws requiring contributions in support of churches and their ministers. He wanted to avoid any language that might "patronize those who professed no religion at all." Huntington took it for granted that the states should aid religion. So did Samuel Livermore of New Hampshire and Elbridge Gerry of Massachusetts.[2]

The options before the Congress were three: (1) no national religion, with the states free to elect establishment as they saw fit; (2) no establishment at either the federal or the state level, with the governments favoring religion but impartial with respect to sects; and (3) no support of religion whatsoever. The last view was held by a minority and at times was supported by Madison. We can trace the formulation that emerged from Madison's initial proposal of June 8 as it evolved through the House version adopted on August 20, to the modified version approved by the Senate, and to the adoption of the final measure by both bodies on September 24 and 25, 1789: "Congress shall make no law respecting an establishment of religion or prohibiting the free exercise thereof." Could the Congress of 1789 have imagined that the establishment clause, clear within the context that produced it, would one day be regarded as sufficiently ambiguous to give rise to policies diametrically opposed to those that history discloses were intended?

I

Returning to the Framers does not solve any contemporary problem. On any issue one can find almost any contemporary view

2. Annals of Congress, 8 June 1789, 1.451; 15 Aug. 1789, 1.757, 758; 15 Aug. 1789, 1.757 (Washington, D.C.: U.S. Government Printing Office).

entertained by one or more of the Framers. The advantage of historical awareness is that it puts to rest a number of claims that are sometimes defended in the name of "original intent." The Constitution, for example, did not create a "wall of separation between church and state." That is Thomas Jefferson's metaphor, and while Jefferson assumed the major role in drafting the Declaration of Independence, he had no part in the drafting of the Constitution. Similarly, Madison's views were his own, not those of Congress. In fact, he did not labor to have his views prevail but worked instead to achieve consensus.

With respect to the establishment clause, as in many other aspects, the Constitution is a work of compromise. The role of religion in society was well understood by the Framers, but the relationship of church and state was not easily resolved. The result of attempts to deal with that relationship was deliberate ambiguity. America was able to live with that ambiguity for approximately one hundred and sixty years, but in the past forty years, as the intellectual and moral foundations of society have shifted, the relationship has become troublesome. Many things assumed by the Framers can no longer be taken for granted. It was assumed, for example, as expressed in the Northwest Ordinance passed in 1778, that "Religion, morality, and knowledge, being necessary to good government and the happiness of mankind, schools and the means of learning, shall forever be encouraged."[3] We may yet believe in the value of education, but it is a technical education divorced from religion and morality. The average college student is untutored in matters of religion, and regards morality as a subjective affair, a code of values one adopts for oneself but wouldn't impose on anyone else.

While attitudes toward religion varied among the states (Massachusetts was perhaps strongest in its insistence that worship be a public affair), most of the Framers regarded religion as a beneficent force in society and judged it by the role that it played in conserving morality and decorum. Washington's attitude, expressed in his Farewell Address, can be taken as representative:

3. *Act of Congress*, 7 August 1789.

Of all the dispositions and habits which lead to political prosperity, religion and morality are indispensable supports. In vain would that man claim the tribute of patriotism who should labor to subvert these great pillars of human happiness, these firmest props of the duties of men and citizens. The mere politician, equally with the pious man, ought to respect and to cherish them. A volume could not trace all their connections with private and public felicity. Let it simply be asked where is the security for property, for reputation, for life, if the sense of religious obligation desert the oaths, which are the instrument of investigation in courts of justice? And let us with caution indulge the supposition that morality can be maintained without religion. Whatever may be conceded to the influence of refined education on minds of peculiar structure, reason and experience both forbids us to expect that national morality can prevail in exclusion of religious principle.

Washington was convinced that government cannot afford to be neutral between believers and nonbelievers.

But to return to the Constitution itself, as Walter Berns has pointed out, "Instead of establishing religion, the Founders established religious *freedom*, and the principle of religious freedom derives from a nonreligious source."[4] Interest in the well-being of religion was determined by the purely secular goals of state. Washington, it should be noted, was a Freemason; Jefferson was a deist, and although he called himself a Christian he did not believe in the divinity of Christ. Although they were not as cynical as Voltaire, their motives for endorsing religion were much the same. Voltaire, it will be remembered, urged the eradication of Christianity from the world of higher culture but was willing to allow it to remain in the stables and the scullery for the pragmatic reason that he did not want his servants to steal from him.

The state requires a certain amount of virtue in its citizens if public order is to be maintained. Religion is a proven vehicle for the inculcation of those moral principles that lead to virtue. At the time of the drafting of the Constitution, most of the new nation's schools were in fact religious. The public, nonreligiously affiliated school became the norm only in the last half of the nineteenth century. And even those

4. Berns, *First Amendment*, 15.

schools were religiously oriented, albeit in a nondenominational, Protestant way. It was in fact the fight over schools that led the Court to initiate a series of glosses on the First Amendment in 1947. Catholics, largely immigrants from the Continent, balked at sending their children to what were, in effect, Protestant public schools. They established their own schools, and in due course began to demand that a portion of their tax dollars be allocated to support them.

In *Everson v. Board of Education*, the Court decided that state aid to religiously affiliated primary and secondary schools was problematic if not unconstitutional, depending on the kind of aid. A 1941 New Jersey statute authorized school districts to subsidize the transportation of pupils to school, but districts were left to decide for themselves whether they wished to underwrite the cost of transporting children to private (including church-related) schools. The Board of Education of Ewing, N.J., decided to reimburse parents for the cost of transporting their children to private schools on public transportation. When this decision was challenged, the trial court sustained the objection on state constitutional grounds, but the New Jersey Court of Errors and Appeals reversed the decision. Eventually the case came to the U.S. Supreme Court.

Writing for the bare 5 to 4 majority of the Court, Justice Hugo Black stated that the establishment clause

means at least this; neither a state or a federal government can set up a church. Neither can pass laws which aid one religion, aid all religions or prefer one religion over another.... No tax in any amount, large or small, can be levied to support any religious activities or institutions, whatever they may be called, or whatever form they may adopt to teach and practice religion.... In the words of Jefferson, the clause against the establishment of religion by law was intended to erect "a wall of separation between church and state."[5]

Having said that, the majority concluded that reimbursement for transportation expenses did not constitute establishment and that the Ewing school district was free to pay for the transportation of private school pupils, including parochial schoolchildren.

5. *Everson v. Board of Education*, 330 U.S. 1 (1947), 15–16.

The "wall" metaphor stuck, however, as did the spurious reading of history incorporated in Black's opinion. Both have proved troublesome ever since. Robert L. Cord has shown conclusively that Black's use of historical documents was selective. Black's opinion followed uncritically the argument of Leo Pfeffer, whose scholarship was by no means disinterested.

II

A peculiar feature of the tripartite American system of government is that interest groups whose projects are defeated in legislative assemblies can nevertheless secure their enactment into law through decisions of an activist court. Legislation designed to ensure the perpetuation of a religious attitude is typically challenged by those who do not see its value. Since *Everson*, they usually receive a favorable hearing in the highest courts.

Whether prayer and Bible reading can take place in public schools were questions that reached the U.S. Supreme Court in the early 1960s. Both cases were decided on the principles first enunciated in *Everson*. The Court ruled negatively in both cases, but the issues were not laid to rest. In 1985 the Court was again confronted with the necessity of ruling on prayer in the schools, this time as a result of a challenge to an Alabama state law that provided for a moment of meditation or silent prayer at the opening of the school day. The Court ruled that the Alabama provision was unconstitutional.

The Court's 1987 decision with respect to the teaching of "creationist science" may be regarded as a symbolic attempt to have God's existence acknowledged in public schools. Be that as it may, a review of the 1962, 1963, and 1985 decisions will tell us much about religious pluralism and education in the United States. The prayer and Bible-reading decisions bring to the fore varying conceptions of education and the role of religion in American life. Of course, they also raise questions about the Court's interpretation of the U.S. Constitution.

On June 25, 1962, the Supreme Court ruled in *Engle v. Vitale* that reading an official prayer in New York public schools violated the Constitution. The prayer had been drafted by the New York Board of

Regents and was recommended for recital by all teachers and children at the start of every school day. The brief nondenominational prayer read: "Almighty God, we acknowledge our dependence upon Thee, and we beg Thy blessings upon us, our parents, our teachers and our country."

By a vote of 6 to 1 the Court held that reading the prayer was "an establishment of religion forbidden by the First Amendment to the Constitution." In the majority opinion, written by Justice Black, the Court asserted that the "prohibition against laws respecting religion must at least mean that in this country it is not part of the business of government to compose official prayers for any group of the American people to recite as part of a religious program carried on by government."[6] The Court went on to say: "There can be no doubt that New York's state prayer program officially established the religious beliefs embodied in the Regents' prayer."[7] In a concurring opinion, Justice William O. Douglas wrote:

By reason of the First Amendment, government is commanded to have no interest in theology or ritual. . . . The First Amendment leaves the Government in a position not of hostility to religion but of neutrality. The philosophy is that the atheist or agnostic—the non-believer—is entitled to go his own way. The philosophy is that if the government interferes in matters spiritual, it will be a divisive force. The First Amendment teaches that a Government neutral in the field of religion better serves all religious interests.[8]

The passages quoted above are more than many religious leaders had to work with when they were called on by the press to comment on the Court's decision. The comments elicited by the press probably reflect the spectrum of opinion to be found in the nation as a whole. Religious leaders held divided opinions. At the time Francis Cardinal Spellman stated flatly: "The decision strikes at the very heart of the Godly tradition in which Americans have for so long been raised."[9] Some Protestants looked upon the decision as favoring a completely

---

6. *Engle v. Vitale*, 370 U.S. 421, 425 (1962).
7. *Engle*, 430.
8. *Engle*, 443.
9. As quoted by the *New York Times*, 26 June 1962, pp. 1, 17.

secular state, in which the basic moral supports of free democracy would be weakened. Others were not disturbed, and some even welcomed the decision. In Chicago, Dean M. Kelly, then director of the National Council of Churches's Department of Religious Liberty, said: "Many Christians will welcome this decision. . . . It protects the religious right of minorities and guards against the development of *public school religion* which is neither Christianity nor Judaism but something less than either."[10]

Some immediately recognized the implication of the ruling, namely, that subsequent rulings would likely prohibit the reading of verses from the Bible in the classroom, a widespread practice in one-third of the United States, particularly in the South, where three-fourths of the public schools at the time held chapel exercises and Bible readings. A national survey conducted shortly before the Court's ruling in *Engle* revealed that 30 percent of all public schools held a morning devotional; between 40 percent and 50 percent of all schools had Bible readings. Approximately 85 percent of all public school commencement services in the public schools had some religious content, and many were conducted in a local church.

A decision on Bible reading approximately one year after the Regents' prayer decision proved that the fears of many were well founded. On June 17, 1963, the U.S. Supreme Court ruled 8 to 1 in *Abington v. Schempp* that state and local rules requiring recitation of the Lord's Prayer and reading of Bible verses at the start of the public school day violated the Constitution's prohibition of an establishment of religion. The majority opinion was written by Justice Clark. Again, the opinions of religious leaders were divided. On the whole, major Protestant organizations expressed their approval of the decision. About a week before the Court's decision, the National Council of Churches issued a statement reminding all citizens that "teaching for religious commitment is the responsibility of the home and the community of faith rather than the public schools."[11] The

---

10. *New York Times*, 26 June 1962, p. 17.
11. *New York Times*, 11 June 1963, p. 12.

Council continued: "Neither the church nor the state should use the public school to compel acceptance of any creed or conformity to any specific religious practices." Eugene Carson Blake, then chief executive officer of the United Presbyterian Church, and Silas G. Kessler said in a joint statement that the ruling had underscored common belief that religious instruction is the sacred responsibility of family and church. In their words: "It must be remembered that the moral and religious heritage of this nation is not dependent for its survival on these decisions. Prayer is cheapened when it is used as a device to quiet unruly children and the Bible loses its true meaning when it is looked upon as a moral handbook for minors."[12] But Bishop Fred Perce Corson, then president of the World Methodist Council, took issue with the Court ruling, declaring that it "penalized the religious people who are very definitely in the majority in the United States."[13]

Catholic reaction to the Bible-reading decision varied, but the assessment of Monsignor John J. Voight, secretary for education of the Archdiocese of New York, was representative of most of the comments:

I deeply regret the Court action. I say this for two reasons: one, because it will bring about the complete secularization of public education in America, which to me represents a radical departure from our traditional and historical religious heritage; and two, because it completely disregards parental rights in education and the wishes of a large segment of America's parents who want their children to participate in these practices in the public school.[14]

Most Jewish leaders, however, looked with favor on the Court ruling.

Confronted with these decisions, a foreign observer may want to know whether they really flow out of the U.S. Constitution itself or are the fruit of a specific legal philosophy unknown to the Founders but prevalent today. Anyone might ask: Do these decisions secure religious freedom, or do they prevent religion from exercising one of its rightful functions? Do they enthrone secularism?

12. Ibid.   13. Ibid.
14. Ibid.

First, there is little doubt that the Supreme Court, in reviewing the practices it found unconstitutional, would not have found them unconstitutional a century earlier. The Court, like any institution, is a product of its time. Its judges are educated in the schools of their generation. They are formed by the legal philosophies prevalent in these schools, and legal philosophies change.

At present there are roughly two schools of thought on how the Constitution should be interpreted. One holds that the Court must ascertain the intention of the Framers of the Constitution and rule accordingly. The other believes that the Constitution is a living document that must be interpreted in light of the needs of the time. According to the second view, the Framer's actual desires need not be ignored, but are less important than what they *would have* intended had they created the Constitution in our own time. This view was publicly articulated by Justice William Brennan when he was a member of the Supreme Court.

One hundred and fifty years ago it would have been impossible to object to prayer in the public schools. A century ago, Catholics had little success in objecting to the Protestant character of American schools. Today, by contrast, a statistically insignificant number of nonbelievers have been able to reverse a tendency in the schools that has been a part of the country's tradition since its founding. It is not our intention to examine all reasons why this has become possible, but one stands out—namely, the change in the intellectual climate of the universities and consequently in the media and the courts. It is these opinion-making centers that have influenced common thinking about law, morality, and religion. These centers have thrown the credibility of religious witness into doubt. The result is a growing body of secularists or nonbelievers. It is the views of this minority that the Court has sought to respect in its recent rulings. In those rulings the Court has forcefully pointed out to the believer the fact that the nonbeliever is a member of the community. The Constitution, the courts have been saying, is not an instrument of majority representation; rather, it is what the Founding Fathers designed for the defense of minorities, however small or unpopular they may be. The

Court seemingly has reached the only decision it could in demanding silence with respect to religious utterances in our public schools.

Another side to the debate is represented by Justice Potter Stewart, who dissented in both the 1962 and 1963 decisions. Dissenting from the majority decision in *Engle v. Vitale* (1962), Justice Stewart wrote:

> With all respect, I think the Court has misapplied a great constitutional principle. I cannot see how an "official religion" is established by letting those who want to say a prayer say it. On the contrary, I think that to deny the wish of these school children to join in reciting this prayer is to deny them the opportunity of sharing in the spiritual heritage of our nation.[15]

Justice Stewart went on to note that Congress begins each of its sessions with a prayer; that the crier of the Supreme Court itself says at every session: "God save the United States and this honorable court"; and that the country's coinage, its national anthem, and its Pledge of Allegiance contain references to God. "Countless similar examples could be listed," he said,

> but there is no need to belabor the obvious. It was all summed up by this Court just ten years ago in a single sentence: We are a religious people whose institutions presuppose a supreme being (*Zorach*). I do not believe that this Court, or the Congress, or the president has by the actions and practices I have mentioned established an "official religion" in violation of the Constitution. And I do not believe that the State of New York has done so in this case. What each has done has been to recognize and to follow the deeply entrenched and highly cherished spiritual traditions of our nation—traditions which come down to us from those who almost two hundred years ago avowed their "firm reliance on the protection of divine providence" when they proclaimed the freedom and independence of this brave new world.[16]

In his subsequent comments on *Abington v. Schempp* (1963), Justice Stewart took roughly the same position. "We err," he said, "if we do not recognize, as a matter of history and a matter of the imperatives of our free society, that religion and government must necessarily interact in countless ways."[17] Justice Stewart wrote:

15. *Engle v. Vitale*, 370 U.S. 421, 425 (1962).
16. *Engle*, 450.
17. *Abington v. Schempp*, 374 U.S. 203, 309.

Religious exercises are not constitutionally invalid if they simply reflect differences which exist in the society from which the school draws its pupils.
They become constitutionally invalid only if their administration places the
sanction of secular authority behind one or more particular religious or irreligious beliefs. To be specific, it seems to me clear that certain types of exercises would present situations in which no possibility of coercion on the part
of secular officials could be claimed to exist. Thus if such exercises were held
either before or after the school day, or if the school schedule were such that
participation were merely one among a number of desirable alternatives, it
could hardly be contended that the exercises did anything more than to provide an opportunity for the voluntary expression of religious belief.[18]

Justice Stewart recognized the practical difficulties the implementation of such a policy might create with Christians of many sects,
Jews, agnostics, atheists, and Muslims in the community, but he expressed his confidence that with inventiveness and good will school
boards could settle the problem locally.

Justice Stewart's dissenting opinion in some respects reflected the
opinion of Erwin Griswold, then dean of the Harvard Law School. In
an address delivered shortly after the *Engle* decision (and thus before
the *Abington* decision) Griswold said that it was unfortunate that the
question involved in that case ever came before the Supreme Court.
Griswold argued that the American people have a spiritual and cultural tradition of which they ought not to be deprived by judges ef-
fecting the logical implications of absolutist notions not expressed in
the Constitution and surely never contemplated by those who put the
constitutional provisions into effect. He went on to say: "There are
some matters which are essentially local in nature, important matters, but none the less matters to be worked out by the people themselves in their own communities, when no basic rights of others are
impaired."[19]

In the same address Griswold raised the key question:

Does our deep-seated tolerance of all religions—or, to the same extent, of no
religion—require that we give up all religious observance in public activities?

18. *Abington*, 317–18.
19. As reported in *America*, 16 March 1963, p. 374.

Why should it? It certainly never occurred to the founders that it would. It is hardly likely that it was entirely accidental that these questions did not even come before the court in the first hundred and fifty years of our constitutional history.[20]

Griswold commented:

This, I venture to say again, has been and is, a Christian country in origin, history, tradition and culture. It was out of Christian doctrine and ethics, I think it can be said, that it developed the notion of toleration. No one in this country can be required to have any particular form of religious belief; and no one can suffer legal discrimination because he has, or does not have, any particular religious belief. But does the fact that we have officially adopted toleration as our standard mean that we must give up our history and our tradition? The Moslem who comes here may worship as he pleases, and may hold public office without discrimination. That is as it should be. But why should it follow that he require others to give up their Christian tradition merely because he is a tolerated and welcomed member of the community.[21]

The judgments of Justice Stewart and Dean Griswold, though not reflected in the decisions of the Court, probably represent the opinion of the majority of U.S. citizens. They strongly suggest that in these two decisions the Court did more than recognize the existence of a large body of nonbelievers. Stewart and Griswold believe that the Court construed the no-establishment clause in such absolutist terms that any governmental encouragement of religion appears to be illegal.

The principles embodied in the 1962 and 1963 decisions were carried to their logical conclusion when the Court ruled in *Wallace v. Jaffree* (1985) that an Alabama statute authorizing a one-minute period of silence in all public schools "for meditation or voluntary prayer" was unconstitutional. The Court held that the statute had the effect of establishing religion and was thus a violation of the First Amendment.

Individual freedom of conscience as protected by the First Amendment, it maintained, embraces the right to select any religious faith or none. Invoking criteria first enunciated in a case known as *Lemon v.*

20. Ibid.
21. Ibid., p. 375.

Kurtzman (1971), the Court declared that the Alabama statute clearly violated the First Amendment. The criteria set forth in *Lemon* were that any statute: (1) must have a secular legislative purpose; (2) must have a principal or primary effect that neither advances nor inhibits religion; and (3) must not foster excessive government entanglement with religion.

In the Court's opinion, the first criterion was not met by the Alabama statute because its purpose was the advancement of religion by returning prayer to public schools. The endorsement of prayer is "not consistent with the established principle that the government must pursue a course of complete neutrality toward religion."[22]

Perhaps the most valuable thing to come out of the 1985 prayer case is the minority opinion of Judge Rehnquist, who shows the absurdity of invoking the "wall" metaphor in light of American history and the intent of the authors of the Constitution's Bill of Rights. In his opinion, use of the wall analogy has led to numerous inconsistencies in Supreme Court rulings since its invocation in *Everson* forty years ago.

Rehnquist draws up an interesting list of the inconsistencies found in the Court's rulings since *Everson*: a state may lend to parochial schoolchildren geography textbooks containing maps of the United States, but it may not lend maps of the United States for use in geography class; a state may lend American colonial history textbooks, but it may not lend a film on George Washington or a film projector to show it with; a state may lend classroom workbooks but may not lend workbooks in which parochial schoolchildren write, thus rendering them nonreusable; a state may pay for bus transportation to religious schools but may not pay for bus transportation from the parochial school to a public zoo or museum for a field trip. Rehnquist bluntly concludes: "The wall of separation between church and state is a metaphor based on bad history, a metaphor which has proved useless as a guide to judging. It should be frankly and explicitly abandoned."[23]

22. *Wallace v. Jaffree*, 472 U.S. 38, 60.
23. Ibid., 107.

Against those who would argue that the Constitution means what judges declare it to mean, Rehnquist urges:

The true meaning of the Establishment Clause can only be seen in its history. ... As drafters of our Bill of Rights, the Framers inscribed the principles that control today. Any deviation from their intentions frustrates the permanence of that charter and will only lead to the type of unprincipled decision-making that has plagued our Establishment Clause since *Everson.*[24]

He reaches a conclusion supported by history:

The Framers intended the Establishment Clause to prohibit the designation of any church as a "national" one. The clause was also designed to stop the Federal government from asserting a preference for one religious denomination or sect over others. Given the "incorporation" of the Establishment Clause as against the states via the Fourteenth Amendment in *Everson,* states are prohibited as well from establishing a religion or discriminating between sects. As its history abundantly shows, however, nothing in the Establishment Clause requires government to be strictly neutral between religion and irreligion, nor does that Clause prohibit Congress or the states from pursuing legitimate secular ends through non discriminatory sectarian means.[25]

The secular purpose prong [of the three-part *Lemon* test] has proved mercurial in application because it has never been fully defined, and we have never fully stated how the test is to operate. . . . The *Lemon* test has no more grounding in the history of the First Amendment than does the wall theory upon which it rests.[26]

Given the historical accuracy and the logical strength of Rehnquist's dissenting opinion, one may be encouraged to believe that a slight shift in the ideological complexion of the Court may lead to an altogether different reading of the Constitution, one that would be favorable to parental control of education. The Supreme Court tends to be the intellectual battleground for the soul of the United States, and its decisions often lead to major transformations in the social order. Thus one can be sure that the debate concerning church–state issues before the Court and the struggle for the control of education will continue. Subsequent rulings of the Court, to the horror of many,

24. Ibid., 113.   25. Ibid.
26. Ibid., 108, 110.

have drawn the logical conclusions of these post–World War II decisions and have led to the banning of even the posting of the Ten Commandments.

Knowing *what is* does not automatically tell us *what ought to be*. The larger question confronting us can be variously formulated: Does society have a stake in the presence or absence of religion? Does it make a difference to society whether men worship or believe in God? Should governments encourage, remain indifferent to, or actively oppose religion? To raise this type of question is not to embrace a romantic interpretation of religion. Given that more than 215 religious bodies exist in this country, one is not apt to look to religion in general as a source of wisdom, or even of moral knowledge. It can be argued that contemporary religion is not good at performing even those functions at which Voltaire thought it excelled best and because of which, from the state's viewpoint, he thought it ought to be promoted. The religious mind, cut off from the resources of the academy, is an impoverished mind.

John Dewey thought that philosophy could do the job vacated by religion, that it could develop a common civic faith that would serve as the necessary foundation for morality and law. But outside the Marxist school of thought, few today would share his confidence. The philosophical community is as divided and unsure of itself as is the religious one.

Western culture may indeed be suffering its death throes, as Nietzsche suggested, but a bright spot as we enter a new millennium is that there has been a measure of soul-searching that has caused us to attend to our roots as a nation. We are in a position to see how far we have drifted from the worldview embraced by our Founding Fathers. In this celebration year, the wisdom of their political outlook has not gone unappreciated. To appropriate those time-transcending principles that guided their action is a short step that neither logic nor experience prevents.

THOMAS ON NATURAL LAW

What Judge Thomas Did Not Say

I

The Senate Judiciary Committee's hearings on the qualification of Judge Clarence Thomas for appointment to the U.S. Supreme Court raised for a worldwide audience questions concerning the role of natural law in the legislative and judicial processes, that is, in the framing and the interpreting of law. The media debate that ensued more often than not led to confusion rather than clarification. Many were left wondering what indeed is "natural law" that views about it should prove so controversial? Given the complexity of the matter, it is not surprising that Judge Thomas could not satisfy his interrogators. What the hearings did show is that law is not created in a vacuum but presupposes an intellectual and cultural history, including philosophical considerations.

I do not want to put words into Judge Thomas's mouth or suggest that I know any more than what is publicly available, but on the basis of evidence it is my judgment that what makes him a good Supreme Court justice is that he shares the outlook of the Framers of the Constitution. He shares with them the principles upon which the Constitution was built, principles that are supported by a time-transcending, natural law philosophy. That he has many detractors is due to the fact that the morality embedded in the Constitution has been repudiated by much of modernity. It is a morality secure in its conception of human nature and in its conception of human fulfillment, a morality that favors the common good over special interests, a morality that recognizes spiritual as well as material goods and the transcendent as well as the temporal end of man. Of one mind with the Framers, a judge, as a member of the bench, will find it easy to be a strict constructionist. Such an outlook will put him at odds with the intellectual establishment or, as Thomas Sowell calls it, "the anointed," but not at odds with the people.

The confirmation hearings were not about qualifications or judicial temperament. They were the clash of two intellectual systems, one embedded in the Constitution, the other its antithesis.

Lord Patrick Devlin, writing in the early 1960s, speculated that if a society's laws are based on a particular worldview and that worldview collapses, the laws themselves will crumble. Ronald Dworkin, in his work *Law's Empire*, argues the converse thesis: in a moral pluralistic society only law can provide the unity required for the social order. The concept "natural law" is but a symbol in this debate; it is not surprising that it arose during the Judiciary Committee's hearings.

The concept of natural law, of course, is an ancient one. We find it in the Greek poets, in the Athenian philosophers Plato and Aristotle, and in the Roman Stoics Cicero and Seneca. The notion is rather simple. There are laws of nature, some of which we have discovered and have articulated for ourselves and for others. A law of nature is simply a report on *what is*. It is a description of a process that under specified conditions remains invariant through time and place. A law of nature is opposed to an accidental generality—for example, all the senators from the southern provinces have deep brown eyes. Examples of other natural laws known to antiquity might include: copper expands when heated, silver is malleable, wine loosens the tongue, to be fruitful the vines must have at least eighty-five days of sun, credibility follows a habit of speaking the truth, a well-ordered household permits leisure. In addition to these homey, prescientific laws, we can add the modern laws of physics, chemistry, and biology and the laws that govern music, painting, architecture, corporate management, and personal fulfillment. They can be stated flatly in the form of declarative sentences, for example, "Bodily health is contingent upon a proper diet"; or as admonitions, for example, "One should observe a healthful diet," "Desiring other people's property will make you miserable," or "Thou shall not covet thy neighbor's goods." Some of the laws that deal with personal self-fulfillment we call "moral laws" as distinct from rules that promote good manners. The Fulbright Scholars Program, for example, is promoting good manners when it suggests to American youths going abroad to bring flowers to the hostess when invited to a dinner party. To be moral, one must be prudent, temperate, just, and courageous. To be just, one must pay homage to the gods, one must honor one's father and one's mother, one must remain faithful to one's spouse, one must respect the terms of any contract into which one has entered. The list goes on and on. Experience teaches that the cardinal virtues of prudence, temperance, justice, and fortitude must be cultivated early in life if one is to lead a successful life.

If natural law is so evident, why is it denied? The denial is of relatively recent origin. It is due partly to the success of modern philosophy and its repudiation of the inherited, namely, the classical and Christian, sources of Western culture. In the seventeenth and eighteenth centuries, Descartes, Hume, and Kant provided major critiques of antiquity that culminated in the movement we know in the English-speaking world as the Enlightenment. The movement taught that given the impossibility of demonstrating God's existence and given the ability of modern scholarship to provide a purely secular interpretation of the miraculous events of the Bible, the inherited had to be reevaluated from the standpoint of reason alone.

One of the lasting results of the eighteenth-century Enlightenment, Anglo-French and German, has been a diminution of respect not only for those institutions symbolized by crown and miter but for the moral authority of the classical tradition itself. The Enlightenment did not set about repudiating all that was inherited, but it did insist that any values that were to be retained had to be justified on purely secular, as opposed to religious, grounds. It took time for the views of the philosophers to reach the marketplace, but reach it they surely did. Since the late eighteenth century the nihilistic tendencies of Western society have proceeded nonstop to the point where the underpinnings—classical and Christian—of Western common law have given way. It is evident that civil law itself is beginning to crumble, with devastating effects for society, for the family, and for the individual. Judge Thomas was caught in a debate between two opposing camps with divergent views regarding the source and function of law.

This is not to deny that a certain superficial appeal to traditional moral norms, often explicitly Christian, still pervades contemporary social discourse. No one proposes any program or any course of action without invoking moral principles. Legislators openly create law in the light of moral principles, and judges are not hesitant to interpret or recast statutes to satisfy the demands of moral claims. This occurs in spite of the fact that prominent philosophers insist that there are no general norms to serve as guides and others tell us that reason can determine means but not ends. Some merely admonish us to be scientific, insisting that an inherited, largely religious, morality is to be evaluated against the data provided by contemporary science. Still others recommend morals by agreement.

II

If these impressions are correct, a reexamination of natural law theory is clearly warranted. When natural law is presented as a set of normative propositions that because of their universality and intrinsic necessity transcend time periods and cultures, it is apt to be rejected out of hand in an age accustomed to looking upon the acquisition of knowledge as an incomplete and ongoing process. But when considered as a meta-ethic, it can be argued that natural law theory has a contribution to make on several fronts. In providing a theory about the determination of moral norms, it speaks to topics such as ethical reasoning, the movement from descriptive to normative assertions, the use of science in ethics, the extralegal grounds for judicial decision, and the societal basis of law.

Natural law, when considered as a meta-ethic, has more the character of advice with respect to procedure than of a set of conclusions.

The advice amounts to this: Proceed with confidence that intelligence can determine in a general way what is good for man. This assertion presupposes the twin convictions that nature is intelligible and that the human intellect is powerful enough to ferret out the secrets of nature. Put another way, natural law encourages the observer to look for regularities in nature, human and otherwise. Regularity indicates structure, and a knowledge of structure will in turn yield functional explanation, which has a major role to play in the determination of norms.

The confidence that nature is intelligible was a distinctive feature of the Greek mind that gave birth to the concept of natural law. Intelligibility for the Greek owed itself to design and was explained variously by an ultimate final cause drawing all things to itself or, in terms of a demi-urgos, a divine life artificer. The Christian Middle Ages took it for granted that nature is the handiwork of God and that things are as they are as a result of a divine plan. In both the Greek and Christian traditions there is the common affirmation that things have natures that disclose tendencies and that both are the product of intelligence. Aristotle, for example, maintained that from a consideration of what a thing is in its tendential aspects, one can determine what is suitable for it, in other words, its good.[1] From a consideration of what man is, one can determine what ends he ought to pursue. For Aristotle, the supreme end of man is happiness, which consists primarily in intellectual activity, all other pursuits being subordinate or instrumental to that one. In practice, to use a contemporary example, this means that one should not spend all of one's leisure on the golf course; one needs to spend some time in one's library as well.

Aquinas adds principally that ultimate fulfillment consists in an eternal beatitude, that is, in union with the divine, a union in which man's intellectual and appetitive faculties find complete satisfaction.[2] For Aquinas, ultimate beatitude is possible even if temporal beatitude of the Aristotelian sort escapes one by reason of chance or the poverty of

1. *Nicomachean Ethics*, 1, chap. 6, 1097ff.; *Physics* 2, chap. 9.
2. *Summa Theologiae*, I-II, Q. 1, arts. 1–6

the human organism. Obviously Thomas's insight is a theological one, based on a revelation and not subscribed to by all. But whereas theology divides, philosophy can still provide unity to discourse. It need not close one to data provided by revelation. Philosophies, of course, also divide, but in principle their divisions are reconcilable.

In these considerations, we can observe the foundation of a natural law methodology. It consists in advice to look to man's nature to determine what is good for him. No conclusions are ready-made. This is evident in both Aristotle and Aquinas, although there is a difference in starting points and emphasis. Aristotle's ethical quest begins with a man already in society with a given set of mores. The culture that has already formed him will play an important role as he systematically works out a moral code. Aquinas's beginning is different but compatible. He begins with the confidence that nature is the handiwork of the divine, with the conviction that the divine intellect is the root of an order that the human intellect is able to perceive. What this order is, as it was for Aristotle, remains to be discovered. Hence, Aquinas emphasizes reason. In his "Treatise on Law," he tacitly identifies law with reason; elsewhere, he develops a methodology that reason is to follow.[3]

It is significant that Aquinas does not attempt to deduce from general principles the content of natural law. It is also significant that he draws no clear-cut distinction between natural and civil law. His famous definition of law, summarized as "an ordinance of reason promulgated by he who has authority in the community,"[4] while formulated to be predicative of all law, is primarily a definition of civil law. There is no hard-and-fast line where so-called natural law leaves off and civil law begins. True, there is this difference: civil law is articulated in some fashion by the state, whereas natural law is not. Yet the difference is not determinative. Natural law may be articulated by a church or by an academic community and may be reflected in the ordinances of a community; by whom it is articulated is not significant.

3. *Summa Theologiae*, I-II, Qq. 90–108.
4. *Summa Theologiae*, I-II, Q. 90, a. 4.

Nor is it significant that the state does not articulate all that is affirmed by the community of scholars, whether called rabbis, bishops, or professors. Deserving of emphasis is the fact that law, natural or civil, is the product of reason's figuring out what is good for the race, men taken individually or as members of a community designed to serve their common interest. This suggests that the principal difference between natural law and civil law is the difference between an intellectually articulated norm and a promulgated statute.

Aquinas, like anyone in the natural law tradition, recognizes that there are certain constants in man and that these can be discerned. These constants are the grounds for those normative enunciations that will remain the same from generation to generation or, for that matter, whenever and wherever man is found. The variables are cultural, economic, and topographical. This is something to keep in mind as Washington or Brussels legislates for varied regions. While the protection of the environment is a good, it may not be possible to legislate for the nation as a whole. The proportion between the constant and the variable is not worked out, but Aquinas is not generous in mentioning constants. The assertion that the natural law is immutable can easily misrepresent Aquinas's position. As he presents his views in the "Treatise on Law," most of the content of the natural law is variable.[5] To employ a few contemporary examples: In home construction, safety is promoted through building codes, but building codes vary from climate to climate. The enduring principles pertain to safety; the variables are topographical. Similarly, in any profession, accepted standards may change as matters become more intricate. In the field of accounting, for example, the enduring principle of fairness or justice will dictate changes in reporting as complexity increases. In the delivery of health care, extraordinary means may become through technological innovation normal care. Thus, a physician may be morally culpable for failing to use a readily available diagnostic device that only a decade earlier may have been a rare and prohibitively ex-

5. Cf. *Summa Theologiae*, I-II, Q. 94, a. 5, where Saint Thomas talks about natural law having changed by addition.

pensive procedure. The codes and procedures mentioned are not merely prudential applications of principles. They are principles or norms themselves, although they fall under principles more general in scope.

Aquinas, in his "Treatise on Law," is affirming principally that law is rooted in something other than the will of the legislator. Where he distinguishes between the immutable and the temporal aspects of law, he is recognizing that in certain basic features man is everywhere alike. But the emphasis in his treatise is on reason as the proper way of finding out what is good for man. In stressing reason Aquinas is more concerned with the method of inquiry than with the content of laws discovered.

It should be clear that not everything that is legislated or determined to be law by a lawmaking court is in fact to be treated as law.[6] (No one believes that a 55-mile-an-hour speed limit is morally binding.) Aquinas will not give the force of law to those enactments that clearly fly in the face of reason and experience. One may assume, however, that when lawmaking bodies are interested in determining the equitable and conditions are propitious, they will in a large measure, perhaps as far as humanly possible, succeed. This is not to ignore that much legislation is a tissue of compromise, often reflecting conflicting and contradictory insights and principles. Free intelligence and goodwill will produce good law—not inevitably, but for the most part. Good positive law is continuous with the dictates of nature, or natural law if you will.

III

The foregoing concept of natural law rests on two ontological pillars: the conviction that there are natural structures, and the conviction that the processes of nature are orderly. In the language of Aristotle, it rests upon the principles of substance and final causality, and the related notions of potency and act.

In an attempt to understand change, Aristotle distinguishes between

---

6. *Summa Theologiae,* I-II, Q. 96, a. 4.

the relatively permanent essence and its modifications.[7] Becoming is understood as the gaining of further actuality. Through its activity a substance emerges from isolation and enters into relation with other substances, either passively receiving their influence to which it is actively open or acting in ways ultimately determined by its essence. Each entity tends toward further actuality beyond what it already has. For Aristotle, the whole of reality is shot through with the distinction between potentiality and actuality, between what is still only able to be and what actually is. The potential is related to the actual as the imperfect to the perfect, the incomplete to the complete.

Equipped with these insights Aristotle could understand not only what a thing is when viewed statically but also what a thing is when viewed dynamically—that is, as subject to change. Change is rendered intelligible in terms of the end of change. That toward which a thing is essentially tending is judged to be its proper good. There is a relation of fitness. Goodness is not to be identified with any goal; it is a fulfillment and thus is founded on the essence and its tendencies. By "good" is meant what is fit for a thing, what is due its nature, the further existence that will complete its basic tendencies and its incidental tendencies as well, so far as these do not conflict with the former. Thus the valid ground for desire is that the thing desired is prescriptively required by the nature desiring it.

A teleological concept of nature, supported by a realistic epistemology, is therefore the basis of the unity of "being" and "ought," of "fact" and "value," of "nature" and "goodness." The ontological and moral orders are ultimately one. A basis for values exists only in the tendency of something incomplete to complete itself. In apprehending a tendency, we grasp something of what the entity is tending toward. The essence of a thing implies the goal of becoming.

Here it is important to acknowledge that essence is not something that we first understand by itself—and from which we infer tendency. We experience beings and infer something of their essences by observing them in the process of fulfilling these tendencies. Things are

7. *Physics*, 5, chaps. 1–2.

always in a state of becoming or development. Essence herein conceived is not an immutable substrate, nor is it subjectively created by interest; nor does it represent a kind of shorthand by which we keep in mind properties or observations we cannot now conveniently articulate.

Essence is rather given in experience and discovered upon reflection. It controls our endeavor to distinguish between the peripheral and the central, to discover the order and cause of the properties that the sciences catalog. In answering the question "What is it?," essence marks the thing off from other entities. And most importantly for value theory, essence in its tendential aspect implies what is suitable to it.

In these considerations, we can observe the groundwork of a theory of the good. It consists in advice: (1) to look to man's nature to determine what is good for him, and (2) to look to social structures, given both through experience and through history, to determine which goods are conducive to man's communal well-being. No conclusions are ready-made. This is evident both in Aristotle and in Aquinas.

I V

It must be recognized that both principles are denied by many contemporary philosophers. Richard Rorty, in his *Philosophy and the Mirror of Nature*, has argued that there are no structures—natural, social, or cognitive—that permit of scientific study.[8] From Rorty's perspective, "human nature" is a fiction. From a materialistic or naturalistic perspective, absent a designer of the universe, there is no ordering to an end other than self-determined ends on the part of human beings. The supposed order of the universe can be explained either by chance or by assuming that any arrangement would necessarily be regarded by the human observer as "ordered."

Is it possible, then, to subscribe to a natural law basis for morality

8. Richard Rorty, *Philosophy and the Mirror of Nature* (Princeton, N.J.: Princeton University Press, 1979).

without first establishing the existence of the orderer, of the eternal lawgiver, of God? The answer seems to be a qualified "Yes." There are many who would find themselves agnostic with respect to the question of God's existence and yet who would like to recognize "that arbitrary will is not legally final," that civil law and conscience are to be measured against an independent scale. History may provide a clue. Natural law has not always been associated with belief in a divine governor or lawgiver, and even where it has been, it can be argued that its characteristic tenets have not been explicitly related to that belief. Aquinas insisted that natural man, without revelation, can know what is good. In her speech before Creon, Antigone insists that there is a higher law to which human ordinance ought to conform. The question of the source of that law remains open. The logical inference may not be drawn or the source never questioned.

Natural law teaching gains considerable force when contrasted with two prevalent views: (1) the morals-by-agreement school, and (2) the pragmatic outlook. I do not take seriously the positivistic view that law is simply what the legislature declares it to be, or the supremacist view that law proceeds simply from the barrel of a gun. Allow me to characterize, first, the morals-by-agreement faction. *Is There a Measure on Earth?* is the title of a work by Werner Marx, not to be confused with Karl Marx.[9] Werner Marx begins with the conviction that one can no longer appeal to a divinely ordained schema or to a religious outlook as a source for moral norms. "We are condemned to think in a realm between tradition and another beginning."[10] His "other beginning" has its roots in Martin Heidegger. Marx wants to create not merely a secularized morality but one without presuppositions in metaphysics. His proposed measure is the adoption, or appropriation, of recognized values such as "love," "compassion," and "the recognition of others." Love, Marx says, includes its weaker forms of "fraternity," "friendship," and "social solidarity." Love possesses the

9. *Is There a Measure on Earth? Foundations for a Nonmetaphysical Ethics*, trans. T. J. Nenon and R. Nenon (Chicago: University of Chicago Press, 1987).
10. Ibid., 7.

traits of a measure; for those who love, it is a valid norm. Although love is possible only in smaller groups, compassion can be present in larger societies. Compassion includes every sort of kindness and concern for others. For those who are filled with compassion, compassion, though experienced as immanent, is absolutely valid as a transcendent norm. "The obligating power of compassion instigates actions without any further reflection whatsoever."[11] In similar fashion, recognition of others is a "moral absolute." "Once one has seen the 'obligatory' character inherent in this form of 'intersubjectivity,' then it works as a binding power . . . [providing] him with a means of distinguishing good and evil and . . . [giving] him a motivation for preferring good to evil."[12] All of this sounds so congenial that the unreflective mind is almost willing to give assent. But Werner Marx's position is far from the moral teaching of a Saint Augustine or of a Saint Benedict. Benedict's *Rule*, for example, was designed to produce harmony in a community within which moral virtue, natural and theological, might be cultivated; it didn't presuppose it. He didn't leave matters to chance or conscience, he laid down rules in the interest of a well-ordered society.

A more subtle version of the morals-by-agreement school is provided by John Rawls. In his recent John Dewey Lectures, Rawls ventures this opinion: "What justifies a conception of justice is not its being true to an order antecedent to and given to us, but its congruence with our deeper understanding of ourselves and our aspirations, and our realization that, given our history and the traditions embedded in our public life, it is the most reasonable doctrine for us."[13] Clearly lost in both Marx and Rawls is a transhistorical set of concepts or judgments against which action can be measured. Both are saying that we can keep the notion of morality just insofar as we cease to think of morality as divinely ordained and instead think of it as the voice of ourselves as members of a community or as speakers of

11. Ibid., 22.
12. Ibid.
13. Unpublished lecture, quoted by Richard Rorty, in "The Contingency of Community," *London Review of Books*, 14 July 1986, p. 13.

a common language. Morals-by-agreement has implications, as Richard Rorty has noted, not only for morality considered in the abstract but for the application of moral principles to concrete situations, that is, for the distinction between morality and prudence. We can no longer think of the difference between the two as the difference between an appeal to the unconditioned and an appeal to the conditioned. Rather the distinction has to be thought of as the difference between an appeal to the interests of our community and an appeal to our private, possible conflicting, interest. An important result of this shift is that it makes it impossible to judge in any objective way. Morality, Rorty has remarked, then becomes a matter of "our practices" or "our intentions." Immorality is the name we give to "the sort of thing we don't do."[14]

Morality thus comes to be identified in the language of John Dewey with "the values we hold dear." But need attention be called to the ambiguity that surrounds the use of the word "values"? The term "values" is employed in many contexts, and even in a single context it can have a plurality of meanings. As used in moral discourse, the term may connote a subjective prizing or, conversely, the recognition of an objective ontological structure. It may be used to designate personal preferences or to refer to social customs. It may suggest an ethical judgment or merely the preferences of the marketplace.

The use of the word "values" to designate moral norms or a set of principles is of relatively recent origin. Contemporary use is in fact foreign to the classical mind, perhaps even to some of the foremost representatives of the modern mind. For the classical mind—and on this point Aristotle may be taken as typical—some things are prized in themselves, that is, as ends; other things are prized for their utility, that is, as means to ends. That which is prized for itself is primarily responsible for the prizing. Prizing is the recognition of worth. To evaluate is to take an ontological measure. Since men are fundamentally the same, they have fundamentally the same requirements, and therefore will measure in fundamentally the same way. Alike in their

14. Rorty, "Contingency," p. 13.

common desire for happiness, men may differ about the means for the attainment of happiness, but there is, nevertheless, enough agreement about ends that there emerges a science that investigates and weighs materials as instruments for the achievement of commonly recognized human goods.

The second contrasting view, the pragmatic one, finds an articulate holder in the person of John Dewey, perhaps the most influential American educator of the twentieth century. Dewey called his moral philosophy "instrumentalism"; it may also be called a "pragmatic naturalism."[15] What constitutes it as a "naturalism" is Dewey's conviction that man has his origin, growth, and decay within nature. Man is through and through physicochemical. Dewey's ontology is obviously a materialism. What makes his moral philosophy "pragmatic" is the conviction that each problem is to be solved in the context in which it arises without invoking transcendent principles. There are no permanent or immutable principles upon which to draw. The implications for education are obvious. The inherited is not to be cherished for the wisdom it provides; rather the inherited is to be challenged. Education is not the cultivation of an appreciation of the best produced through the ages; it is rather the employment of critical intelligence which is to be turned on the received. Theistic metaphysics and biblical religions are prime targets for the use of critical method. From Dewey's perspective, history and ancient languages are not as important as was once thought since the weight given the ancients has been diminished. More important than classical studies is the pursuit of the social sciences whose testimony is apt to bear upon the problem to be solved here and now. Inquiry should be future-oriented not past-directed.

Dewey's process philosophy renders obsolete an appeal to a natural order independent of the mind. There are no natural structures, nor can one say there is order in nature. Inquiry for Dewey creates the

---

15. For an extended study of the pragmatic naturalistic outlook, see Jude P. Dougherty, *Recent American Naturalism* (Washington, D.C.: The Catholic University of America Press, 1960).

structures it deals with; the mind imposes, not discovers, order in nature. A naturalism or materialism can recognize neither a lawgiver nor a *telos* to nature. There is no first efficient cause, nor is there a final cause. Man takes the materials presented by nature and makes of them the best he can. If there is no divine lawgiver and no transcendent end, in Dostoevsky's words, is "everything permitted"? Are we inevitably led to the "now" society? Dewey himself, of course, would not embrace so crass a hedonism. Rather he holds out as the noblest aim one can embrace the goal of making society a better place for future generations.

V

By way of conclusion, it must be recognized that the moral outlooks that divide on issues such as contraception, premarital intercourse, adultery, abortion, in vitro fertilization, homosexuality, and euthanasia have more than one source. Certainly one is intellectual. First, it makes a difference how one conceives the end of man. If temporal fulfillment is all there is, one has to achieve happiness in this life. But views with respect to immortality may not be the deciding factor. Few would affirm that we are so obtuse or that nature is so unintelligible that we cannot figure out what leads to human fulfillment in the long run. On basic moral goals, divergent schools are likely to be in agreement even though they may be in disagreement about the ultimate end of man. Until the middle decades of this century communities could ban pornography and discourage premarital sex, divorce, and homosexuality. But the unity of thought required for such concerted action gave way as ideas long dormant in the academy reached the marketplace. The ability of nineteenth-century rationalism to reverse time-tested codes forces us to confront another aspect of human behavior, one known to antiquity but too often ignored by moralists, namely, a built-in disorder in human nature. Aristotle recognized that man is the only animal in nature with two sets of faculties warring against each other. Saint Paul was aware that "the good I would, I do not." Aristotle's puzzlement was answered for Paul in the Hebrew Scriptures. It must be admitted that philosophers themselves can be driven by extraphilosophical impulses just as a temporizing conscience is willing to embrace questionable theory to justify congenial behavior.

If a moral consensus is today a rarity, if in the West we seem to have lost our intellectual bearings, it may in part be the result of a willful rejection of a heritage that would call into question favored practice. There is a long line of texts in Western literature that address the relation of morality to law, texts that are as relevant today as when they were first written. Ancient descriptions of human nature, discussions of happiness, of virtue, of means and ends, of personal and social goals, and of law are as instructive today as they were when they first appeared. The twentieth century may be more conscious of method than the Greeks, but the ancients, no less than we, distinguished among the ontological source of principle, principle itself, the application of principle, and the role of observation in both determining and applying principle. Iconoclastic denunciations of the inherited have not served us well. Cicero, reflecting on the qualifications for leadership in the commonwealth, made a knowledge of and respect for tradition a prime requisite for office.[16] Livy recommended much the same for his period when he wrote of a failing Rome.

I invite the reader's attention to the much more serious consideration of the kind of lives our ancestors lived, of who were the men and what the means, both in politics and war, by which Rome's power was first acquired and subsequently expanded. I would have him trace the processes of our moral decline, to watch first the sinking of the foundations of morality as the old teaching was allowed to lapse, then the final collapse of the whole edifice, and the dark dawning of our modern day when we can neither endure our vices nor face the remedies needed to cure them.[17]

In many texts Saint Thomas gives custom the force of law.

The critical movement that has culminated in today's rejection of the past itself needs to be scrutinized. As Karl Lowith has pointed

---

16. *On the Commonwealth*, trans. C. H. Sabine and S. B. Smith (Indianapolis, Ind.: Bobbs-Merrill, 1950), 7.

17. Titus Livius, Preface to his *History* (Cambridge, Mass.: Loeb Classical Library, Harvard University Press, 1924), 1.5

out, criticism can be exercised with reference to what unites things or what separates them.[18] Critical reflection on the common experience of mankind will inevitably challenge a deviant now. The norms that are apt to be recognized as universal are none other than those time-transcending guidelines for the attainment of the human good, norms known since antiquity as "natural law."

18. *From Hegel to Nietzsche: The Revolution in Nineteenth-Century Thought*, trans. David E. Green (New York: Columbia University Press, 1964), 328.

PART II

THE LAW AND SOCIETY

* * *

EIGHT

COLLECTIVE RESPONSIBILITY

I

There are two things that I wish to do in this brief presentation. First, I will sketch in a general way the philosophical temperament that has in recent decades influenced the framing of law; second, I will single out for special treatment the idea of "collective guilt," which I take to be one of many concepts that first gained currency in the philosophical world before its use in the law. Particular attention will be paid to the use of the notion of collective guilt in corporate law.

It is commonly acknowledged that if a society's laws are based on a particular cultural outlook and that outlook collapses, the laws themselves will crumble.[1] Ronald Dworkin, in his work *Law's Empire*, argues the converse thesis that in a morally pluralistic society only the law can provide the unity required for social order.[2] For Dworkin, law receives its moral force precisely because it provides this unifying function. He recognizes that Western society is ideologically split, with the consequence that its laws no longer flow out of a common view. Law tends to be created as a tissue of compromises between self-interested factions and consequently provides the only set of agreed-upon principles that may serve for concerted action. The open question, of course, is whether law pragmatically created

1. Lord Patrick Devlin, *The Enforcement of Morals* (London: Oxford University Press, 1965).
2. Ronald Dworkin, *Law's Empire* (London: Fontana, 1986).

will either serve the common good or foster the noblest of human tendencies.

Alasdair MacIntyre, in *Whose Justice, Which Rationality?*, makes the point that theories of justice and practical rationality are but aspects of an allegiance given to a much larger intellectual tradition.[3] He speaks of the illusion of the autonomy of philosophical thought. "Philosophical theories," he argues, "give organized expression to concepts and theories already embodied in forms of practice and types of community. As such they make available for rational criticism and for further rational development those socially embodied theories and concepts of which they provided an understanding."[4] One can be, suggests MacIntyre, an Aristotelian or a Humean, but one cannot be both. Furthermore, one cannot be either without appropriate social organization or without a congenial *polis*. The conditions for the administration of Aristotelian justice are different from the conditions for Humean justice.

Although such issues are rarely accorded public debate, the forums in which they are occasionally aired are those provided by the U.S. Supreme Court and the Senate Judiciary Committee. It is principally in briefs submitted to the Court that ideas that touch upon the fundamental aspirations of life and that affect the culture of the nation and its modes of governance are contested. No one denies that judge-made law has become a powerful force in shaping the nation's culture, perhaps more so than the enactments of legislative assemblies, either at the national or the state level. So-called interest groups with legislative agendas take it for granted that they are more likely to have their aims implemented through the process of judicial review than through the enactments of legislative assemblies. Litigation is instigated with deliberation; "forum shopping" is standard practice as activist organizations seek judges of like mind. The bench itself tends to reflect the intellectual trends of the very same academy that inspires the interest groups to take action.

3. Alasdair MacIntyre, *Whose Justice, Which Rationality?* (Notre Dame, Ind.: University of Notre Dame Press, 1988).

4. Ibid., 390.

In recent decades most of the moralism has come from the left and has had as its objective the alteration of accepted modes of procedure. Whereas any legislation is apt to be the result of mutual concession, judge-made law often reflects the purely utopian ideas of the academy. Social theory fabricated by intellectuals who are untouched by life in the work-a-day world can be compelling in its clarity and with ease can be translated into law by an activist judiciary. To understand the drift of contemporary courts, one has to probe beneath current legal theory and in a MacIntyre fashion place such theory in a larger cultural, should I say, philosophical context.

MacIntyre is not alone in his judgment that law, whether created by legislative or judicial action, is but one strand in a single fabric called an "intellectual tradition." Peter W. Huber, in discussing changing conceptions of "liability," recognizes as much when he identifies a concerted effort on the part of a handful of legal scholars, largely for philosophical reasons, "to repeal the common law of torts."[5] Ted Honderich convincingly shows the legal implications of accepted theories of psychological determinism and their tendency to instantiate liberal rather than conservative policies in the social order.[6]

Two other works of interest to both philosophers and lawyers are those written by Peter A. French and Larry May.[7] French writes on collective and corporate responsibility, providing a systematic rationale for holding corporations not merely civilly but criminally accountable. May argues that many social groups that lack tight organizational structures can be said to be collectively responsible for the joint actions of their members, and argues similarly that social groups are capable of being harmed even when individual members are not aware of the harm. "In unorganized groups," writes May,

5. Peter W. Huber, *Liability: The Legal Revolution and Its Consequences* (New York: Basic Books, 1988).

6. T. Honderich, *A Theory of Determinism: The Mind, Neuroscience, and Life Hopes* (Oxford, U.K.: Clarendon Press, 1988).

7. Peter A. French, *Collective and Corporate Responsibility* (New York: Columbia University Press, 1984); Larry May, *The Morality of Groups: Collective Responsibility, Group-Based Harm, and Corporate Rights* (Notre Dame, Ind.: University of Notre Dame Press, 1987).

"solidarity and other relationships allow the group to have action and interests even though no decision-making structure for the group exists."[8]

These are only a few of many philosophical works that consciously attempt to alter common thinking about the law and the objectives of legislation. One easily forms the impression from a survey of recent legal theory that much discussion is not dispassionate in a professional way but has gone beyond a descriptive stage of theory and of plausible outcomes to one of outright advocacy. The literature is not without its effect. U.S. corporations are increasingly the victims of the new modes of thought as zealous prosecutors couple philosophical discussion with vague federal statutes to transform civil regulations into criminal law. Countless state and local regulations similarly have been criminalized. In holding corporations accountable for regulatory violations, many prosecutors no longer require evidence of malicious intent, the traditional condition of criminal conduct. Dubious or not, the notion of "corporate criminal liability" is one that hands over to an unreasonable prosecutor a powerful capacity for mischief. If a corporation can be exposed to criminal punishment for even a good-faith error of judgment, traditional common law in important respects has been abandoned.

With this impression as a backdrop, I wish to examine the philosophical wellsprings of certain ideas, particularly the notion of collective guilt, that have crept into legal theory with consequences for civil law. Many examples could be pursued. Need we be reminded that a rejection of the traditional understanding of what it means to be a person was accomplished in the philosophical community before it became the basis of *Roe v. Wade*. Similarly, the rationale undergirding the use of capital punishment was eroded in the social sciences before the Supreme Court invalidated most state laws that theretofore had permitted its use. When retribution, for philosophical reasons, ceased to be regarded as a plausible goal, and the deterrent effect of punishment was thrown into doubt by social science,

8. May, *Morality of Groups*, 180.

capital punishment became difficult to defend. Consequently, it is rarely employed even where new statutes have been written to make it legally permissible. Interestingly, whereas the retributive purpose of punishment is generally eschewed in criminal law, Peter French is happy to employ it in civil law, at least when it comes to punishing corporations.

Tort law is yet another area where shifting philosophical sands have undermined legal structures. Traditional notions of liability depend on the acceptance of the principles of causality and free will. With the ascendancy of various psychological and sociological determinisms, tort law has changed dramatically. At one time the law was fairly clear: one had to be causally responsible in some way to be held accountable. Today any loss is thought to demand compensation, and if it is not available from the wrongdoer, the burden of compensation is thought to be distributable to the community. Notions such as "responsibility," "causality," and "intention" obviously do not play the role they once did. Social objectives have become paramount, superseding legitimate accountability or fault. The ancient starting point of tort law—"the loss lies where it falls"—has been replaced by "the loss lies with the community." Another example of changing intellectual outlooks influencing the Supreme Court is found if one reviews the opinions of the Court over the past forty years as it has interpreted the religion clauses of the First Amendment. As the academy has become progressively secular, severing its ties with a Christian past, the Court has turned the First Amendment, which was designed to *protect* religion, into something that *handicaps* its influence.

This is not to ignore the fact that many changes are the result of the political activism of groups that have effectively lobbied the Court, but activism alone cannot account for success. Before judicial change can take place, the intellectual soil first has to be made receptive. It is manifestly easier to change the minds of those associated with the interpretion of law than it is to change the minds of those responsible for legislative enactments. The split between the intellectuals and the people on basic social issues is notorious. Thus a handful of social scientists by carefully placing in a variety of law journals more or less the same article, with statistics changed to fit the locale, purporting to show the uselessness of capital punishment as a deterrent, managed though sympathetic courts to have the Supreme Court void most state laws. One is forced to make the judgment that in the English-speaking world we have witnessed in the decades since the 1960s a concerted effort to change social structures by changing the law. The new law is the product of a "new" way of looking at things. I say "new" guardedly since the new is little more than an Enlightenment way of looking at things. MacIntyre uses Aristotle and David Hume to symbolize the difference between the old and the new.

II

While many of these philosophical underpinnings beg attention, I turn now to the principal theme of the present inquiry, namely, the notion of "collective guilt." Surprisingly, it goes unexamined in a number of contexts where one would expect the use of critical intelligence. Peoples, generations, classes, races, industries, geographic regions, professions, and religious bodies are held accountable, not in some vague "public opinion" sort of way, but before courts of law. From tort law to affirmative action policy, blame is often assigned to groups, sometimes to groups no longer in existence, and sometimes to mere conceptual entities. Restitution is not infrequently extracted from groups or from the heirs of groups without their responsibility for harm having been established.

Corporate defendants have been assessed damages even after proving that they could not possibly have caused the harm. Take the following case: From the 1940s to 1971 approximately two million women took the synthetic hormone diethylstilbestrol (DES) to prevent miscarriages and morning sickness during pregnancy. The drug had been approved by the U.S. Food and Drug Administration (FDA) and was marketed by some three hundred pharmaceutical companies, often under generic labels. In 1970 researchers reported cancer and other problems among the daughters of DES users. The FDA banned the drug in 1971.

The cases quickly went to court. The mothers of many DES plaintiffs couldn't remember which brands they had used. Courts in several states made the assumption that all DES pills were essentially the same and created a market-share test so that damages could be assessed against the drug makers in proportion to their share of sales. In *Hymowitz v. Lilly* the highest New York court went further, applying the market-share concept of responsibility to a drug manufacturer that could prove that the defendant's mother did not use its pill.[9]

The questions forced upon us are these: Can there be collective complicity and therefore collective liability without personal or corporate guilt? Can a corporation be held liable where there is no evidence that it or anyone else knew of any risks connected with the product?

Broad notions entertained in the framing of law are almost always the by-product of previous academic discussion. Before the concept of "market share" became current, certain philosophical discussions of collective guilt, collective responsibility, and punishment had to occur. While this is not the place to examine the history of all these concepts, little inquiry is needed to show that the notion of "collective guilt" is an ancient one. Discussions of that notion can be found in classical and medieval literature, as well as in contemporary literature.

The ancients no less than we recognized that societies are generated out of collective beliefs and traditions that are passed on unconsciously by individuals. Emile Durkheim, the student of history and influential social theorist of the late nineteenth century, thought that traditions can exist in groups even when they are not instantiated by any individual. In his *Rules of Sociological Method* (1895) he even accords ontological status to social traditions and social relations independent of individual members of the group.[10]

In a now-famous article, written shortly after the close of World War II, Karl Jaspers attempted to deal with the guilt of the German

9. *Hymowitz v. Lilly and Co.*, 73 N.Y. 2nd 487, 539 N.E. 2nd 1069, 541 N.Y.S. 2nd 1941 (1989).

10. Emil Durkheim, *Rules of Sociological Method*, trans. S. Soloway and J. Mueller, ed. E. Carlin (New York: Free Press, 1964), 7.

people.[11] The horrors perpetrated in the concentration camps were by then generally known. What had been suspected could now be graphically documented. Jaspers raised the question of guilt in the context of demands for restitution. To what extent were the German people as a whole culpable, and to what extent could one expect atonement? The issue Jaspers raised was not that of the responsibility of the German state. No one questioned national accountability or the requirement of "reparations." Jaspers was probing much deeper. Though his essay was entitled "Moral Guilt," Jaspers was aware that the vast majority of the German-speaking peoples were not morally responsible for the atrocities committed under the Third Reich. If the vast majority of the German people were neither legally nor morally guilty, could the German-speaking peoples yet be held accountable? In an effort to sort things out, Jaspers introduced the notion "collective guilt at a psychic level." Insofar as the German people shared a common language and a common culture, and insofar as they were nourished by a common literature, common music, and distinctive patterns of civic behavior, they could be said to be a collective. In Jaspers's analysis there existed enough solidarity to produce a national psyche that in some sense could be held accountable such that one generation could make claims on another. Jaspers recognized the difficulty of defending a notion of psychological guilt apart from legal or moral guilt. With Aquinas, he could agree that "no man can do an injustice except voluntarily."[12] Though he did not, he could in other respects have appealed to Aquinas for at least partial support of his view.

Saint Thomas's position on collective guilt might startle the modern reader. He writes: "When the whole multitude sins, vengeance must be taken on them." He even speaks of the virtue of revenge. The moral virtue of fortitude disposes one to vengeance. Of the two vices opposed to vengeance, cruelty is the excess; being remiss is the

11. "Moral Guilt," reprinted in *Crimes of War*, ed. R. A. Falk, G. Kolko, and R. J. Lifton (New York: Vintage Books, 1971), 476ff.

12. *Summa Theologiae*, trans. Fathers of the English Dominican Province (New York: Benzinger Brothers, 1947), II–II, Q. 59, a. 3.

defect.[13] The severity of vengeance should be brought to bear upon the few principals if they can be identified. "Sometimes even the good are punished in temporal matters together with the wicked, for not having condemned their sins."[14] But Saint Thomas enters this qualification: "A man should never be condemned without fault of his own to an inflictive punishment such as death, mutilation or flogging, but he may be condemned . . . to a punishment of forfeiture, even without any fault on his part, but not without cause." For example, in the crime of high treason, a son loses his inheritance through the sin of his parent.[15] Saint Thomas also writes: "It is a natural law that one should repent of the evil one has done, by grieving for having done it, and by seeking a remedy for one's grief in some way or other, and also that one should show some signs of grief."[16] Charity demands that a man should both grieve for the offense and be anxious to make satisfaction. "Now amendment for an offense committed against another is not made by merely ceasing to offend, but it is necessary to make some kind of compensation."[17] Clearly Jaspers is reaching for the same solution. While Jaspers does not use the word "charity" in his analysis of German guilt and restitution, his analysis leads him to a similar notion. Thomas in many contexts appeals to the principle of charity where modern authors are apt to invoke the concept of "right."

For the discussion that follows it is important to lay bare a number of distinctions and assumptions. No one denies that guilt implies responsibility. Responsibility in turn presupposes freedom to act or not to act. In speaking of freedom, it is necessary to distinguish: (1) freedom in a moral sense from freedom under the law, and (2) the legal sense of guilt from its moral sense. One can be held *accountable* before civil law without being *morally responsible* for harm. Civil law itself recognizes this truth when it takes into consideration motivation and extenuating circumstances and sometimes allows them to mitigate

---

13. Ibid., Q. 108, a. 1, ad. 5. 14. Ibid., Q. 108, a. 4.
15. Ibid., Q. 108, a. 4, ad. 2. 16. Ibid., III, Q. 84, a. 7, ad. 1.
17. Ibid., Q. 85, a. 3.

guilt. The continuity between the moral and the civil is so fast that in practice the distinction is often blurred or even ignored. Moral outrage is not infrequently thought to be immediately translatable into law. Appeals for the creation of law typically invoke danger to health or damage to the environment, or they cite some other material or social disadvantage if action is not taken, but they are nonetheless appeals to the moral order.

Another insight that must be kept in mind is that action follows judgment and judgment is made necessarily within a cultural context. How one views a proposed course of action depends in part on one's education, that is, on the distinctions one has learned to make and the principles one invokes habitually. Certain courses of action that may acceptable in the West are unthinkable in the East and vice versa. In the West some may see nothing wrong with the merchandising of pornography or with divorce or abortion. The same is not true in an Islamic society. It would be precarious to attribute moral guilt to those who act in the light of conscience, even if that conscience judged by a time-transcending moral code seems to be ill-informed, but this does not mean that holders are unaccountable for their beliefs in all respects. From any point of view, one has the obligation to form a correct conscience.

Also recognized is the principle that not all law binds in conscience. Good civil law tends to explicate or elaborate the moral order. Thus, building codes, traffic regulations, and rules governing securities trading are in some sense moral dictates before they become statutes. Law that flouts common perceptions of right and wrong is not regarded as moral. This distinction between civil law and moral law, though sometimes challenged from the academy, is universally recognized. The distinction cuts both ways. A corporation that operates wholly within the law may yet be guilty of moral infraction. The sale of pornography, the creation of advertising that deliberately manipulates the truth, or media distortion on behalf of partisan causes are examples to the point. One can claim that the manufacturing of shabby merchandise that mimics the genuine article and is marketed to the ill-educated or unsuspecting is a kind of

moral infraction. Some would extend moral guilt to those who manufacture tobacco products or distilled spirits or who make coats from
animal pelts. No one would hesitate to attribute moral guilt to a corporation that knowingly manufactures a defective and potentially
dangerous product, quite apart from any civil penalty that might be
inflicted.

But, granted immorality on the part of a corporation, where does
moral guilt lie? Are all associated with the corporation collectively
guilty? If not, how far down the corporate ladder does responsibility
extend? To the worker on the assembly line? To the wholesaler? To the
retailer? To the shareholder? If guilt follows knowledge, it may be that
only a few in the testing laboratory or in the executive suite are privy
to the information that a given product is potentially troublesome or
could be modified with additional cost to diminish risk. Although the
corporation, before the law, can be held accountable for negligence, it
is difficult to believe that the average worker in the plant or billing office, unless the company has a record of dubious performance, is in
possession of the knowledge that would imply criminal complicity.
There are exceptions, of course. We all have read stories of whistle-
blowers who have brought to light questionable practices, sometimes
to the gratitude of management. Where corporate guilt is determined, it is not likely that all workers would be held accountable either by an irate group of stockholders or before a court of law. When
a specific individual, in violation of corporate policy, has been guilty
of harm, it makes little sense to hold the corporation criminally liable, subject to punitive damages, which ultimately are collectively
shared by innocent shareholders.

Readiness to accept the notion of "collective guilt," no doubt,
stems from the number of egregious cases where societies taken as a
whole seem accountable. The twentieth century provides numerous
examples of societies acting, if not as wholes, at least with sufficient
unity to implement morally unacceptable policy—for example, Germany under Hitler and the Soviet Union under Stalin, two governments that systematically eliminated so-called enemies of the state.
One also thinks of South Africa's apartheid system that limited full

civic participation to whites, the antebellum American South's enslavement of blacks, and the postbellum South's system of segregation laws. To what extent are we willing to blame the German or Soviet peoples for the atrocities committed within the borders of their nations? Can the nineteenth-century immigrant cooper working within his shop in Minneapolis be blamed for slavery in Mississippi or for postbellum segregation statutes enacted all over the South? The way we talk about these matters is often misleading. We speak of "sharing in the greatness of a nation," or we may say that we "take pride in belonging to a scholarly family," but we must be careful not to hypostatize abstractions or make them bearers of value. As H. D. Lewis pointed out in his seminal article "Collective Responsibility," linguistic devices that make for succinctness of expression are to be recognized for their metaphorical and elliptical meaning and not taken as literal truth.[18] A family group or a nation, I am willing to argue, cannot be the bearer of guilt; in neither is there sufficient unity or participation in the deliberative process to warrant accountability.

Corporations are different. They are not mere aggregates of people but have a metaphysical-logical identity. Otto von Gierke has suggested that the law in conferring on the corporation the status of a legal person is merely recognizing a prelegal social condition. The corporation is the offspring of certain social actions and possess a de facto personality that the law declares to be a juridical fact.[19] Brian Tierney traces the notion of corporate personality to medieval canon law and its doctrine of agency. "In Roman law," writes Tierney, "an individual or group could appoint an agent to negotiate with a third party, but the result of the transaction was to establish an obligation between the third party and the agent, not directly between the third party and the principal. In canon law, when a corporate group estab-

18. H. D. Lewis, "Collective Responsibility," *Philosophy* 23, no. 84 (1948): 47. See also Joel Feinberg, "Collective Responsibility," *Journal of Philosophy* 65, no. 21 (1968): 674–88, and Virginia Held, "Can a Random Collection of Individuals Be Morally Responsible?," *Journal of Philosophy* 67, no. 14 (1970): 471–81.

19. *Political Theory of the Middle Ages*, trans. F. W. Maitland (Cambridge, U.K.: Cambridge University Press, 1900).

lished a representative with *plena potestas* that group was directly obliged by the representative's acts, even when it had not consented to them in advance."[20] The ancient Roman principle *Quod omnes tangit ab omnibus approbator* (What touches all is to be approved by all) was replaced by one that allowed a representative to act on behalf of all. Thus commitments made in the name of an organized group may persist even after the composition of the group and its "will" changes. If a group reneges on a commitment, the fault may be that of no individual member, yet the liability for breach of contract, falling on the group as a whole, will distribute burdens quite unavoidably on faultless members.

Peter A. French, in his extended analysis of corporate responsibility, maintains that for a corporation to be treated as a moral person, it must be possible to attribute to it a corporate intention. This is different from attributing intentions to the biological persons who comprise its board of directors or its top-level management.[21] Corporations, at least major corporations, have internal decision-making structures, and this is reflected in their organizational charts and in their established methods of creating corporate policy. In many cases, one can even describe the basic beliefs of a corporation from which specific actions flow. The moment policy is sidestepped or violated, it is no longer the policy of the company. Maverick acts cannot be described as having been done for corporate reasons. Thus it is possible to distinguish between individual staff negligence and corporate negligence. Executives voting to adopt certain objectives when required by the corporate structure to vote, in fact, constitutes the corporation's deciding to do something. A corporate officer who ignores corporate policy, possibly in the name of expediency, may be morally accountable while the corporation itself is innocent of moral blame, although corporate civil accountability may be unavoidable.

20. B. Tierney, *Religion, Law, and the Growth of Constitutional Thought* (Cambridge, U.K.: Cambridge University Press, 1982), 23.
21. French, *Collective and Corporate*, 39.

The *Exxon Valdez* oil spill provides a case study. The question yet to be answered is the following: Is the poisoning of Prince William Sound a simple matter of a captain and his ship or of a corporation and its policies? The former skipper of the *Valdez* was criminally charged. Normally, in spite of the National Wildlife Federation's urging federal prosecutors to "go after the individual who is responsible at the top,"[22] one would not expect Exxon to be charged with criminal as opposed to civil wrongdoing. The law offers a way to punish corporations through liability suits. It is usually thought that the possibility of a large judgment against the malfeasance of a company is adequate inducement to establish operational policies sufficient to minimize risk. In the *Valdez* case evidence is yet to be produced that Exxon as a corporation was remiss. Its criminal prosecution may be more a political move than one dictated by legal principle. The *Valdez* oil spill and its aftermath also illustrate a willingness on the part of some to extend blame beyond the principals at hand. This is seen in the suggestion that the Coast Guard be held accountable for not warning the ship that it was heading for a reef. While hasty finger pointing is not evidence of the collapse of law, the readiness to attribute guilt apart from any causal connection has to be confronted. One is amused how outdated is the oft-quoted remark of Baron Thurlaw. The once Lord Chancellor of England is reputed to have said, "Did you ever expect a corporation to have a conscience when it has no soul to be damned and no body to be killed?" But times have changed. Corporations are expected to have souls and can be sentenced to death by juries.

Although responsibility belongs essentially to the individual, responsibility can be shared, both morally and before the law. To the extent that one shows the mind-set and objectives of the group, one participates in the group's guilt. If one subscribes to a doctrine of natural slavery and is in full sympathy with segregationist laws, one is intellectually united to others of like mind and can be accused of moral failure. But to be held legally accountable is another matter. Here we must distinguish between active and passive participation.

22. *New York Times*, 11 February 1990, Sec. E, p. 6.

Active participation entails full responsibility; *passive participation* indicates less responsibility. It is possible to be part of a community that through its leadership is bent upon injustice of one sort or another and yet be in no way responsible.

In a democracy it is necessary to distinguish among the nation, the body politic, and the state. A *nation* is created by a common language and culture and may be broader than the political boundaries that demarcate countries. A *body politic* is coextensive with geographical boundaries although suffrage may not be universal within those boundaries. The *state* is the topmost governing body, and even though it must ultimately receive its authority from the people, it may not at every turn reflect the desires of the majority, let alone the people as a whole. A nation is more like an aggregate, and there is reason to argue that moral responsibility predicates cannot rightfully be ascribed to aggregate collectives. An aggregate may act, but without a decision-making organization it can be aware neither of its action nor of the moral nature of that action.

Even where representative government prevails there are severe limitations on the power of the individual to modify the actions of the state. It is easy to envisage a situation where dissent or protest would result in severe penalties. The obligation to work for change in policy varies from situation to situation and depends on one's station in life. Mental reservation is always possible, but active resistance may be self-defeating. It is idealistic in the extreme to attribute guilt to the whole although sanctions may unavoidably be imposed on the whole from without and indiscriminately affect guilty and nonguilty alike. The sanctions that one country may morally inflict on another depend on the gravity of the matter. They range from war to tariffs and import quotas.

With respect to the ontology of groups, a group is created by a common final cause. A group has no being except in the intentional order. Ends may be shared to varying degrees. Personal responsibility follows interior assent to the end and may not be coextensive with legal accountability. While one may not have options with respect to membership in a nation or in a body politic, one does exercise choice with respect to lesser communities or organizations. It is commonly acknowledged that one has to be careful with respect to the organizations one joins or to which one lends one's name. Again, accountability follows intention.

If this analysis is correct, one can speak of "collective guilt" only if certain conditions are met, that is, only if one can identify a common intention, a common purpose, which is the product of a deliberative mechanism, and only if one is successful in enumerating those who belong to the collective. One can allow for different degrees of accountability, but accountability must be demonstrated. Tenuous connections are connections, but they are nevertheless "tenuous." They may be both morally and legally compelling, but, on the other hand, they may not be. Circumstances dictate our judgment. The "collective" need not be a person in the legal sense.

I find inconsistent deterministic approaches, psychological and sociological, which, on the one hand, seem to deny personal responsibility but, on the other, insist on collective responsibility. Deterministic approaches usually fail to recognize the subtlety of decision making. Decisions are always made within a context, but how that context is presented or is allowed to influence decisions is self-determined. This is seen negatively in our ability to opt out of a distasteful milieu, if not physically, at least psychologically. In a pre-Solidarity address to his fellow countrymen, Karol Wojtyla warned of the dangers of a psychological migration, a failure to engage oneself politically.[23] His admonition may be taken as a recognition that one can be remiss with respect to an obligation to influence the collective, and in being remiss one can share responsibility for the harm that may ensue from its action. But his analysis also points to a fundamental freedom. We control how things are presented to us. We choose to be engaged by putting the matter at hand in a certain light; appetency follows cognition.

One has the impression that the notion of "collective guilt," like

---

23. *Sollicitudo Rei Socialis*, promulgated 30 December 1987. *Origins* 17, no. 38 (1988): 656–57.

the notion of "right," is used principally to extract concessions or reparations from groups judged to be guilty. This is particularly oner-ous when one generation is charged with the wrongs of another and is confronted with demands to compensate members of a generation who were not born when the wrong occurred. Of course, claims may be made across generations if lineage and causality can be estab-lished. If an individual can inherit both positively and negatively, something similar is true with respect to natural structures such as family and country and artificial constructs such as corporations. But most of the time what is inherited is a melange. While egregious fault cannot be ignored nor attendant hardship dismissed, the social mi-lieu is rarely black or white. Reason must prevail in sorting out re-sponsibility and therefore accountability. One cannot be guilty either before civil law or the divine throne for infractions one has not com-mitted. One cannot be part of a collective without intent. When col-lective guilt is invoked, whether it be called "market share" or "corpo-rate accountability," prudence dictates that one examine not only the causal record that will determine responsibility but the motives of the accuser. The concept "collective guilt" may be more a political or a distributionist banner than a useful moral insight.

NINE

ACCOUNTABILITY WITHOUT CAUSALITY

Tort Litigation Reaches Fairy-Tale Levels

I

"Tort Litigation Reaches Fairy-Tale Levels" is the caption given to a letter to the editor recently published by the *Wall Street Journal.* The writer, of course, was not the first to notice.[1] By one estimate tort awards represent 2.3 percent of the U.S. gross national product, about eight times the comparable rate for Japan. Another study reports that U.S. liability insurance rates are twenty times those of Europe.[2] Complaints about the drift that tort law has taken have come from many quarters as sellers are found strictly liable for environmental cleanups, as industries are held liable for "unsafe" products, and as physicians are obligated to pay enormous sums for insurance protection against malpractice awards. (While usually a matter of federal and state regulations rather than tort law, liability for environmental infractions proceeds from the same expanded duty of care that drives current tort concepts.) Questionable court rulings are occurring with enough frequency that it is apparent to anyone who follows American legal practice in even a cursory way that major shifts in legal theory are occurring. Tort law is, of course, but one facet of a vast legal

1. The 78th American Assembly, held from 31 May to 3 June, 1990, was devoted to "Tort Law and the Public Interest." Seventy men and women representing a spectrum of leaders from the defense and plaintiff's bars, industry, insurance, medicine, science, government, the judiciary, and academia met to assess the drift of tort law in America.

2. William Fay, *Washington Times,* 24 August 1991.

system, a system built upon an ancient philosophy of law and notions concerning the function of law in society.

It is not simply, as one would expect, that a difference exists between the nineteenth- and twentieth-century jurisprudential outlooks. G. Edward White in his 1980 book *Tort Law in America* reports a major shift in discussions of tort law between the 1950s and the 1970s.[3] He finds that typical law review articles in the 1950s were tightly argued analyses of case law leading to the discovery of applicable principle, whereas in the 1970s tort literature was supplanted by broad and abstract analyses based on sociological and economic perspectives. "The novel quality of recent casebooks," says White, "is their tendency to speculate broadly on the function of tort law as a whole."[4] He cites one textbook that calls for "a critical examination of fundamental ideas underlying tort liability" and another that discusses "three competing perspectives" concerning its rationale.

The 1970s literature that White views with some alarm because of its "non-legal, theoretical perspective" has been amplified as philosophers and social theorists have written works bearing titles such as *A Sociological Theory of Law* (1985), *Marxism and Morality* (1985), *Ethics and the Rule of Law* (1984), *The End of Law* (1984), *Marxism and Law* (1982), *The Concept of Socialist Law* (1990), *Collective and Corporate Responsibility* (1984), and *Postmodern Jurisprudence* (1991).[5] White suggests that shifting legal perspectives may be the result of the law's groping for a secular foundation to replace its former theistic underpinnings.[6]

---

3. G. Edward White, *Tort Law in America* (Oxford, U.K.: Oxford University Press, 1980), 212ff.

4. Ibid., 215.

5. N. Luhmann, *A Sociological Theory of Law* (London: Routledge & Kegan Paul, 1985); Steven Lukes, *Marxism and Morality* (Oxford, U.K.: Clarendon Press, 1985); David Lyons, *Ethics and the Rule of Law* (Cambridge, U.K.: Cambridge University Press, 1984); Timothy O'Hagan, *The End of Law* (Oxford, U.K.: Basil Blackwell, 1984); Hugh Collins, *Marxism and Law* (Oxford, U.K.: Clarendon Press, 1982); Christine Sypnowich, *The Concept of Socialist Law* (Oxford, U.K.: Clarendon Press, 1990); Peter French, *Collective and Corporate Responsibility* (New York: Columbia University Press, 1984); C. Douzinas et al., *Postmodern Jurisprudence* (London: Routledge, 1991).

6. White, *Tort Law*, 214.

Lord Patrick Devlin, writing in the early 1960s, speculated that if a society's laws are based on a particular worldview and that worldview collapses, the laws themselves will crumble.[7] Ronald Dworkin, in his work *Law's Empire*, argues the converse thesis: that in a moral pluralistic society it is only the law that can provide the unity required for social order.[8] For Dworkin, law receives its moral force precisely because it provides this unifying function. Recognizing that Western society is ideologically split, Dworkin argues that law no longer flows from a common view of man and the social order. Instead, law tends to be created as a tissue of compromise between self-interested parties, and consequently it provides the only set of agreed-upon principles that may serve as norms for concerted action. Alasdair MacIntyre reminds us in *Whose Justice? Which Rationality?* and again in *Three Rival Versions of Moral Inquiry* that rival intellectual traditions are not only incompatible but also give rise to different legal structures.[9] The conditions of the administration of Aristotelian justice, he maintains, are different from the conditions of the administration of justice based on the principles of David Hume.

It may be noted that the issue is not one of cultural pluralism. It is not that we are confronted with a variety of cultures—Islamic, Oriental, and Western—vying for allegiance; rather, the conflict is between two modes of Western thought, reducible, roughly, to the Roman and common law tradition, on the one hand, and its repudiation, on the other. At one level, the conflict is between two differing conceptions of law and two differing conceptions of the role of law in society. At a deeper level, the conflict is between two views of human nature. The virtue ethics and the common-good morality of the natural law tradition advance one view; the materialisms and determinisms, social and psychological, of the nineteenth century advance another.

7. Lord Patrick Devlin, *The Enforcement of Morals* (London: Oxford University Press, 1965).

8. Ronald Dworkin, *Law's Empire* (London: Fontana, 1986).

9. Alasdair MacIntyre, *Whose Justice, Which Rationality?* (Notre Dame, Ind.: University of Notre Dame Press, 1988), and *Three Rival Versions of Moral Inquiry* (Notre Dame, Ind.: University of Notre Dame Press, 1990).

Theories respecting the purpose of law date to antiquity; clear expressions are to be found in the pre-Socratics and in Plato. In the *Laws*, Plato identified the purpose of law with instruction, instruction both of the individual and of society. The legislator's method, Plato observed, is not essentially different from that of a physician, for law is nothing other than a prescription for a well-ordered society. Law is both a communication and an institutionalized way to regulate and direct human behavior. Communal interests demand that codes of behavior be formulated and observed. A well-ordered society is likely to be a beneficent one.

A beneficent social order is undoubtedly the goal of the many who aim to change our way of thinking about the objectives of law. It was the goal of Karl Marx when he delivered his famous critique of bourgeois law. Marx was convinced that the bourgeois law of his day was the product of the capitalist ruling class, a class that created the law to sustain its mode of economic organization. Marx's critique focused on nineteenth-century tort law, which he thought tempered entrepreneurial risk with a doctrine that places the risk of accidents and product defects on the user. His blueprint for the establishment of a socialist order called for the overthrow of the status quo in favor of laws that would promote his egalitarian conception of society. He recognized that before the revolution could occur, the groundwork for it had to be laid. First, the belief structures that prevail have to be shown to be historically contingent; this he found to be easy, for they can be shown not always to have existed in their present form. Once contingency is recognized, the door is open to change; legal structures, just and unjust, are thus seen to be alterable. It may take courage and cunning to organize with others the struggle against the received, but once the ideological structure is in place, the practical may be advanced. Although the failure of Marxism as an economic theory has been clearly observed in the economic collapse of Eastern Europe and the Soviet Union, its inadequacy remains to be demonstrated in other areas.

One of the most notorious expressions of Marxist legal theory is found in the theory that currently goes under the banner "critical

legal studies," although it has antecedents in the outlook known variously as "legal realism," "legal positivism," and "legal activism." I do
not wish to exaggerate the influence of the critical legal studies
movement on the courts. The judicial system on the whole works
well, with the courts invoking solid case law in the everyday satisfaction of their mandate. Yet there seems to be a subtle battle for the soul
or conscience of the nation taking place within the American academy today, with the critical legal studies faction forming one battle
group at war with the Western cultural tradition. Like Marx, the
"Crits" recognize that law reflects, constitutes, legitimizes, and en-
forces commonly perceived notions of right and wrong, excellence
and decay. In the promotion of their own ends, they seek command
posts in the courts and in the law schools, and when it becomes possible, they do not hesitate to instantiate law that reflects their social
objectives. In their hands law has become a political instrument.

No one can deny the discretionary nature of court decisions, but
to flatly deny that objectivity and justice are desiderata, as many do, is
to fly in the face of the traditional notion of the role of law in society.
It is bad enough that the critical legal studies faction tends to reduce
the framing of law to a political function, but the political objectives
in question are usually not those chosen by any democratic referendum. The objectives sought are framed by an intellectual elite often
contrary to the judgment of the common man. Activist judges, drawing upon purely academic intelligence, find confirming legal rationalizations for their choices; ignore or distort contrary arguments, authorities, facts, and social realities; and in so doing transform the
inherited culture that serves daily life. The battleground extends over
areas such as class, race, sex, the Constitution, crime, personal injury,
and business.

In support of the judgment that the critical legal studies movement is but a thinly disguised socialist program, I turn to Robert W.
Gordon, who provides a profile of the kinds of persons who comprise its ranks:

Some of us [were] law teachers with humanist intellectual concerns and liberal (civil rights and anti-war) political involvements in the 1960s and 1970s;

others, radical activists of the 1960s who identified with neo-Marxist versions of socialist theory or feminism or both; still others primarily practitioners, many of whom are associated with the National Lawyers Guild and who work in collective law practices, legal service offices, or a variety of other progressive jobs.[10]

The aim of the movement, reports Gordon, is to challenge the underlying rules, principles, and purposes that gave the inherited law its character.

It is clear that what is in conflict are belief systems. Many of the social aims endorsed by the moderate faction of critical legal realists are shared by others, but the categories invoked in their defense are usually those of classical and biblical wisdom, which stand in contrast to the categories most cited by the "critical realists," categories provided by Marx, Sartre, Foucault, Lukàcs, Derrida, Habermas, and Lévi-Strauss.

If I am correct in assuming that alternative views of human nature are at the root of this conflict, it may be useful to examine some of those thought patterns. A theoretical aim of law that the Crits regard as compatible with ancient conceptions is the correction of social imbalance and the righting of natural inequity. Thus law is used to remove inequalities, to redistribute income, and to remove as far as possible the ill-effects of natural handicaps. The question that needs to be discussed is: Should this be an aim of law, particularly of judge-made law?

No one, not even those critical of the activist movement, will argue that social objectives cannot be established by law or that law must be in accord with viewpoints shared by all. Yet goals can be inappropriate for a multiplicity of reasons. For one thing, legislative- or court-instituted objectives may not have been well thought out. For another, many worthy ends may not be attainable in practice, given the propensities of human nature. Take welfare legislation as an example. It may be that apart from the temporary alleviation of misfortune, ben-

---

10. Robert W. Gordon, "New Developments in Legal Theory," in *The Politics of Law*, ed. David Kairys (New York: Pantheon Books, 1990), 414.

eficiaries are not helped by government largesse. Furthermore, laws that redistribute income may be a disincentive when it comes to the creation of wealth. There is evidence, in fact, that laws created in the interest of the poor, which bring into being massive bureaucracies, ultimately work to the detriment of those whom they seek to assist. Laws, for example, that enforce rent control undoubtedly have the effect of reducing the housing supply. As a matter of historical record, the activism of courts that struck down or diminished residency requirements for welfare benefits changed the character of many of our major cities.

If there are questionable social effects of even well-intentioned lawmaking that passes through the legislative process, the subversive effect on the common good of special-interest lawmaking through the channel of the courts needs little comment. So-called interest groups with legislative agendas take it for granted that they are more likely to have their aims implemented through the process of judicial review than through the enactments of legislative assemblies. Litigation is instigated with deliberation; where permitted, forum shopping is standard practice as activist organizations seek favorable state law and/or judges of like mind.

However, activism alone cannot account for success. Before a judicial outlook can be changed, as Marx rightly noted, the intellectual soil first has to be made receptive. As Marx was well aware, it is manifestly easier to change the minds of those associated with the interpreting of law than it is to change the minds of those responsible for legislative enactments. Unfortunately, the split between the intellectuals and the people on basic social issues is great. Thus, to use one example, a handful of social scientists, by carefully placing in a variety of law journals more or less the same article, with statistics changed to fit the locale, purporting to show the uselessness of capital punishment as a deterrent, managed though sympathetic courts to have the Supreme Court void most state laws. It is doubtful that any public referendum would have voided most laws regarding capital punishment. Examples of this sort could be multiplied. One cannot avoid the judgment that in the English-speaking world we have wit-

nessed in the decades since the 1960s a concerted effort to change social structures by changing the law. The new law is the product of a
"new" way of looking at things. I say "new" guardedly since the new is
little more than an Enlightenment way of looking at things. MacIntyre uses Aristotle and David Hume to symbolize the difference
between the old and the new.

Although such issues are rarely accorded public debate, the forums in which they are occasionally aired are those provided by the
U.S. Supreme Court and the Senate Judiciary Committee. In briefs
submitted to the Court and in hearings before the Senate committee, ideas that touch upon the fundamental aspirations of life and
that affect the culture of the nation and its modes of governance are
contested. While a generation ago the judgment may have been contested, today no one denies that judge-made law has become a powerful force in shaping the nation's culture, perhaps more so than the
enactments of legislative assemblies, either at the national or the
state level. The bench itself tends to reflect the intellectual trends of
the very same academy that inspires the interest groups to action.
Whereas any legislation is apt to be the result of mutual concession,
judge-made law often reflects the purely utopian ideas of the academy. Social theory fabricated by intellectuals who are untouched by
life in the work-a-day world is compelling in its clarity and with ease
can be translated into law by an activist judiciary. To understand the
drift of contemporary courts, one has to probe beneath current
legal theory and place such theory in a larger cultural, or should I
say philosophical, context. Philosophers have not been hesitant to
advance their own objectives through discussions of law and the social objective of law. If one looks carefully, one may be surprised to
find the number of articles by philosophers that appear in legal
journals.

Law, whether created by legislative or judicial action, is but one
strand in a single fabric called an "intellectual tradition." Peter W.
Huber, in discussing changing conceptions of "liability," recognizes as
much when he identifies a concerted effort on the part of a handful
of legal scholars, largely for philosophical reasons, "to repeal the

common law of torts."[11] Ted Honderich convincingly shows the legal implications of accepted theories of psychological determinism and their tendency to instantiate liberal rather than conservative policies in the social order.[12] Two other philosophical works of interest to legal theorists are those written by Peter A. French and Larry May.[13] French writes about collective and corporate responsibility, providing a systematic rationale for holding corporations not merely civilly but criminally accountable. May argues that many social groups that lack tight organizational structure can be said to be collectively responsible for the joint actions of their members, and he argues similarly that social groups are capable of being harmed even when individual members are not aware of the harm. "In unorganized groups," writes May, "solidarity and other relationships allow the group to have action and interests even though no decision-making structure for the group exists."[14] The last mentioned works are only two that challenge traditional notions of accountability. Liability follows causality, negligence presupposes a free act. But these principles are challenged not only by French and May but by many others.

The literature is not without its effect. U.S. corporations are increasingly the victims of the new modes of thought as zealous prosecutors couple philosophically derived principles with vague federal statutes to transform civil regulations into criminal law. Numerous state and local regulations similarly have been criminalized. In holding corporations accountable for regulatory violations, many prosecutors no longer require evidence of malicious intent, the traditional condition of criminal conduct. Dubious or not, the notion of "corporate criminal liability" is one that hands over to an unreasonable

11. Peter W. Huber, *Liability: The Legal Revolution and Its Consequences* (New York: Basic Books, 1988).

12. Ted Honderich, *A Theory of Determinism: The Mind, Neuroscience, and Life Hopes* (Oxford, U.K.: Clarendon Press, 1988).

13. Peter A. French, *Collective and Corporate Responsibility* (New York: Columbia University Press, 1984); Larry May, *The Morality of Groups: Collective Responsibility, Group-Based Harm, and Corporate Rights* (Notre Dame, Ind.: University of Notre Dame Press, 1987).

14. May, *Morality of Groups*, 180.

prosecutor a powerful capacity for mischief. If a corporation can be exposed to criminal punishment for even a good-faith error of judgment, traditional common law in important respects has been abandoned. In April 1991 the U.S. Sentencing Commission voted to send Congress draft guidelines for sentencing corporations and other organizations convicted of federal offenses. J. M. Kaplan reports that "under the guidelines, convicted corporations could face mandatory fines of staggering amounts—as high as $290 million dollars in some circumstances, and even higher."[15]

II

With this impression as a backdrop, it is my intention to focus upon the notion of "causality" and other notions crucial to tort litigation, such as "*mens rea*," "free agency," and "collective responsibility."

Tort law is important because it affects not only the litigants but the economic productivity of a region or a nation, consequences that the redistributionists who use it to achieve their own ends rarely take into account. Alarming, too, is the contemporary tendency to award punitive damages and to substitute criminal prosecution for civil actions in cases of tort. Through criminal instead of civil prosecution the state is, in effect, extending its protective role to the workplace, to the environment, and to the market.

Many examples of accountability without causality can be mentioned. A few well-publicized cases may serve to illustrate a number of key principles. The first case never reached the courts. Fear of adverse publicity and of a negative ruling led Johnson & Johnson to settle the Tylenol case out of court. Claiming that there was no way it could have anticipated a criminal's tampering with its product, Johnson & Johnson nevertheless settled claims resulting from the deaths of seven Chicago-area people. Lawyers for the families concerned had contended that the company's McNeil Consumer Products unit, Tylenol's manufacturer, should have known that its capsules were vulnerable to tampering and should therefore have acted to protect

15. J. M. Kaplan, *Corporate Conduct Quarterly* 1, no. 1 (1991).

consumers. The criminal actually responsible for the deaths has so far gone undetected.

To take another case, a federal appeals court in Atlanta ruled that financial institutions can be held liable for toxic cleanup of tainted properties where they have taken over that property as a result of defaults on loans.

A third class of cases may be illustrated by two examples. In recent years a number of courts have imposed collective liability on manufacturers when plaintiffs have been unable to identify which company sold a particular defective product. In some instances corporate defendants have been assessed damage even after proving that they could not possibly have caused the harm. Take one example. From the 1940s to 1971, approximately two million women took the synthetic hormone diethylstilbestrol (DES) to prevent miscarriages and morning sickness during pregnancy. The drug had been approved by the U.S. Food and Drug Administration (FDA) and was eventually marketed by some three hundred pharmaceutical companies, often under generic labels. In 1970 researchers reported cancer and other problems among the daughters of DES users. The FDA banned the drug in 1971. The cases quickly went to court. The mothers of many DES plaintiffs couldn't remember which brands they had used. Courts in several states made the assumption that all DES pills were essentially the same and created a market-share test so that damages could be assessed against the drug makers in proportion to their share of sales. In *Hymowitz v. Lilly* the highest New York court went further, applying the market-share concept of responsibility to a drug manufacturer that could actually prove that the defendant's mother did not use its pills.[16] In a similar case a Cleveland jury in federal court awarded $650,000 in punitive damages to the estate of a merchant seaman who died in 1988 at the age of sixty-one from mesothelioma, a form of lung cancer believed to be caused by asbestos.[17] Until

16. *Hymowitz v. Lilly and Co.*, 73 N.Y. 2nd 487, 539 NE 2nd 1069, 541 N.Y.S. 2nd 1941 (1989).

17. As reported by Amy Stevens and Amy Dockser Marcus, "Law," in the *Wall Street Journal*, 14 May 1991, B5.

the 1970s merchant ships were built using asbestos. The seaman had sailed between 1944 and 1969 with thirteen different companies. All thirteen became defendants. Their common defense was that they did not know any more about the dangers of asbestos than anyone else.

A recent case goes a step further. An intermediate appeals court in the state of New York has ruled that the several makers of multipiece tire rims, one of which had been implicated in a wrongful death, could be jointly sued even though two of the three manufacturing companies charged could prove that their product was not involved. The court ruled that the plaintiffs could introduce evidence that the companies acted in concert through an expressed agreement or a tacit understanding to prevent public awareness of the propensity of multipiece tire rims to explode and to prevent government action that would have prevented their use.[18]

The questions forced upon us are these: Can there be collective complicity and therefore collective liability without personal or corporate guilt? Can a corporation be held liable where there is no evidence that it or anyone else knew of any risks connected with its product or practice?

Broad notions entertained in the framing of law are almost always the by-product of previous philosophical discussion. Before the concept of "market share" became current, certain philosophical discussions of collective guilt, collective responsibility, and punishment had to occur. Traditional notions of liability depended on the acceptance of the principles of causality and free agency. With the ascendancy of various psychological and sociological determinisms, those principles were challenged. There was a time when the law was fairly clear. In some way one had to be causally responsible to be held liable. The new theory would have it that any loss requires compensation. If the compensation is not available from the wrongdoer, then the burden of compensation is thought to be distributable to the community. Diluted then are notions such as "responsibility," "causality," and

18. As reported by Amy Dockser Marcus, "State Court Allows Industrywide Liability," in the *Wall Street Journal*, 25 March 1991, p. B5

"intention." Social objectives supersede legitimate accountability or fault. The ancient starting point of tort law—"the loss lies where it falls"—is replaced by "the loss lies with the community."

The traditional notion of tort law held it to be an instrument of corrective justice. Its intent was the restoration of the status quo that existed before any infringement of a person's right. Aristotle called this "rectificatory justice." The plaintiff in a tort action, it was thought, should recover because of an unlawful interference with his right, not because of any more general public goal of the state.

In our own day damages are routinely awarded to victims who previously would have been barred from recovery, for example, charity hospital patients, social guests, trespassers, and those who are contributorily negligent. Employers or manufacturers engaged in abnormally dangerous activities are frequently defendants, even when the danger was antecedently apparent to all parties. Rarely in nineteenth-century law would one encounter damages awarded for intangible injuries, but today tort damages are awarded for physical pain, disfigurement of body, fear, damage to emotional relationships, and loss of consortium.

The transformation of tort law has taken place over a period of time. Many torts, particularly the most serious, are caused by corporate entities, both public and private. Collectives can cause much greater damage, whether through momentary events, such as the Bhopal disaster, or ongoing activities, such as the manufacture and sale of asbestos as an insulating material, the marketing of thalidomide, or the dumping of toxic waste. Holding corporations civilly accountable for wrongdoing even when the fault is traceable to a maverick employee is in accord with traditional notions of accountability. Corporations are not mere aggregates of people but have a metaphysical-logical identity. Otto von Gierke correctly suggested that the law in conferring on the corporation the status of a legal person is merely recognizing a prelegal social condition.

Traditionally, when obliged to determine liability, a court would distinguish between proximate and remote causes. It was recognized that an intervenient or supervenient cause might break the causal

chain. Furthermore, nineteenth-century judges tended to allow recovery only if defendants were morally culpable and victims wholly
innocent. So much confidence was placed in judicial procedure that
in the heyday of ordinary language philosophy H. L. A. Hart was
prompted to study legal language and decisions of the court in order
to gain some insight into the nature of causality. That study became
the influential book *Causation in the Law*.[19] First published in 1959, it
was reprinted four times; the second edition appeared as recently as
1985. Hart found from his study of British common law and the judiciary system of the United States that courts inevitably claim that
they are using the ordinary man's conception of causality in determining legal responsibility.

The causality issue is, of course, not new. It was discussed in the
nineteenth century in terms not unlike those found in some contemporary literature. The nineteenth-century debate between Nicholas St.
John Green and Francis Warton is instructive for both the issues confronted and their commonsense resolution by Warton. Green at that
time was a young instructor at Harvard Law School and a member of
the famous Metaphysical Club of Cambridge, when it included people
like William James, Chauncey Wright, and Oliver Wendell Holmes.
Green many have been the first to directly challenge the orthodox legal
notion of objective causation. In an *American Law Review* article of
1870 Green challenged both the notion of "objective causation" and
the notion of "causal chain."[20] Echoing John Stuart Mill, Green wrote,
"[T]o every event there are certain antecedents. It is not any one of
this set of antecedents taken by itself which is the cause. . . . No one by
itself would produce the effect. The true cause is the whole set of antecedents taken together."[21] The legal implications are obvious. If no distinction is made among occasion, condition, and cause, the true mechanism responsible for the effect is impossible to determine. Turning his

19. H. L. A. Hart, *Causation in the Law*, 2d. ed. (Oxford, U.K.: Oxford University
Press, 1985).

20. Reprinted in *Essays and Notes on the Law of Tort and Crime* (Menasha, Wis.:
George Bonta, 1933), 211.

21. Ibid., 11–12.

attention to the metaphor "causal chain," Green offered a political interpretation: when a court says this damage is remote, all it means is that under the circumstances it does not think the plaintiff *should* recover. Green was convinced that the court manipulated the terms "proximate" and "remote" to accomplish its policy objectives in contract cases and in negligence cases. Like Marx, he believed that law was simply an instrument of the ruling class whose values it instantiated.

Francis Warton saw that Green's doctrine was incompatible with the principles of both the Roman and the Anglo-American common law traditions. In his 1874 work *A Treatise on the Law of Negligence*, Warton argued that men become prudent and diligent by the consciousness that they will be made to suffer if they are not prudent and diligent.[22] But if the law bypasses the agent truly responsible in search of what we today would call the "deep pocket," then the deterrent effect of punishment is negated. Law can never be content with the mere cataloging of antecedent events. A leveling of all antecedents to the same parity denies man's moral primacy and responsibility. The law must be able to distinguish between physical and moral forces. In an interesting aside, Warton notes that the court may draw upon multiple experts but warns that their reports will not make the key distinctions that lead the court to decision. It remains the function of the court to determine what is and what is not the result of responsible causation. The fact finder, usually the jury, must ultimately decide what the expert's report means.

Since a cause is not the sum of all antecedents, a jurist must discriminate between such antecedents as are produced by responsible volition and those not so produced. Warton maintained that nothing that is not the result of the action of a free agent can be viewed as a cause. "Action" may be an act of commission or one of omission. Negligence, or breach of positive duty, can be as culpable as any positive action:

22. Francis Warton, *Treatise on the Law of Negligence* (Philadelphia: Kay & Brother, 1874). The St. John Green–Worton debate was brought to my attention by Morton J. Horwitz; see his "The Doctrine of Objective Causation," *The Politics of Law*, ed. David Kairys (New York: Pantheon Books, 1990), 203–4.

The law when any injury is done, betakes itself to consider whether there is any rational being who could if he had chosen, have prevented it, or who either seeing the evil consequences, or refusing to see them, has put in motion, either negligently or intentionally, a series of mechanical forces by which the injury was produced. This is the basis of the distinction between conditions and causes.[23]

A negligent person exercises no will at all. The moment he wills to do the injury or breaches his duty, he ceases to be negligent and becomes criminally liable. In the case of contributory negligence, the plaintiff by intervening breaks the causal connection between the injury received by himself and the defendant's negligence.[24]

In discussing negligence, Warton draws attention to two views: (1) the first holds a person liable for all the consequences that flow in an ordinary sequence from his negligence, that is, the normal view of accountability; and (2) the second holds a person liable for all the consequences that could be foreseen as likely to occur.

The second view opens a Pandora's box of philosophical questions. If we can't predict the actions of others viewed as individuals, can we predict the action of others taken as a class? Is behavior so governed by natural laws that certain actions, including negligence, can be accurately predicted? Warton's answer is based on his understanding of human nature and its propensities: "To require us to act in such a way that no negligence on our part may be the conditions of negligence on the part of strangers, would require us to cease to be."[25] If we do nothing, we are apt to omit something we ought to do.

If we do something, owing to the imperfection of all things human, there will be some taint, no matter how slight, of imperfection in the thing we do. Yet whether in doing or omitting, we touch more or less closely multitudes of persons each with a free will of his own, each with idiosyncracies with which we have no acquaintance, each of whom may by some negligence cross our path and make action on our part which is innocuous in itself injurious.[26]

The consequences of making one man liable for another's fault would lead to mischief. Where would such vicarious liability end,

23. Warton, *Law of Negligence*, 90.   24. Ibid., 130
25. Ibid., 134.   26. Ibid., 134–35.

Warton asks? "The consequence of this would be that capital would be obliged to bear the burden, not merely of its own want of caution but of the want of caution of everybody else."[27] Afraid that the law, if interpreted as Green affirmed, could be used to destroy the economic underpinnings of society, Warton wrote: "Here is a capitalist among these antecedents; he shall be forced to pay. The capitalist, therefore, becomes liable for all the disasters of which he is in any sense the condition, and the fact that he is held liable, multiplies these disasters."[28] If Green's view were to prevail, Warton continues, "No factory would be built. . . . Making the capitalist liable for everything, therefore, would end in making the capitalist, as well as the non-capitalist, liable for nothing; for there would soon be no capitalist to be found to be sued."[29]

Warton saw that in divorcing responsibility from liability, capital is likely to be either destroyed or compelled to shrink from entering into those large operations by which the trade of a nation is built up. He could have had an instance like the *Exxon Valdez* prosecution or the Monsanto case in mind when he wrote: "We are accustomed to look with apathy at the ruin of great corporations."[30] Convinced that no corporation could be ruined without grave social effects, he argued for a limit to entrepreneurial liability. He rejected the "foreseeable test" doctrine because it could only be made on a statistical basis. From a statistical point of view, all risks are predictable in the aggregate. In a world of randomness where there is no necessary connection between particular causes and particular effects, all that can be done is to statistically correlate acts in the aggregate with consequences in the aggregate. Moral causation and free agency are replaced by probabilities and statistical correlations.

In conclusion, two things need to be said. Warton's views remain as viable today as when they were first enunciated. Although his causal

27. Ibid., 136.
28. *A Suggestion as to Causation* (Cambridge, Mass.: Riverside Press, 1874), 11.
29. Ibid.
30. "Liability of Railroad Companies for Remote Fires," *Southern Law Review* 719 (1875): 729–30.

analysis of responsibility cannot be gainsaid, what he did not envisage was the widespread adoption of liability insurance based on probabilities and statistical correlations which he rightly thought could not say anything about the individual. Needless to say, Warton's basic position is challenged by the tendency to look upon misfortune, whether inflicted by nature, by lack of self-discipline, or by accident, as somehow a social problem that ought to be rectified. If one begins with the principle that all loss should be compensated, the temptation is to search for a corporate or other affluent defendant at the expense of blurring the causal chain or placing all antecedents on an equal footing where there is no recognition of the distinction among occasion, condition, or cause. When massive awards do occur, the community is ultimately forced to bear the burden as the damages assessed are passed on to the consumer by means of higher prices.

Warton, and the legal tradition he represented, assumed certain general principles, namely (1) that causes can be discerned; (2) that to the extent that they can be identified, responsibility can be assigned; and (3) that accidents do occur in which no one is at fault in any sense. An accident, by definition, is an unintended event, the intersection of independent causal chains. Warton recognized that lack of intention may or may not mitigate liability; the prudent-man test he would not abandon. Still, in any transaction there are at least two parties; intelligence must be assumed on all sides. Put another way, both buyers and sellers have reason to beware, lest hidden and unknown dangers become a reality.

Much has happened both in law and in the marketplace since Warton's day. Whereas lack of caution or misuse of product in the nineteenth century would not have been allowed to serve as a basis for a claim, given shifts in legal theory, corporate leaders recognize that both judges and juries are likely to be swayed differently today. By and large, the market has responded intelligently. Since most products, quite apart from misuse, are liable to failure or breakdown, any prudent manufacturer has to take the probability of failure into account. No enterprise, business or professional, whether engaged in manufacturing or in providing services, can afford to be without product-liability or malpractice insurance. Drawing upon experience and probability statistics, liability insurance, in effect, mediates between the actual world of lived experience and the predictable world of aggregate risk. Warton's concepts of human nature, causality, and responsibility are not incompatible with the insured's assumption of inevitable failure. No doubt he would accept that, but he would not allow into the courtroom mere logical possibility to be used with hindsight. The "prudent man acting with all available foresight" is a principle he would undoubtedly seek to preserve. Warton would understand but lament the growing need for ever increasing amounts of liability insurance, recognizing that insurance no less than a jury award shifts the financial burden to the public, albeit indirectly. He would adamantly resist the employment of judge-made law or even legislation to redress natural inequities or to disavow fault.

If Warton represents one side, the critical legal studies faction represents another side in a debate that promises to be an ongoing one in legal circles. The fundamental debate is, of course, between two anthropologies, a classical view of human nature represented by Aristotle in antiquity and a socialist one represented by Marx in the nineteenth century.

Philosophies do in fact matter; they determine how we think about law and the ends of law—that is, the role of law in society.

ON THE JUSTIFICATION OF
RIGHTS CLAIMS

I

There are times when the large brush stroke is appropriate, when a Chagall-like impression serves better than the detail of a Vermeer. In an effort to gain insight into the nature of "right," I have chosen to sketch rights theories in a general way and to focus upon the notion of entitlement. If a librarian were to catalogue the flood of literature that the past decade has produced on the subject of "human rights," a number of broad categories would suggest themselves. There is the theological or religiously inspired literature that assumes the dignity of the human person and proceeds to draw its conclusions in the light of that premise. There is the philosophical literature that cannot assume the dignity of the human person and hence must variously defend that premise, although many philosophers effectively presume it through inattention to fundamental principles. Both types of inquiry are to be distinguished from political tracts which, although they may appeal to principle, are frequently long on rhetoric and amount to nothing more than assertions or declarations of political programs.

It is not the political use of the concept of "rights" that is the focus of this essay. The "rights" that ought to be enjoyed by the people of the Philippines, of El Salvador, of Spain, or of Nigeria cannot be decided in the abstract but only contextually, for reasons that will be evident as this text progresses. Justification of political rights presupposes principles; it is those universal principles and their justification that are the focus of this inquiry.

In discussing rights, the theologian does not seem to be in a privileged position. Although he knows that man is made in the image and likeness of God and that man's eternal destiny is personal union with God, the truths that follow from that knowledge are not self-evident but have to be ascertained with the aid of relevant observation and philosophical reasoning. Furthermore, the theologian or the religious mind usually seeks to convince the person of no belief and thus resorts to philosophical argument, if not in the first round, then in the second. Thus it is appropriate to concentrate on the philosophical literature. Ecclesiastical pronouncements themselves can be measured against natural reasoning. Assuming accord, they acquire greater strength when their supervenient character is made manifest.

Philosophical approaches to the topic are multifarious. One can immediately recognize theistic and nontheistic strains. In North America and Europe the later occupies center stage. Anglo-American philosophy tends to be nonmetaphysical, assuming fundamental principles and pragmatically justifying this or that specific right. Rarely does the analyst attempt to ground rights in considerations of human nature or in theories of the state. Phenomenologists and existential philosophers tend to be more metaphysically aware than ordinary-language philosophers. Thomists and other natural law theorists are perhaps the most inclined to ontologically ground the concept of rights. That said, it is better not to generalize but to concentrate on the work of specific philosophers.

I choose to characterize two approaches which, although they do not represent the entire spectrum, nevertheless represent important strains. They are the classical natural law tradition and the contemporary analytic, largely utilitarian, approach.

II

Within the classical natural law tradition, one finds few discussions of "rights" as such. There is, instead, considerable discussion of the common good, of justice, of the ends of government, of obligation, and of beneficence.

For Aristotle, those rights we are today calling "human rights" are a part of the generic category "political rights." All rights presuppose society and are dependent on the presence of established social structures. Rights cannot be discussed in the abstract, nor can they be presumed to be unchangeable. The same doctrine is found in the Stoics. Stoic natural law teaching is based on a doctrine of divine providence and on an anthropocentric teleology. It admits that there is a universally valid hierarchy of ends, even though there are no universally valid rules of action. Knowing the proper ends of government, one does not know anything of how and to what extent those ends can be realized here and now under these circumstances. For both Aristotle and the Stoics, normally valid rules may be justly challenged in extreme situations. Political freedoms may be a blessing or a curse. If the very existence of a society is at stake, there may be a conflict between the requirements of self-preservation and the requirements of commutative and distributive justice. In extreme situations, public safety is the highest law. A decent society, for example, will not go to war except for a just cause, but what it will do during a war will depend to a certain extent on what the enemy—possibly an unscrupulous and savage enemy—forces it to do. For both Aristotle and the Stoics, one can say that in all cases the common good must be preferred to the private good. But this does not say more than "justice must be observed." The free society presupposes virtue in its populace. The root of legitimacy is not consent or contract, as it is to become after Hobbes and Rousseau, but proved beneficence. This outlook of Aristotle and the Stoics is reflected in nearly every period of Western philosophy, notably by Aquinas, by Montesquieu, and by Burke, and in the twentieth century by Jacques Maritain and Yves Simon. It is this classical philosophical tradition that has provided the underpinnings of much of nineteenth- and twentieth-century Catholic social teaching.

To turn attention to specifically Catholic social teaching in the recent past, one of its features is its emphasis on the material conditions required for personal growth, moral and otherwise. A key principle of Catholic social teaching is the conviction that the modern state has obligations in justice to ensure the prosperity of all in the commonwealth. It stresses the rights of the worker, the obligations of employers, the communal nature of natural resources. One statement that proved influential in North America in the early part of this century is that of John A. Ryan, the author of *The Church and Socialism* (1919) and an influential member of the "brain trust" that gave direction to Roosevelt's New Deal. Ryan was primarily a sociologist, although in the work just mentioned he draws upon both philosophical and theological sources to aid his analysis. Like Leo XIII before him, Ryan believes that a sense of independence, manliness, self-reliance, self-respect, and economic power can only come from the possession of property: "No system of insurance, nor any scale of wages, can provide a man with those psychic goods which are an integral element of normal life, and which are second in importance to food, clothing and shelter."

The Catholic Church, insists Ryan, is not a social reform organization, nor is social betterment her main function. Her mission is to bring men to religion and to make them virtuous. But men cannot be virtuous without essential material goods. The Church thus has a stake in the material conditions of society. Ryan presupposes the need for and the actual presence of decency in the mercantile class, and for that he was called by his critics an idealist. Men, he thought, cannot be virtuous unless they practice justice and charity in all the relations of life, including those of an economic character. Christian principles concerning the dignity and sacredness of the individual human person, the essential equality of all persons, the brotherhood of men in Christ, and the dominion of the moral law over the industrial as well as the other actions of men are principles that he expected the Church to teach and principles that he expected to be widely accepted.

Ryan was well aware of the baser tendencies of and the limitations of human nature. He admits that men will never set up and maintain a regime of social justice until they become convinced that the supreme law of life is the moral law, but he is more confident that men can be brought to virtue than he is in the effectiveness of legislative coercion. The most cunningly devised social statutes, he argues, will not compel men to act justly in their economic relations unless they are impelled by a living and enlightened conscience. And the voice of conscience will ordinarily have little effect if it is not recognized as the voice of God. Neither legal ordinances nor humanitarian appeals will be effective without the assistance and direction of religion.

Property owners, he continues, do not have the right to do what they please with what they call their own, for they are only stewards of their possessions; hence, when they have made reasonable provisions for their own needs, they are obliged to use reasonably what remains for the benefit of their neighbor. As Pope Leo XIII affirmed, men "are not free to choose whether they will take up the cause of the poor or not; it is a matter of simple duty."

Whenever the general interest of any particular class suffers or is threatened with mischief that can in no other way be met or prevented, the public authority must step in. This intervention is not limited to material interests. The community, for example, has the right to resist the propagation of lies or calumnies, the right to resist those activities that have as their aim the corruption of morals, and the right to resist those who aim to destroy the state and the foundations of common life.

It is worth noting that Ryan's approach is characterized not by considerations of rights but by considerations of the commonwealth. John Finnis, in his investigation *Natural Law and Natural Rights*, uses the metaphor of a "watershed" in the history of natural rights theory, with Suarez standing on one side and Hobbes on the other. Finnis notices that the vocabulary employed in talking about the matter shifted in the seventeenth century from "liberty" and "obligation" to "rights" and "due." On the classical side of the watershed, emphasis is placed on freedoms and benefits essential for the maintenance of life and on the security, development, and the dignity of the individual; whereas, on the modern side, the vocabulary of rights introduces a way of talking about what is just from a special angle, namely, the viewpoint of those to whom something is due and who would be wronged if denied that due. The shift in meaning is so drastic, Finnis believes, that it carries the rights holder and his rights altogether outside the juridical relationship that is fixed by law. Finnis quotes a revealing passage in Hobbes: "*Jus* and *lex,* right and law[,] ... ought to be distinguished; because right consisteth in liberty to do, or to forbear; whereas law determineth and bindeth to one of them; so that law, and right, differ as much, as obligation and liberty: which in one and the same matter are inconsistent."

In his *Grundlage des Naturrechts,* Fichte delineates the features of the two approaches. A moral commandment shows us what we morally must do. Civil laws, by contrast, are concerned with rights; they open opportunities for action that need not be pursued. Moral commandments present obligations; civil laws present options. Moral commandments depend on goodwill, the will to do what is conceived as obligatory; the commands of civil law depend upon the compulsion of the community regarding individual acts, not individual motives. Fichte reduces all rights to civil rights. General moral principles and goodwill are too shapeless to give bone for the moral life either of the individual or of the group. Definite conclusions and decisions are required. These are reached by deliberation and effort and not by natural inclination. It is through judicial ordinances that a community is held together.

To return to my theme, I have drawn at length from John A. Ryan, not because his views are representative of current tendencies in Catholic social thought, but because they represent a period in which there was little talk of rights but much thought about the common good which was regarded as the site of, or condition for, the enjoyment of social goods.

The tradition of Ryan has been perpetuated in North America largely through the writings of Jacques Maritain, one of several architects of the United Nations "Declaration on Human Rights," and through the writing of his more prominent disciples John Courtney Murray and Yves Simon. For Maritain, the recognition of personal rights has its origin in the conception of man and of natural law established by centuries of Christian philosophy. The first of these rights is that of the human person to make his way toward his eternal destiny along the path which his conscience has recognized as the path indicated by God. Maritain distinguishes between natural rights and civil rights. Examples of natural right include freedom of conscience, the right of a person to raise a family, the rights of the family vis-à-vis the community itself, the rights of spiritual families, and the right of suffrage. Rights of *civic persons*, or political rights, spring directly from positive law and from the fundamental constitution of the political community, and they vary from community to community.

The most fundamental political right, Maritain holds, is "the right of the people to take unto itself the constitution and the form of government of its choice. . . . Such a right is subject only to the requirements of justice and natural law." Other rights of the civic person include "political equality," assuring to each citizen his status, security, and liberties within the state; equality of all before the law, implying an independent judiciary power that assures to each one the right to call upon the law and to be restrained by it alone if it has been violated; equal admission of all citizens to public employment according to their capacity; and free access of all to the various professions, without racial or social discrimination.

I am willing to argue that the classical tradition remains strong in North America, even though it is largely ignored by those trained in Anglo-American analytic techniques. Even theologians who have abandoned Saint Thomas and the Scholastic tradition find it hard to do without natural law theory. Catholic thinkers obviously do not have a monopoly on the tradition. Leo Strauss's *Natural Law and History* has enjoyed a large readership, and Strauss himself has generated a school of followers. From one viewpoint, some of the best analytic work has unconsciously reconstructed or recaptured certain key elements of the classical tradition.

Anglo-American analytic approaches tend to begin with rights claims and work back to their justification rather than to begin with theories of self-fulfillment or with broad social philosophies, showing their implication. While much of the literature, if judged from a classical perspective, seems ahistorical or rootless, one finds in it nonetheless many precisions and distinctions that can be appropriated by the natural law philosopher. The list of rights that has attracted attention is lengthy, and some of the rights that are brought under scrutiny are anything but basic. How can a social philosopher discuss "the right of a rejected friend to be heard"? But if there is little agreement on the length of the list, there is nevertheless some agreement on fundamental rights of a social and political kind.

Profound and valuable discussions of rights are found in monographs and essays by David Braybrooke, Ronald Dworkin, Joel Feinberg, Alan Gewirth, John Rawls, and W. J. Stankiewicz. John Finnis, perhaps the leading Catholic in the natural rights debate, provides the strength of one who has mastered both the classical and the analytical traditions. Other philosophers who represent the Catholic moral tradition and who ought to be mentioned are Germain Grisez, John Noonan, and Ralph McInerny.

As mentioned, a large portion of contemporary Anglo-American rights discussion proceeds without regard for a metaphysical justification. Some authors deliberately avoid the grounding of rights in order to leave open the question of their proper justification, whether theistic or nontheistic, natural law or utilitarian, conventional or normative.

While there is no agreement with respect to the grounding of rights, few dissent from the observation that rights must be contextually defined. No inquiry proceeds for any length of time without the investigator reaching the conclusion that rights are relative to a social system. As Braybrooke has pointed out, "[W]hat presses for mentioning as rights depends partly on what sorts of dangers, obstructions, and inferences actually exist." Braybrooke comes to the somewhat cynical conclusion that rights are simply "devices for advocating welfare." He would say that there are no rights in the abstract, that is, in isolation from society. A right is an opportunity guaranteed by the state to the individual to enjoy the social benefits and values of that society. Although Braybrooke is not sympathetic to the natural law tradition, he still regards rights claims as a standard for social self-criticism. A man invoking his rights is positioned to defend his privacy, secure his property, and obtain the use of public facilities. A government's policies regarding rights may be made the test for distinguishing good government from bad.

Human dignity and equal claims for respect are the fundamental principles assumed by Ronald Dworkin. He writes: "The important thing about rights is that they give the right-holder an especially strong justification for acting in a certain way or for demanding a certain benefit, a justification which is independent of and which will generally triumph in competition with collective goals, such as welfare, prosperity, or security."

According to Joel Feinberg, one of the most prolific English-speaking writers on the topic, "To have a right is to have a claim to something and against someone, the recognition of which is called for by legal rules or, in the case of moral rights, by the principles of an enlightened conscience." To have a claim is to produce a set of reasons based on legal rules or on moral principles. Feinberg thinks that much can be learned about the nature and value of claims by attending to the activity of claiming. We can speak of someone having a claim without knowing who that claim may be against. A natural need is the basis of a claim even though that need may be unfulfillable at the moment. A person in need is always in a position to make a claim even when there is no one in the corresponding position to do anything about it. Moral and legal rights, writes Feinberg, are parallel in character. What differentiates them is the kind of norm from which they derive validity. Moral rights are prior to and independent of any legal or institutional rules. In my judgment, no natural law philosopher could disagree or put the matter more clearly.

The range of views from among Anglo-American philosophers is extensive, and the literature is vast. There have been several attempts to survey that literature comprehensively, notably by Tibor Machan and by Rex Martin and James W. Nickel in a joint article. There is no need for me to duplicate those efforts. What might be useful is an examination of a typical justification of rights.

III

A list of "fundamental" human rights cannot be very long. Right implies another's obligation. A human being cannot be said to have rights vis-à-vis nature. Nature owes man nothing except in the sense that God has ordained nature to man as its end. From a purely materialistic point of view, the fact that man has emerged is due to chance, and chance can eradicate the human race just as it gave it birth. Right presupposes a relationship. The relationship is one where the claimant has some lien on the one obligated.

Examples of rights that tend to be universally acknowledged begin with the child's right to life and with the claims it can make on its parents. These claims extend from sustenance in infancy to educational support in childhood and young adulthood. Parents may be said to be obligated to nurture, care for, and educate their offspring, but the mode of the fulfillment of their obligation varies. Education beyond simple skills for self-maintenance is relative, depending upon social structures and the social rank of parents within the community. Where there is community, whether it be that of the tribe or the modern state, the family and individuals have a just claim upon the common wealth, assuming that as units within that large society they have made some contribution toward the common store. The claim of the individual is proportionate to the fortunes of the whole and to his contribution to that whole. He may rightly claim a contributor's just share. But claims made upon the whole have to be justified. A child cannot claim to share in the deliberative process; similarly, it is not self-evident that suffrage ought to be universal. In the beginnings of the American Republic, suffrage was limited to property owners since they were thought to have a larger stake in the outcome of deliberations. Given the social structure of that time, the arrangement was not self-evidently unjust.

A means to a livelihood is generally conceded to be another fundamental right. But by whom is such a means to be provided? In industrial as well as agrarian societies, ownership of property is a condition for or the means to a livelihood. For the majority, labor is the only source of income available for life's necessities. In an agricultural society what is produced is directly the consequence of labor. In the crafts, entitlement is similarly related to productivity, although raw materials necessarily make their claim against returns. In an industrial society, raw materials, labor, and marketing techniques all diminish claims to the full value of the product. The rights of a laborer who participates in the creation of a product are defended as claims that are earned. The owner is enjoined in justice to recognize those claims and not exploit the laborer because of the owner's superior position. While the state may extract taxes for its just purposes, it is usually acknowledged that a person has a right to the fruits of his labor, that a person has a right to property.

I bring these matters to the fore to suggest that the right to a living wage is not a natural right but a social right. It is one contingent upon there being a social order in which manufacturing or trade produces a structure in which labor results in entitlement. "Entitlement" is perhaps a better word than "right," since it connotes the true source of claim. A number of questions can be raised. Is one entitled to benefit without contribution? Can the ill-born or the unfortunate enter claims against the community? Is one entitled to health care? The notion "He has a claim on our charity" implicitly distinguishes between a genuine claim in justice and a claim based on humanity. Yet charity is over and above justice. Where a just claim cannot be entered, where the potential beneficiary is not entitled, he may nevertheless require certain treatment by another. The other is obligated, but not contractually or legally. The donor is obligated by his own manhood and its requirements for virtue. We even recognize that the performance of charitable works without seeming to perform them may require considerable skill, but that modesty enjoins the attempt.

The thesis I am arguing is that rights must be grounded. If they are not simply to be claims, the grounding has to take a form something like the analysis above. That is, it must establish first universal principles from a consideration of human nature and its *telos*. If rights are to have a universal character, they will have to be closely identified with indispensable human needs, apart from social considerations.

Otherwise, we are talking about the rights of an individual in a social setting, and that becomes a matter for politics. The affirmation of political rights may be necessary, but it then becomes a matter of assessing the requirements of communal and individual good within a given nation or region. Such affirmations require a large measure of experience, detailed knowledge of cultural history, economic resources, and political possibilities pertaining to the nation or region in question. Few outsiders can appraise situations judiciously. Universal declarations of rights, when they move from the level of generic principle to the advocacy of specific policy, are fraught with danger.

This essay has focused on the grounding of rights and on the notion of "entitlement." If I may be permitted an aside, one of the dehumanizing aspects of the welfare state is that it tends to do away with both entitlement and charity. When claims can be entered against the community without regard for their basis, when they are divorced from a consideration of labor or material contribution, when all members of society are regarded as equally entitled, the productive are penalized. The converse notion of "care even when not entitled" is then lost. No merit is recognized in the act that goes over and above because no extraordinary care is acknowledged. It is important that the notion of charity be kept in both personal and civic dispensing. State aid is no less charity than personal assistance. The indigent cannot make claims in the same sense as the productive.

With respect to political rights, enfranchisement is contextual. Within certain social orders, property may be legitimately demanded as a condition of suffrage. No one argues for the enfranchisement of children. Within the context of the modern democratic state, adult enfranchisement is a necessity. In some parts of the world, other forms of government may work as well. That form of government is best that works best. Hence, I would make no particular brief for democracy. Just social orders existed long before modern democratic governments came into being. There is much to be said for democracy with its system of checks and balances. Democracy is required as a condition, or at least as a safeguard, for some of the freedoms and economic benefits that twentieth-century man takes for granted. While structures such as the separation of powers into legislative, judiciary, and executive are not contingent upon democracy, it is hard to see how a free-market economy can exist without a democracy. The merits of a free-market economy may be debated, but most of the claims made against the world community by third world or underdeveloped countries are made only because that free market has generated a surplus in some. Certain political and economic claims can be made only on the assumption of a benevolent world economic order.

The context in which most human rights claims are made is the context of individuals demanding greater freedoms or benefits from their governments or third world nations placing claims upon the so-called developed countries. The economic and political are intertwined, and even the political life of a single nation, when world powers vie for dominance, has to be seen in a global context.

From any vantage point, human rights considerations drive home the notion that there is an order or law above the state, which in some sense universally prevails without regard for context.

ELEVEN

THE NECESSITY OF PUNISHMENT

I

Nearly every report or bulletin published by the Bureau of Justice Statistics, U.S. Department of Justice, provides material for serious reflection if not cause for alarm. Studies reported in the past decade reveal that of prisoners released for the first time from state institutions, those sentenced for homicide had served a median term of only 42 months; those sentenced for rape or sexual assault a mere 36 months. Other studies surveying the criminal history records in eleven states, covering a period of three years, found that in a sample of prisoners released within a given year, 62.5 percent were rearrested for a new felony or serious misdemeanor.[1]

These studies show either that the penalties attached to homicide and sexual assault are insignificant or that we do not regard the taking of life or assault as serious crimes. They also show—not that anyone needed to be reminded—that prisons do not reform. The recidivism evident from these and other studies suggests that the criminal justice system does not protect the public. A society that cannot bring itself to punish the criminal element within it is doomed to insecurity and chaos.[2]

---

1. It may be noted that in 1997, the last year for which statistics are available, 74 persons were executed in the United States. At year's end 1997, 3,335 prisoners were under sentence of death. Of the 38 states with capital punishment statistics, 36 provide for review of all death sentences regardless of the defendant's wishes. See T. L. Snell, "Capital Punishment 1997," Bureau of Justice Statistics, Department of Justice, *Bulletin*, December 1998.

2. The 1997 study reveals that among inmates under a death sentence on 31 December 1997, for whom criminal history information was available, 65 percent had past fel-

In the middecades of this century the conviction that criminals ought to be punished was successfully challenged by many social scientists in both Western Europe and North America. For reasons that we intend to explore, punishment was equated with "retribution," an attitude that was judged to be psychologically if not morally inappropriate. Social theorists were not reluctant to suggest that those who would punish, be it an individual or social group, were simply deficient in their ability to cope with an unpleasant situation.[3] The perceived need to punish was equated with a desire for revenge, and revenge itself was presented as passion in need of control. The moral authority of those who would impose punishment was thereby questioned. Advocates of meaningful sanctions became the guilty ones, the ones in need of therapy. This dark view of the motives of those who seek sanctions is often coupled with a romantic view of the reformability of the criminal. The same social scientists present the criminal as an unfortunate victim of a social order on which he has a claim. We can find bodies of legal scholars and even organizations of judges reflecting this outlook as they propose model penal codes for their jurisdictions.[4]

Obviously the issue of whether to punish or not to punish is not simply a problem for social scientists. There is a philosophy of punishment that one explicitly or implicitly brings to the subject and that determines the comprehension and use of the data uncovered by the many studies of crime and criminal justice systems.

---

ony convictions, including 9 percent with at least one previous homicide conviction. Among those for whom legal status at the time of the capital offense was reported, 42 percent had an active "criminal justice status." Nearly half of these were on parole, and about a fourth were on probation.

3. It is surprising to find enunciations of this outlook in the academy. As L. E. Goodman points out in his study *On Justice: An Essay in Jewish Philosophy* (New Haven, Conn.: Yale University Press, 1991), since biblical times a characteristic feature of retribution has been its lack of animus. It is to be distinguished from vengeance and cruelty. Punishment is justified rationally and is pronounced by a judge in accord with due procedure; it is not grounded in emotion. "The notion of punishment as an alternative to passion," writes Goodman, "is as ancient as the idea of law. Penal law as an institution is a moral containment of both crime and passions it arouses" (73).

4. E.g., see Council of Judges of the National Council on Crime and Delinquency, *Model Sentencing Act*, 2d ed. (1973), and the American Law Institute, *Model Penal Code* (1970).

Some legal scholars have suggested that the received rationale for punishing is not even philosophical but religious. Others have suggested that there may be a deep natural strain in human propensities to punish, of which the religious outlook, with its sanction of heaven and hell, is but a manifestation. That argument is muted by the fact that societies untouched by biblical religion have employed sanctions parallel to those found in the West.

To limit discourse to the West, one finds in the Hebrew and Christian traditions ample discussions of punishment and its purpose. To some extent those discussions are paralleled in the pagan world. Pagan antiquity had no reluctance in meting out death. If a father could determine whether his infant child could be exposed, he could certainly put to the sword or enslave a captured enemy. The criminal element of ancient Rome was subject to execution even for what today would be judged relatively minor offenses, and in the process of yielding his life the condemned might be obliged to entertain the spectators at the Coliseum. The Hebrew Scriptures are full of violence: the adulteress could be stoned to death; no sympathy whatever was lavished on the murderer or the rapist.

The right of the state to defend itself against serious physical threat, affirmed in the classical period, remained uncontested through the ages. Any overt attack could be met with force, and in the case of external enemies the resulting counterforce might entail war, with the subsequent execution or enslavement of the vanquished. In the domestic sector, certain crimes were recognized as serious enough to merit execution. At various periods in the history of the West, even after Christianity came to prevail, capital offenses were numerous. The common good was thought to entail drastic measures to ensure its maintenance.

The death penalty itself partook of a larger notion of "punishment." It didn't exist simply to thwart a threat. The notion of punishment rested not only on the assumption that the culprit freely performed the criminal deed but on the conviction that he incurred a debt to society. Where an order had been broken, justice required retribution. The offense was not simply to be acknowledged and then forgiven. The restoration of the order broken demanded a commensurate act in recompense. A grave crime entailed a serious penalty. To major crimes such as treason, murder, rape, and armed robbery, the supreme penalty was attached. In identifying certain crimes as capital, states implicitly placed a value on the object destroyed by the crime.

When in the nineteenth century the theistic context for punishment began to fade and even its deterrent effect was challenged, Emil Durkheim consciously formulated a purely secular rationale for the imposition of sanctions.[5] For Durkheim, a crime is a serious affront against the "collective conscience," that is, the common morality that holds men together at points where its sentiments are both strong and precise. The "collective conscience" need not be correct or be dictated by any natural order. It is sufficient that the values it promotes be firmly held by the community. Thus punishment, for Durkheim, is grounded in the hostility excited by violations of the common morality. Punishment is "a passionate reaction of graduated intensity" to offenses against the collective conscience. We punish, says Durkheim, primarily as a symbolic expression of the outraged common morality. If we didn't punish, there would be a breakdown in social solidarity.[6] But what if morals change? Durkheim responds that it is not necessary to conserve a penal rule because it once corresponded to the collective sentiments. Rules should be preserved only so long as the sentiments to which they correspond are still "living and energetic."[7] For Durkheim, punishment sustains the common morality not mainly by repressing immoral conduct, but principally by giving vent to a sense of outrage; if this vent were closed, the common conscience would lose its energy and the cohesive morality would weaken.

Durkheim was as prescient as he was influential. Within the present century we have witnessed the law change as moral perceptions have

---

5. Emil Durkheim, *The Division of Labour in Society* (New York: Free Press, 1964), 77ff.

6. Ibid., 96, 104.

7. Ibid., 107.

changed. Absent the notion of "sin," something happens to the notion of "punishment." To use a parochial example, but one for which parallels can be found in any Western nation, the U.S. Supreme Court in its famous decision in *Coker v. Georgia* struck down the death penalty as a punishment for rape.[8] Such a decision would have been unthinkable in a previous period, but in our day, given the demystification of sex, the denigration of traditional morality, and the pervasiveness of a psychological determinism, the decision is not surprising. The Court simply constitutionalized the prevailing values. The death penalty for rape, it has been argued, derived its force from sexual morality. Attitudes toward sexual purity have ceased to be primary in the contemporary pattern of values, and the Court cannot be faulted, so the argument goes, for recognizing this reality.

By the mid-twentieth century the emphasis Durkheim placed on the venting of collective conscience came under attack from his fellow sociologists. The trend was global. Throughout the early part of this century, punishment had been discussed in the light of three purposes: (1) retribution (2) deterrence, and (3) reformation. In the 1960s and 1970s sociologists discovered that punishment, even capital punishment, did not deter. Evidence was usually produced in the context of a movement to abolish capital punishment. In the United States William C. Bailey, who may be taken as a representative of that movement, wrote: "Neither the certainty of execution nor the severity of imprisonment have been found to be effective deterrents to homicide."[9] Of the remaining two reasons for punishing, retribution and rehabilitation, the last mentioned, after a century or more of experience, is now seen by all to be chimerical; no one believes that reformatories reform. That places all the weight on "retribution."

II

Since social theorists often profess not to understand the rationale that calls for retribution, it may be useful to examine the thought of

8. 433, U.S. 584 (1977).
9. William Bailey, "Abolishing Capital Punishment," *Law and Human Behavior* 2, no. 3 (1978): 259.

two intellectual giants concerning this subject. One is Thomas Aquinas, representing at once the classical and a Catholic intellectual tradition; the other is Immanuel Kant, representing the Enlightenment tradition. Both Aquinas and Kant stand apart from the contemporary debate. We will question Aquinas first. Does the notion of punishment presuppose a theistic context? If not, then what is the natural law rationale for punishment? Under what conditions is punishment to be employed? To be avoided?

Aquinas's notion of punishment may be said to be the traditional one. Punishment consists in the infliction of some pain, suffering, loss, or social disability as a direct consequence of some action or omission on the part of the person punished. Punishment may occur in the form of death, physical assault, detention, fines, loss of civil and political rights, or banishment.[10] There must be a statutory, contractual, or familial relationship between the punisher and the punished. The legitimacy of the actions of the punisher is the primary distinction between punishment and other forms of coercion and constraint. Unless the agent who inflicts the pain or deprivation has authority to do so, his action constitutes a form of assault. Punishment is usually personalized in the sense that it is applied to individuals. Collective punishment, for Aquinas, is of dubious moral standing.

Punishment may be inflicted by various social institutions, for example, family, church, guild, and civil or military society. Aquinas took Roman law as his model. Roman law acknowledged the authority of the *pater familias* whose authority extended over all members of the household, including those who had married into it, free servants, and slaves. In Aquinas's day the master craftsman had similar authority over his apprentices, as did the masters of a university over their students. That authority was subject to the rule of civil law but more importantly to the rule of reason. Furthermore, within Christendom appeals for mercy could be made for the modification of punitive

10. The principal texts for Saint Thomas's doctrine on punishment are *Summa Theologiae*, I-II, Q. 87, a. 1, and *Summa contra Gentiles*, III, chaps. 146–49.

sanctions. Taken for granted was a theology that recognized the elements of sin, guilt, absolution, and penance. One can find in medieval literature extended theological treatises devoted to the relationship between guilt and punishment.

Brian Tierny has shown that many notions advanced in these treatises were subsequently incorporated into legal doctrine in the British common law, particularly that of *mens rea* which holds that there can be no crime without intent.[11] For centuries the doctrine of *mens rea* enabled English common law to protect those whose actions, although intrinsically unlawful, were committed without malice. Also characteristic of medieval theology is the doctrine that punishment must be related to the offender's sense of responsibility or comprehension of the gravity of the offense. Roman law established age seven as the age of culpability. This idea was carried over into the Church, with the result that confession was not required until that age. Penance following confession was constructed to fit the degree of responsibility by the penitent. A condition of expiation was the penitent's honest resolve to sin no more. As with confession, the "penance" became an important part of sentencing in common law. With the destruction of the unity of Christianity, punishment assumed a new rationale. By the middle of the eighteenth century a fundamental reexamination was well under way.

It should be noted that the word "sin" for Aquinas does not have a distinctive religious connotation, although it implies a moral infraction. "Sin" means any infraction, any deviation from a prescribed order—be it familial, civil, or the order of nature. To perform any evil deed is to sin. "Because sin is an inordinate act, it is evident that whoever sins, commits an offense against an order, wherefore he is put down in consequence by that same order, which repression is punishment."[12] "Accordingly," continues Aquinas, "man can be punished in a threefold manner corresponding to the three orders to

---

11. Brian Tierney, *Religion, Law, and the Growth of Constitutional Thought* (Cambridge, U.K.: Cambridge University Press, 1982).

12. Thomas Aquinas, *Summa Theologiae*, trans. Fathers of the English Dominican Province (New York: Benzinger Brothers, 1947), I-II, Q. 87, a. 1.

which the human will is subject."[13] First, a man's nature is subject to the order of his own reason; second, it may be subjected to the order of another who governs him in spiritual or in temporal matters, as a member of either the state or of the household; third, it is subjected to the universal order of the divine government. Now each of these orders is disturbed by sin, for the sinner may act against reason, against human law, and against divine law. Wherefore, he is liable to a threefold punishment: one inflicted by himself, for example, remorse of conscience; another inflicted by man; and a third inflicted by God.

Obviously punishment for Aquinas is not an evil. He who sins by that sin incurs the debt of punishment. Some punishment is what today we could call "psychological punishment." Aquinas uses the words "tribulation" and "anguish" to describe those interior effects of sin. Some sin punishes, so to speak, by confirming the person in sin; one deception leads to another, with the result that the habitual sinner becomes hardened. This, says Aquinas, is an accidental effect of the initial deviant act.[14] While nature punishes in the foregoing way, it is evident that infractions against the social order have to be dealt with by that order. The head of a household has the obligation to punish for the good of the household; so, too, does the state. Justice requires punishment, and a society that does not appropriately punish is itself unjust.[15]

Punishment, says Aquinas, must be proportionate to the infraction. This must be true of human judgment as we know it to be true of divine judgment. Punishment may have the side effect of deterrence or be intended primarily as a deterrent. Aquinas writes: "Even the punishment that is inflicted according to human laws is not always intended as a medicine for the one who is punished, but sometimes only for others: thus when a thief is hanged, this is not for his own amendment, but for the sake of others, that at least they may be deterred from crime through fear of punishment."[16] Thomas quotes

---

13. Ibid.
14. Ibid.
15. Ibid.
16. Ibid., a. 2.

Proverbs 19.25: "The wicked man being scourged, the fool shall be wiser."

Thomas also discusses another aspect of "the good of punishment," this time clearly from a theological perspective. God has destined every human being for eternal happiness with Him. But when the creature is held back from this end because of his own failure, God nonetheless fulfills in him that amount of goodness of which he is capable:

He is said to will the salvation of all ... but because some work against their own salvation, the order of His wisdom does not admit of their attaining salvation in view of their failure. He fulfills in them in another way the demands of His goodness, damning them out of justice.... As a result, falling short of the first order of His will, they thus slip into the second. And although they do not do God's will, His will is still fulfilled in them.[17]

Aquinas continues, "The failure constituting sin by which a person is made deserving of punishment here and now or in the future, is not itself willed by God, but merely permitted."[18]

It should be emphasized that for Aquinas punishment is not an end in itself. Its object is requital *(justitia vindicativa)*, as well as deterrence and education. For a modern utilitarian like Jeremy Bentham, "all punishment is a mischief." The only justification for punishment is a plausible belief that greater evils will thereby be averted. Aquinas does not deny this function of law, but the regulation of conduct through threat of punishment is not primary. The threat of punishment is useful because there is no guarantee that all citizens at all times will honor those laws of the state or community. Aquinas is quick to mention obvious conditions. To have this regulatory effect, the law must be predictable in its administration. The citizen must know what the law requires, but also how the law will punish violations. Not all that is sinful need be punished by civil or criminal law. Deviant behavior, or disrespect for the laws of nature, carries with it its own natural sanctions.

17. Thomas Aquinas, *De Veritate*, trans. R. W. Schmidt (Chicago: Henry Regnery, 1954), Q. 23, a. 2.
18. Ibid.

Presupposed is a doctrine of free will and the conviction that one's character is the product of one's own choices. This presupposition is obviously at variance with many contemporary psychosocial perspectives, especially those that are materialistic and behavioristic in their sources. The determinist regards human activity as the immediate outcome of biological drives, urges, motives, and states, and more remotely as the product of historical forces. According to modern doctrine, the individual is essentially formed by determinants over which he has no control, his behavior being the inevitable consequence of anatomy and conditioning.

On the topic of capital punishment, Aquinas considers two kinds of objections to the use of the death penalty: (1) those based on biblical texts, and (2) those based on social considerations.[19] While the scriptural arguments have no impact in philosophical debate, they are nevertheless interesting. Arguments based on Sacred Scripture, says Aquinas, frequently refer to the biblical admonition "Thou shalt not kill" (Exodus 20.13 and Matthew 5.2) or to the parable of the cockle and the wheat (Matthew 3.38–40) in which the criminal is likened to the cockle that should not be removed until harvest. The wheat-and-cockle metaphor suggests that the criminal should not be removed from the world by execution but kept for eternal punishment.

Aquinas dismisses these arguments as frivolous. In countering the first he uses additional passages in Scripture to show that they do not lead to the conclusion supposed. Of the first, he says,

Indeed, in the law which says "Thou shalt not kill" there is the later statement: "Wrongdoers thou shall not suffer to live" (Exodus 22.18). From this we are given to understand that only the *unjust* execution of men is prohibited. This is also apparent from the Lord's words in Matthew 5. For after He said: "You have heard that it was said to them of old: 'Thou shalt not kill' (Matthew 5.21), He added: 'But I say to you that whosoever is angry with his brother,' etc. From this He makes us understand that the killing which results from anger is prohibited, but not that which stems from a zeal for justice. Moreover, how the Lord's statement, 'Suffer both to grow until the harvest,' should

19. *Summa contra Gentiles*, trans. Vernon J. Bourke (Garden City, N.Y.: Hanover House, 1956), III, chap. 146, 9.

be understood is apparent through what follows: 'lest perhaps, gathering up the cockle, you root up the wheat also together with it' (Matthew 13.29). So, the execution of the wicked is forbidden wherever it cannot be done without danger to the good. Of course, this often happens when the wicked are not clearly distinguished from the good by their sins, or when the danger of evil involving many good men in their ruin is feared.[20]

To the argument in favor of rehabilitation, Aquinas admits that as long as the criminal lives, there is the possibility of the criminal's reformation, but that possibility does not preclude execution, for, speaking generally, "the danger which threatens from their way of life is greater and more certain than the good which may be expected from their improvement." Aquinas recognizes that criminals at the point of execution are usually given the opportunity to turn to God and to repent. But as experience teaches, criminals are frequently so stubborn that even at the point of death their hearts do not draw back from evil. Thus it is possible to make a highly probable judgment that incarcerated they would still not come away from evil to the right use of their powers. Reformation as a result of imprisonment is not to be expected.

In the *Summa* II-II Q. 64, a. 6, Aquinas raises a question interesting in itself but also one with important implications. His answer shows a respect for the force of statutory law and the value of due process. Today we would call him a "strict constructionist." Article 6 of the above text asks "Whether it is ever lawful to kill the innocent?" Thomas considers the situation in which a judge, who is bound to judge according to the evidence, condemns a man whom he knows to be innocent, but who is convicted by false witnesses, and a second example in which an executioner, who in obedience to the judge puts to death the man who has been unjustly sentenced. Thomas's solution is this:

If the judge knows that a man who has been convicted by false witnesses is innocent, he must, like Daniel, examine the witnesses with great care, so as to find a motive for acquitting the innocent: but if he cannot do this he should remit him for judgment by a higher tribunal. If even this is impossible, he

20. Ibid.

does not sin if he pronounces sentences in accordance with the evidence, for it is not he that puts an innocent man to death, but they who stated him to be guilty.

If Thomas thinks a judge does no wrong in knowingly condemning an innocent person to death, is it not reasonable to infer that he would find blameless a judge who, mistakenly, but in accord with due process, condemns an innocent person to death? Similarly, says Aquinas, the hangman may carry out the order in good conscience where there is no "manifest injustice" or "inexcusable error."

III

Immanuel Kant is later to cover the same ground and reach many of the same conclusions, but there are some differences. Not deterrence, says Kant, but justice requires the punishment of the offender. If we were to punish an offender to deter others we would be guilty of using him as a means to achieve ends that he does not share. "Judicial punishment can never be used merely as a means to promote some other good for the criminal himself or for civil society . . . for a human being can never be manipulated merely as a means to the purposes of someone else."[21]

According to Kant, when criminals are punished because they deserve their punishment and not to deter others, they are treated as ends in themselves, and not as means. Their human dignity is affirmed. Thus punishment becomes an end in itself, a moral good, not a means. Kant, like Aquinas, conceived of the evildoer as nevertheless a rational person who would recognize the punishment as deserved and who would intellectually consent to its implementation. It is assumed that the offender, if he had designed the social institution under which he were convicted, would have included the very laws that he violated and mandated the punishment to which he is sentenced. Punishment thus attains ends that offenders themselves im-

---

21. Immanuel Kant, *Grundelegung zur Metaphysik der Sitten* (1798), *Metaphysics of Morals*, part 1, trans. by John Ladd as "The Metaphysical Elements of Justice" (New York: Harper & Row, 1965), 331; Ladd, p. 100.

plicitly share. In consenting to their deserved punishment, offenders share in its purpose and thus are not used as a means to the ends of others.

Kant rejected utilitarian grounds for punishing, including rehabilitation and deterrence. Kant realized that criminals may not, in fact, feel good about their punishments; but, he argued, if they were intelligent beings, reasoning correctly, they would share his view. Kant is adamant in separating punishment from utility. "The law concerning punishment is a categorical imperative, and woe to him who rummages around in the winding paths of a theory of happiness looking for some advantage to be gained by releasing the criminal from punishment or by reducing the amount of it."[22] If the crime is one of murder, retribution requires that the criminal be judicially condemned and put to death:[23]

Even if a civil society were to dissolve itself by common agreement of all of its members, . . . the last murderer remaining in prison must first be executed, so that everyone will duly receive what his actions are worth and so that the bloodguilt thereof will not be fixed on the people because they failed to insert or carry out the punishment; for if they fail to do so, they may be regarded as accomplices in this public violation of legal justice.[24]

Kant rejects the view of those "moved by sympathetic sentimentality and an affectation of humanitarianism" who would abolish capital punishment.[25]

IV

What lessons may be drawn from these considerations? Given the views of Aquinas and Kant on punishment, it would be difficult to argue that informed social thought requires an abolitionist mindset. Furthermore, given the common employment of the death penalty in Western and non-Western countries alike, it would be erroneous to link capital punishment with a given theological viewpoint. Nor is it necessary to limit the defense of capital punishment to

22. Ibid.   23. Kant, "Metaphysics," 333; Ladd, 102.
24. Ibid.   25. Kant, "Metaphysics," 335; Ladd, 105.

purely utilitarian reasons. That justice requires punishment quite apart from any deterrent value is a judgment to be found outside of Western sources.

It is only upon the denial of certain Western intellectual principles that the rationale for punishment has been challenged. It is acknowledged that some social theorists build their case against the effectiveness of capital punishment on empirical grounds, but that evidence is admittedly far from conclusive and is constantly challenged. For one thing, there is no way to measure how many crimes have been deterred by the threat of punishment.[26] Studies that compare one nation with another or one state with another, as in the United States, or utilize a "before" and "after" approach in a given jurisdiction, fail to acknowledge a common culture in which punishment is still associated with crime. Although students of the criminal system may be able to document the uncertainty and rarity of the deterrent power of punishment, for most of the populace the assumption that crime will be punished is enough to deter.

Ultimately the abolitionist must invoke principle. The principles that are assumed by many social theorists include a psychological determinism, a moral relativism, a negative judgment with respect to Western history and culture, and an idealism with respect to the perfectibility of man. Those who defend the abolition of capital punishment are usually at war with their own heritage, often symbolized by Christianity. In recent decades they have met no major academic opposition. But given the legal implementation of their outlook and the consequent crumbling of punitive sanctions, society as a whole has suffered to the point that a significant opposition has now arisen.

The current debate is sometimes framed as a debate between parties designated "utilitarians" and those called "retributionists." But there are reasons for rejecting these abstract characterizations. They are largely the product of an analytic or conceptual inquiry that robs actual positions taken by individual philosophers of their complexity.

---

26. Cf. E. Van den Haag, "On Deterrence and the Death Penalty," *Journal of Criminal Law, Criminology, and Police Science* 60 (1969): 141–47.

Pure positions are hard to find. A utilitarian is thought to be one who stresses the deterrence aspect of punishment; a retributionist, one who grounds his arguments in consideration of justice. Aquinas, of course, was both. Any natural law argument of the type associated with Aquinas looks in part like a utilitarian argument because it evaluates human action in terms of the ultimate end of life. Furthermore, natural law arguments recognize freestanding structures apart from the mind and are aware that behavior adverse to the nature in question can bring about its own disintegration, quite apart from any social sanctions. Thus Aquinas can talk about the observable effects of sin in the party whose habitual choices run contrary to those warranted by nature.

The relevance of Aquinas and Kant to the contemporary debate is the systematic philosophical support they give to principles derived from and employed by common sense and until recently embodied in Western legal practice. Though radically different in their metaphysical outlooks, their knowledge of unchangeable human nature and its requirements is unsurpassed and remains unchallenged by the data uncovered by contemporary empirical study.

TWELVE

PROFESSIONAL RESPONSIBILITY

I

Few would deny that Immanuel Kant is one of a small band of great knowers. Among his lasting contributions to the study of philosophy is his *Metaphysics of Morals*. His discussion of virtue, of one's duties toward one's self and toward others, is time-transcending. Kant is convinced that "a doctrine of virtue is . . . something that can be taught."[1] But virtue cannot be taught merely by concepts of duty or by exhortations. Instead, it must be exercised and cultivated by effort. One cannot straightaway do all that one wants to do. But the decision to embark on a virtuous path "must be made all at once and completely."[2] To form a habit is to establish a lasting inclination apart from any maxim. The emphasis is on "inclination," but Kant was not opposed to the enunciation of maxims, provided they issued from systematic and empirical inquiry. Kant's emphasis on dialogue in the methodical treatment of virtue has found favor with many contemporary moralists as they prepare textbooks and anthologies. This is no more evident than in discussions of morality as it pertains to the professions, particularly the medical, legal, and academic professions. The following discussion focuses upon the concept of professional responsibility in a generic way. It suggests, in a Kantian manner, virtues appropriate to the professions singled out for treatment.

1. *The Metaphysics of Morals*, trans. Mary Gregor (Oxford, U.K.: Oxford University Press, 1995), 266.
2. Ibid.

Professional responsibility is a composite of virtues. It is a moral requirement coextensive with the authority and power conferred by office. I cannot think of a moral virtue that a responsible professional ought not to have, but there are certain virtues associated with the professions which in their absence may cause particular consternation. I will focus on these in a moment. But first let me explain what is commonly meant by "profession" and then by "responsibility."

Although we are inclined to use the word *profession* loosely, not every occupation is rightly called "professional." The etymology of the term and its historical usage may be of some help in securing a manageable definition. The term traditionally was assigned to those callings in which one "professes" to have acquired some special knowledge, useful either by way of instruction or guidance and secondarily to those arts or services that depend upon such knowledge. In antiquity this was thought to rule out purely commercial, mechanical, agricultural, or other similar occupations. Three time-honored professions, theology, law, and medicine, were accorded the designation "learned." Although antiquity recognized only a short list of professions, contemporary claims to professional status are numerous indeed and one would be foolhardy if one attempted to arbitrate what is and what is not rightly called a profession. Obviously, the list of professions recognized in antiquity may be expanded by a kind of analogy to many modern occupations. Given our ability to define them, these occupations have status commensurate with their intellectual component, their importance to the community, and their history. We normally do not look upon an electrician or a plumber as a professional, although we respect tradesmen and their crafts. A profession obviously entails a theoretical dimension.

The word *responsibility* itself may give us a clue. Although the etymology of the word may be obscure, there is reason to believe that it comes from the Latin *respondeo*, similar to the French *répondre*, as in "réspondez s'il vous plait" (RSVP; respond, if you please). In its Latin origin, it implies an amenability, a disposition to answer to a call. To be responsible is to be answerable. "Responsible" as an adjective denotes what Aristotle called *phronimos*, reasonableness and reliability. As a moral quality it is not confined to any particular situation but designates a disposition and perhaps a role.

Professional responsibility entails not only a disposition, but a cluster of virtues. Some of these relate to the profession, some to the person qua person. Professional integrity depends in part on the maintenance of appropriate skills at the highest level. To be au courant, one must be abreast of the current literature in the field, and perhaps be a regular attendee at conventions and other updating sessions. While the maintenance of professional skills is of the highest priority, technique alone is rarely sufficient for success in the long run. There is an obligation to know the truth about one's profession. One needs to know something about its history and where it fits into the larger schema of knowledge and activity. The value of an acquaintance with the history of the profession may vary from one discipline to another, but some knowledge of lineage is required for identity. So, too, is a regard for the future. The professional has an obligation to those who would succeed him. The very notion of "profession" implies continuity through time—past, present, and future. Indeed, one can write a history of medicine, of law, or of the priesthood. We can and do discuss or speculate about the likely future of engineering or nursing as a profession. The perception of long-range needs will determine our action now.

It is hard to imagine any endeavor that may be called "professional" that does not involve this learned or cognitive dimension. In the traditionally recognized professions of theology, law, and medicine, a premium was placed on learning. The obvious relation between learning and achievement is seen historically wherever we find the knowledgeable sought for judgeships, administrative positions, or bishoprics. From Ambrose to Kilwarby to Scalia we find examples. So, too, learning is one defining element in contemporary professions unknown to antiquity.

Just as there are many varieties and many degrees of authority and many mechanisms for conferral of such authority, one achieves responsibility in many ways: by virtue of elected or appointed office, certainly, but in other ways, too. By virtue of authorship, the parent is responsible for the child, even *in utero*, and those who are parents may wonder whether that responsibility ever ceases. Kinship evokes a kind of responsibility quite apart from legal and even moral responsibility. Within the modern corporation, from the building engineer to the chief executive officer, there are levels of responsibility and even within those levels there may be degrees of responsibility. Similarly, within a profession, there are degrees of responsibility.

II

To develop a theme I just mentioned, it is evident that the professional's first obligation is to pursue excellence in his calling. He has an obligation not only to master relevant technique (and in some professions ever-changing techniques), but to master the theoretical dimension of his work. The recognition of those truths that bear upon the fundamental features of his work and of the relation of that work to life as a whole is a part of the speculative and practical wisdom required of the professional. *Praxis* is grounded in *theoria*. One needs normative principles in order to judge and to evaluate. These are most likely to come from sources outside the empirical present. Experience garnered from the past is indispensable if one is to recognize that there are certain laws governing nature and human behavior that remain invariant through generations, indeed through millennia. In almost every profession, to be steeped in its history is to possess a vantage point. One cannot claim status as an economist without having read Adam Smith.

In some disciplines and consequently in some professions a knowledge of the history of the discipline is more important than it is in others. Human nature, like nature itself, has not changed from antiquity. Whereas the natural sciences have advanced on the back of developments in technology, there have been no technological innovations that have brought us closer to an examination of human nature. Thus it behooves us to read and reread works such as Aristotle's *Nicomachean Ethics* and his *Politics*, Cicero's *The Commonwealth*, and Augustine's *The City of God*. If standards are not to be trivial, they will in some sense have to transcend the present and rest upon the best judgments available to the race. If practices are to be judged, if the manners and customs of a profession or even of a people are to be evaluated, there will have to be a means of achieving a perspective that will enable such assessments to take place. Livy said as much for the Rome of his day, which by the first century B.C. was already conscious of its past: "What chiefly makes the study of history wholesome and profitable is this, that in history you have a record of the infinite variety of human experience plainly set out for all to see, and in that record you can find for yourself and your country both examples and warning."[3]

Concerning the nature of law and the responsibilities of the magistrate, Cicero remains a guide. For Cicero, the highest expression of professional life is the care of the public, a vocation he accepted for himself. In *De Officiis*, distinguishing between community service and individual advancement, he makes a high-minded distinction between the *bonum honestum* and the *bonum utile*, identifying the former with the common good and the latter with individual interest.[4] What is just serves the *res publica*. Just as self-interest should not be placed above the common good, the calculations of special interest groups should not be placed above the good of the common wealth. Cicero's emphasis on communal responsibility is so strong that he has often been used to justify overstepping the bounds of law in the pursuit of the common good.

Following Cicero's line of argument, both wisdom and prudence are requisite for he who would assume responsibility in the commonwealth. He who would work for the common good must be able to distinguish between what is truly good and that which has only apparent usefulness. A person in authority must strive always to be just, but it must be acknowledged that, measured against the standard of absolute good, many of his actions will fall short. The just or equitable man is principled and bears in mind long-range effects. The pursuit of

3. Titus Livius, Preface to his *History* (Cambridge, Mass: Loeb Classical Library, Harvard University Press, 1924), 1.7.

4. Cicero, *On the Commonwealth*, trans. C. H. Sabine and S. B. Smith (Indianapolis, Ind.: Bobbs-Merrill, 1950).

utility, disengaged from any notion of *honestum,* threatens the viability of society. Self-preservation depends on the commonwealth; the defense of society is thus the highest priority.

The contemporary relevance of this Ciceronian treatise does not escape us. The rule of law takes precedence, but the principles upon which the law rests are themselves derivative. They presuppose a philosophy and a tradition. Recognition of a divine order is explicit in Cicero. He emphasizes the requirement of learning and respect for the inherited; he takes for granted the commonness of the human condition and on it bases his respect for the lessons of history. Every commonwealth, he proclaims, if it aims to maintain itself in being, requires its tradition. The same can be said here and now of our own commonwealth and of its organizations and professions.

Evidence of the exercise of professional responsibility is to be found in every age. Take the three learned professions. The oath attributed to the ancient Greek physician Hippocrates, adopted throughout the centuries as a guide for conduct in the medical profession, is one still used during graduation ceremonies at many universities and schools of medicine. The first in the book of *Aphorisims* attributed to Hippocrates reads, "Life is short, and the art long; opportunity fleeting; experiment dangerous and judgment difficult."[5] One can say the same of many professions. Their art is indeed "long," meaning they have a history. Often the opportunity to act, regrettably, is fleeting. In times of crisis who does not recognize that the tried and the true provides a standard? And who has not experienced that the prudential judgment is fraught with danger; there are no rules respecting the application of rules. Hippocrates cannot be gainsaid.

The oaths, codes, and rules of professional conduct that have been adopted by the major professions over the centuries may be taken as an expression of collective responsibility. The Hippocratic Oath is only the most famous. Rabbinical codes antedate Christianity. Rules and codes governing the conduct of ecclesiastics from the

---

5. "Medicine, History of," *The New Encyclopedia Britannica,* 11.827.

early centuries of Christianity still prevail or have their contemporary counterparts. Saint Benedict's *Rule* is the epitome of common sense. Legal fraternities offer another example of the adoption and even the enforcement of codes of practice.

The legal profession in the United States as early as the eighteenth century developed a code of conduct relevant to professional activities. For many years this code was unwritten, but in the late nineteenth century some jurisdictions began to adopt written codes by rule of court. Shortly after the turn of this century the American Bar Association (ABA) proposed a series of written canons which, updated in 1970, almost universally have been adopted throughout the United States. The current *Code of Professional Responsibility* is divided into three parts: (1) canons, or axiomatic statements, expressing general standards of professional conduct; (2) ethical considerations deemed relevant; and (3) disciplinary rules, which are regarded as mandatory in character, and which have the force of law in most jurisdictions. The 1970 *Code* was amplified by the "Model Rules of Professional Conduct." Adopted by the ABA in 1983, it may be considered to be a gloss on the earlier code. Citing just a few of the canons will suggest their nature. Canon I asserts that a lawyer should assist in maintaining the integrity and competence of the legal profession; Canon IV, that a lawyer should preserve the confidences and secrets of a client; Canon V, that a lawyer should exercise independent professional judgment on behalf of a client; Canon VIII, that a lawyer should assist in improving the legal system; Canon IX, that a lawyer should avoid even the appearance of professional impropriety. These canons may be viewed as rules of reason that are applicable analogously to other professions.[6]

Responsibility follows upon authority and the power commensurate with it, but authority is achieved in a multiplicity of ways. *De jure* authority is achieved by virtue of appointed or elective office, but other kinds of authority need to be recognized. Print and visual media are cases in point. The authority of the media is in part self-conferred

---

6. *Multistate Professional Responsibility* (New York: SMH, 1987), 17–84.

(the *New York Times* proclaims itself to be "the paper of record"), and in part conferred by a readership, or by "viewers like you," as the expression goes.

An important type of authority is that which comes with the mastery of a discipline or a technique, one that is sometimes called "epistemic" authority. And while epistemic authority is self-generated, once recognized it carries with it commensurate responsibility. The acknowledged authority cannot be loose or careless in speech or in print. The less informed depend upon the precision and carefulness of the acknowledged master. Any sloppiness allowed in the line of reports, judgment, or advice is thought to be a betrayal. People do and must rely on authorities.

What we take to be true of an individual's responsibility is also true of a group or of a profession as a whole. Advertisers often attempt to transfer epistemic authority from its recognized domain to the endorsement of a specific product. The "man in the white lab coat" is a familiar television personality. In the late 1930s when a group of scientists for reasons of national security wanted to get President Roosevelt's attention, they drafted a letter for the signature of one of the best known mathematical physicists (Einstein) of the day. The physicist's authority was sufficient to gain the attention sought. Epistemic authority was recognized, and the message conveyed was acted upon. As we know, the Manhattan Project changed the course of the war in the Pacific.

But beyond *de jure* authority and that based on cognitive skills, there is another kind of authority, often called "moral" or "charismatic," although the two may not be the same thing. The person who with rhetorical skill can dramatically call attention to a moral principle can often wield a tremendous amount of power. While we may be hesitant to call this professional, it is a power frequently found in one who holds office—for example, Dr. Benjamin Spock in the medical profession, Mahatma Gandhi in the political order, or Mother Theresa in the social order. The authority of John Paul II, to the extent that it carries beyond the Church he leads, may be considered as a further example.

There is yet another kind of authority, recognizable, but difficult to define. It flows from an affective disposition, Kant's bottom-line "goodwill," you may say, which leads to "caring," "solicitude," or "concern" and the assumption of responsibility, for example, for one's co-workers, fraternity, or community. Something like this is found in an extended family where members may have very little contact with each other over the course of a year, but respond in an emergency with surprising solicitude. The responsible daughter, brother, or aunt, though separated by distance and the benefit of frequent visits, nevertheless assumes duties that neighbors and even close friends do not recognize as obligations. The recognition of duty to one's kinfolk is certainly an exercise in responsibility, although not of professional responsibility. Still the same disposition has effects in civic order and in one's profession. Cicero located the foundation of a desire for justice in our natural inclination to love our fellow man.[7] Kant recognized that a sense of duty and self-control are the personal moral dispositions that make concerted or communal action possible. Our moral sentiments dispose us to act, but not in any particular direction; they arise in the context of our natural sociability and are affected by the prevailing culture. On the downside, it takes little experience to recognize that without the guidance of a body of settled norms sentiment can wreck havoc. Under the disposition of sympathy or in the name of fairness, a society can destroy itself. Without a standard or a hierarchical ordering of ends, all claims tend to be equated. Without the recognition of time-transcending moral norms, decisions are likely to be ad hoc, resulting in an incoherent pattern of action. Responsible action, personal or communal, entails accountability, even when motivated by compassion. We may not be accountable to any person or authority but still recognize our accountability to an independent moral order. Who or what defines that order is another topic. In the East, it may be a Confucian tradition; in the West, it is likely to be carried by Christianity. Philosophy has been notoriously weak in carrying moral norms.

7. *Laws* 1, 5, 16.

Of some professions we expect exemplary behavior. Physicians for the most part still take the Hippocratic Oath, members of the bar undergo scrutiny for moral uprightness, and there are clearly defined codes of behavior for military personnel. Clergy, most of all, are held to very high moral standards.

III

A responsible person acts within a context. Moral agency implies free will, intentionality, and a moral order independent of one's making. As a manifestation of his freedom, a moral person does not deny agency but accepts responsibility for his actions. His involvement, whether for good or bad, brings praise or blame. Recognizing accountability, the moral agent thinks about what he is doing and acts for reasons that he thinks are professionally proper rather than for reasons he would be ashamed to acknowledge. Considerations of accountability militate against the thoughtless or impulsive act. With sufficient thought, one takes care to perform those acts that must be done and not to leave anything undone that needs to be done. If anything goes amiss, the moral agent must be prepared to put things right again. A responsible person is one who can be left in charge, one who can be relied upon to perform, one who will not leave the job undone or be distracted from the business at hand. The responsible person honors obligations in the absence of rewards for doing so and in the absence of sanctions for failure.

Assuming responsibility may not be the most pleasant of undertakings. Acting from responsibility can lead to the charge that one is unfriendly, unsympathetic, or worse. Yet a person would be imprudent who is so unfailingly sympathetic as to give aid and comfort to even the most devious of supplicants. When placed in competition with one's natural sociability and the desire to be liked, responsibility may lose out. We are inclined to ambiguity in an effort to protect the feelings of a friend or those of the disadvantaged. Yet the responsible person will pursue the difficult good, even if this means that he is the bearer of bad news or the instrument of discipline.

The right course of behavior is not always self-evident. There is a distinction to be made between wisdom and prudence. In deliberating, the relevant principle may be clear, but the application of that principle is something else. Thus when we decide, in difficult cases at least, we take to thought. We weigh considerations pro and con and assess the balance of the competing options. Once we have reached a decision, we are prepared to explain and justify it by citing the principles we have observed and by offering reasons for coming down one way rather than another. Sometimes our decision seems more inevitable than it really was. In looking back on it, we forget the negative factors that could have led us to decide the other way. This lapse of memory is not to be confused with a lack of freedom.

The process we know only too well from personal decisions. As J. R. Lucas reminds us in his admirable book-length study of responsibility, "Reasoning about practical affairs is dialectical, that is, two-sided. It is not a matter of drawing conclusions which must, on pain of inconsistency, be conceded once the premises are admitted, but a matter of argument and counter-argument."[8] The prima facie case is mentally rebutted. The perfectly reasonable argument may be effectively countered on further consideration. We recognize that claims about reality are inherently corrigible. We may always want more information, but as often as not a decision has to be made on the information available. Sometimes it is more important to act than to be absolutely sure that one is taking the proper course of action.

This leads us to another consideration. Since reasons are inherently sharable, actions that are implementations of reason are sharable, too. I can take responsibility for an action without depriving you of responsibility for it, too. I can be held responsible for an action you performed without your being any less responsible. We may be collectively responsible. If I ask you, or suggest to you, or recommend to you to do something, I can be held responsible, although that does not of itself exclude your being responsible, too. To take a similar scenario, suppose I am not the originator of the action but merely go along with it. My assent may be ephemeral; we

---

8. *Responsibility* (Oxford, U.K.: Clarendon Press, 1993), 59.

may be associated in a common enterprise, we may be close colleagues or members of the same family. When policy is debated it is
reasonable to assume that each of us has an obligation to speak out,
and when we have not done so, it may be inferred that we approve of
what is done. In the professional order it may be necessary to become
engaged in the drafting of resolutions that are to be promulgated in
the name of the profession. It may be necessary to challenge groups
within a profession from authorizing documents immoral in themselves or inappropriate to the role of the organization. In some instances resignation from the professional organization may be the
only means to register dissent.

One cannot be responsible for everything that may flow from
one's action. A man is responsible for all the consequences that he can
reasonably foresee as flowing from his act. The professional moral
agent has an obligation to deliberate about likely outcomes. Conversely, in judging the moral action of another, one must take account of its intent. But intent is not everything. Good intentions will
not redeem the intrinsically immoral act. Circumstances may color
responsibility, both in a positive and in a negative fashion. In fact we
are often blamed for things beyond our control; and conversely we
are sometimes given greater credit than we deserve. In the matter of
intention we must look beyond the horizon. *Utile* may not be the
same as *honestum.* In collective action it makes no difference whether
the consequences flow from one's own act taken by itself or in con-
junction with the acts of others. As Lucas puts it, "Responsibility is
not like pie. There is always enough to go around; and the size of each
piece is independent of the number of persons involved."[9]

Professions as a whole can be responsible or irresponsible. Positive
and negative illustrations abound. One may wonder if the American
Medical Association behaved responsibly when, in 1994, under pres-
sure from the Gay and Lesbian Medical Association, it reversed a
time-honored policy by calling for a "non-judgmental recognition of
sexual orientation by physicians." The same may be asked of the prior

9. See "Shared and Collective Responsibility," *Responsibility*, chap. 5, 75–85.

action of the American Psychiatric Association, which until 1973 regarded homosexuality as a treatable form of mental illness.[10]

Examples of professional irresponsibility can be multiplied. Clergymen take sexual advantage of the young, psychiatrists of the helplessness of their patients, lawyers of the ignorance of their clients, professors of the innocence of their students. Many fail not only to observe professional codes of behavior but jeopardize themselves before criminal law as well.

Perhaps the most notorious flouting of professional standards is to be found in the media. Media personnel often identify themselves as members of "the fourth estate." By any definition they certainly qualify as professionals. A survey completed by S. Robert Lichter and Stanley Rothman (1980) reported the moral and political views of more than 240 persons whom they describe as not aspirants to stature as but as members of the elite media in the United States. Among the many outlooks they uncovered, they found that members of the media, on the whole, recognize the tremendous influence they have but nevertheless think that they should have even more influence. This sought-for influence is obviously of a tutorial sort. It is not based on money or political power but on the information and ideas the media transmit to social and political leaders and to the public.[11]

One would be innocent indeed if one thought that the media is without a social or cultural agenda. Lichter and Rothman found that for the leading journalists they interviewed, liberal views on contemporary social and political issues overwhelmingly prevailed. According to Lichter and Rothman,

The pointed views of the national media elite are not mere wishes and opinions of those aspiring to power, but the voice of a new leadership group that has arrived as a major force in American society. Cosmopolitan in their origins, liberal in their outlooks, they are aware and protective of their collective influence. The rise of this elite has hardly gone unnoticed. Some hail them as the public's tribunes against the powerful—indispensable champions of the

10. American Psychiatric Report, *Washington Times*, 22 December 1994, p. A9.
11. *Public Opinion*, October–November 1981, p. 60.

underdog and the oppressed. Others decry them for allegiance to an adversary culture that is chiseling away at traditional values.[12]

There are few sides of life with which the media does not deal. One would think that wielders of such a power would acknowledge and accept the responsibility to be truthful in word and image, avoiding, among other vices, distortion, character assassination, and propaganda designed to alter public attitudes, yet the reverse seems to be true. In the judgment of those who professionally follow the media, we rarely find a scrupulosity in the pursuit of truth, a willingness to admit error, or a consciousness of consequences.

Fourteen years after their initial study, Lichter and Rothman, joined now by Lichter's wife, returned to study the media, focusing this time exclusively on television in the United States. While their 1980 study was nonjudgmental, their 1994 study does not refrain from moral assessment. In their judgment, television has fallen from whatever moral balance it may have formerly possessed. They base their assessment on evidence found regarding an excessive depiction of violence, a failure to disapprove of or question premarital sex or sex under any circumstances, and the lampooning of anyone who criticizes homosexual lives.[13]

Rescinding from the media, who has not experienced sometimes heroic efforts of individual physicians, teachers, and members of the clergy who have acted not only in the line of duty but also beyond the call of duty. But most of the time professional responsibility is exercised in a pedestrian manner. Two minor examples come to mind to illustrate what I take to be professional responsibility. "Deaccessioning" is the bureaucratic term used by museums of art when they decide to sell a holding to enhance their endowment, often to make a specific purchase or to meet operating expenses. The art world as a whole seems uncomfortable with the deaccessioning practice, which often entails the betrayal of the intent of a long-

12. S. R. Lichter, L. Lichter, and S. Rothman, *Prime Time: How T.V. Portrays American Culture* (Washington, D.C.: Regnery, 1994).
13. Ibid.

deceased patron. In an exercise of professional responsibility, the American Association of Museums and the American Association for State and Local History have explicitly condemned the practice, although both associations recognize that there may be very legitimate reasons for deaccessioning.

A second example: The medical profession through its pharmaceutical component has instituted practices which in the delivery of medication look to long-range outcomes, side effects, and the compatibility of multiple prescriptions. Computer programs signal danger. For the busy physician it may become a failsafe mechanism. The cynic many say the system was introduced to avoid litigation but more likely it is an expression of professional and collective responsibility, with manufacturer, physician, and pharmacist cooperating to ensure favorable outcomes.

I V

Physicist Erwin Schrödinger once wrote to his colleague Hans Reichenbach: "In the end, one has to keep it clear that all specialized knowledge has significance only in relation to one's sense of the whole."[14] What is true of physics can be said of the vocation of any professional. The professional's expertise, objectives, and responsibility are one thing, but the profession exists within a larger social or cultural context. Presumably the profession exists not to enhance its practitioners, although it may certainly do so, but to serve a community or society at large. Its standards fall within that society's conception of good, that is, the goals communally pursued. Plato's remark, "What is honored in a community will be cultivated there," comes to mind. Any profession may be corrupted when inappropriate, perhaps idealistic, goals are held out for its members. Can a nation or regime be corrupted? The answer seems to be "Yes." One can think of Germany

---

14. Erwin Schrödenger, letter of 25 October 1926, University of Pittsburgh Archives. "Denn schliesslich muss man sich darüber klar sein, dass alle Spezialerkenntnis überhaupt *nur* im grossen Zusammen-hang des Weltbildes Bedeutung und Interesse hat." Quoted with permission of the University of Pittsburgh; all rights reserved.

under Hitler, the Soviet Union under Stalin, and Cuba under Castro. Under those regimes it is easy to find numerous examples of the subordination by professionals to political aims. In the field of philosophy we have the famous capitulation of Heidegger to the Nazi regime. Chemists, physicists, and engineers on all sides of the conflict we know as World War II responded to the demands of the war machine. This response reflected self-interest in some cases, no doubt, but one can believe that for the most part the response was patriotic.

This leads me to my final point. The professional needs to attend to the larger scheme of morality. Like anyone else, the professional cannot avoid the Socratic quest for wisdom, to know oneself in relation to self, to nature, to others, and to God. Professional responsibility entails not only a mastery of technique but attention to what Russell Kirk called "the permanent things." The permanent things are the locus of any endeavor. In expressing the time-transcendent they are often the guide to communal and personal fulfillment.

PART III

FAITH AND REASON

* * *

THIRTEEN

EDITH STEIN

The Convert in Search of Illumination

I

Earlier this year I had the opportunity to spend several weeks in Salamanca, the seat of a university whose charter dates to 1215. One of its most distinguished twentieth-century rectors was Miguel de Unamuno, known the world over as a philosopher, poet, dramatist, novelist, and essayist. In Salamanca I had the time to read Unamuno and to study his life. Born in 1864 in the Basque coastal city of Bilbao, Unamuno at age sixteen left his native city for Madrid. One of his biographers notes that shortly after he arrived in Madrid, this formerly pious youth stopped going to Mass.[1] What he took up is not fully disclosed, but he began reading German philosophy: Schopenhauer, Kant, Hegel. He learned English in order to read Herbert Spencer, the prophet of evolutionary progress, who was the faddish intellectual in those years. The upshot of his studies was that he lost his faith. Unamuno eventually married his childhood sweetheart, and the couple had eight children. When he was in his early thirties, they lost their third child. The experience was shattering for him. It brought Unamuno to his knees and to a life of contemplation and prayer, although he never returned to the practice of his faith. Though Unamuno was culturally and emotionally a Mediterranean Catholic, he

---

1. Allen Lacy, "Introduction," in *The Private World*, by Miguel de Unamuno, trans. A. Kerrigan, A. Lacy, and M. Nozik (Princeton, N.J.: Princeton University Press, 1984), xii.

never developed a Catholic mind. Years later, as an influential academic and politician, he was trusted neither by the Catholics nor by the secular-minded. His literary legacy remains ambiguous, a kind of reverent humanism without adequate foundation.

Unamuno was fifteen years of age when Leo XIII promulgated his famous encyclical *Aeterni Patris*, a document that recommended to the Catholic world the study of Saint Thomas, both as a philosopher and as a theologian. Leo XIII was aware that the critical philosophy of the Continent, not to mention the empiricism of Scotland and England and the various materialisms that commanded the allegiance of intellectuals throughout the West, provided no foundation for the Catholic faith. To one of the Catholic faith, belief makes sense not only for the understanding it provides, but also because it forms a continuum, adding to what one knows to be the case from experience and reason. Leo XIII recognized that some philosophies open one to the faith, just as some philosophies close it down as an option. Immanuel Kant, for example, may be the perfect philosopher for some forms of Protestantism, but he can never become an adequate guide for the Catholic mind. With his dictum, "I have destroyed metaphysics in order to make room for faith," he reflects the tradition of Luther and Calvin, whose doctrine of original sin held that, as a consequence of the Fall, intellect was so darkened that it cannot unaided conclude to the existence of God. Faith for Luther and Calvin is a leap in the dark. Kant said, in effect, given the limited ability of the human mind, it must always be so. By contrast, the Catholic tradition insists on the reasonableness of belief. Revelation adds to the store of natural knowledge, completing it just as grace perfects nature. The Catholic mind is woven out of threads provided by Jerusalem, Athens, Rome, and medieval Paris.

II

Picture now a young woman schooled in the German philosophy of the period, newly a student of Husserl, discovering Catholicism. Edith Stein was born twelve years after Leo XIII urged the study of Saint Thomas. She was eventually to experience the fruit of the Thomistic revival. Edith's path to Saint Thomas was complex. It began with philosophical study that eventually led, through her acquaintance with Max Scheler, to an appreciation of Catholicism. That is the same Max Scheler on whom Karol Wojtyla wrote to earn his doctorate in philosophy.

Reared in a conservative Jewish home, Edith Stein, not unlike Unamuno, abandoned her faith as an adolescent.[2] Between the ages of thirteen and twenty-one she considered herself to be an atheist. Intellectually precocious from childhood, as a university student she found herself dissatisfied with the dominant German philosophy of her time, the same philosophy that had separated Unamuno from his religious heritage. By accident she discovered the two volumes of Husserl's *Logical Investigations*.[3]

The *Logical Investigations* consists of six investigations preceded by a prolegomena published as volume 1. The prolegomena are a sustained critique of "psychologism," the doctrine that reduces logical entities, such as propositions, universals, and numbers, to mental states or mental activities. Husserl insists on the objectivity of such targets of consciousness and shows the incoherence of trying to reduce them to activities of the mind. The rest of the work examines signs and words, abstraction, parts and wholes, logical grammar, the notion of presentation, and truth and evidence. Husserl's distinction between intuitive presentation and symbolic intention enables him to discuss in a realistic manner not only perceptual objects but categorical objects such as states of affairs, relationships, causal connections, and the like. Husserl maintains that we can have an intellectual grasp of such things by means of an intuition. An intuition occurs when we articulate an object as having certain features or relationships. The formal structure of a categorical object is reflected in the grammar we use to say something about it. With respect to material objects, we intend them either emptily or intuitively, but even when

2. Sister Teresia de Spiritu Sancto, O.D.C., *Edith Stein* (London: Sheed & Ward, 1952), 16.

3. Edith Stein, *Life in a Jewish Family*, trans. J. Koeppel, ed. L. Gelber and R. Leuven (Washington, D.C.: ICS, 1986), 218ff.

they are intuitively given, they retain aspects that are absent. Consequently, perception itself must be regarded as a mixture of empty
and filled intentions. Identity itself is similarly a mixture, given to us
when we see that the object we once intended emptily is the same as
that given to us now. As my colleague Robert Sokolowski explains this
doctrine in an article prepared for the *Cambridge Dictionary of Philosophy*, "Such identities are given even in perceptual experience, as
the various sides and aspects of things continue to present one and
the same object, but identities are given more explicitly in categorical
intuition, when we recognize the kind of partial identity that exists
between a thing and its features, or when we directly focus on the
identity a thing has with itself."[4]

Husserl's realism came as an antidote to both Kant and Hegel, affirming the existence of objective truth and the existence of a knowable world apart from the mind. Husserl himself, partially trained in
Vienna, was indebted to two Austrians, Franz Brentano and Bernard
Bolzano, both trained as priests, both steeped in the Scholastic philosophy of the Thomistic revival.

Thus at age twenty-one Edith left Breslau for Göttingen where she
hoped to study with Husserl whom she had already come to regard as
the philosopher of our time. It was in Göttingen that she met Max
Scheler, a Jew who was an on-again, off-again Catholic. Scheler
opened her eyes to the fact that one could be a philosopher of rank
and a believing Christian. It would be ten years before she entered the
Church, but under Scheler's influence she discovered what she called
"the phenomenon of Catholicism." Husserl taught her phenomenology as a method. She used the method to look closely at the world
and into herself, but always in a detached way.

Long before her baptism she began to study Saint Thomas. Later,
on the advice of the Jesuit philosopher-theologian Erich Przywara,
she began the translation of Saint Thomas's *Questiones Disputate de
Veritate*. It was that translation that brought her into intimate contact

4. For a systematic study of Husserl, see esp. Robert Sokolowski, *The Formation of
Husserl's Concept of Constitution* (The Hague: Martinus Nijhoff, 1964) and *Husserlian
Meditations* (Evanstan, Ill.: Northwestern University Press, 1974).

with the mind of Saint Thomas; but to say that she admired his style would be to leave a false impression. The Scholastic practice of stating a thesis, listing the objections to the thesis, defending the thesis, and then answering the objections to the thesis would, in her judgment, discourage the modern reader. Thus she dispensed with the objections and their answers and got to the meat of Thomas's own systematic thought on the topic. To each question she appended an analysis showing the contemporary bearing of the discussion, with particular emphasis on the metaphysical and epistemological issues involved. She was writing for a literate audience, not for scholars. Martin Grabmann provided an introduction. Father Przywara was to say of it, "It is St. Thomas and nothing but St. Thomas throughout, but he is brought face to face with Husserl, Scheler and Heidegger."[5] The translation gained for her a reputation as a student of Saint Thomas, and she was invited to lecture on his thought.

But it wasn't Thomas alone who prepared her for her reception of the Catholic faith. Husserl and Thomas both opened the way. Husserl's realism opened her to theism, and from Thomas she acquired a Christian outlook. But it was Teresa of Avila who led her to the final step. Visiting the home of Hedwig Conrad-Martius in the summer of 1921, she read *The Life of Saint Teresa of Avila*, an autobiography. Upon finishing the work in the early hours of the morning, she put the book down, proclaiming to herself this is "Truth."[6] Thomas's *De Veritate* was about "truth" in the abstract; Teresa gave her truth concretely.

The same morning she set out to buy a catechism and missal. Frau Conrad-Martius relates that she had the impression that Edith attended Mass daily from the night of her encounter with Saint Teresa. Edith studied both the catechism and the missal, and one morning after Mass she followed the priest into the sacristy and asked to be baptized. Surprised at the abruptness of her request, he informed her that she would have to take instructions. Her response was "Quiz me," which he did. Needless to say, she had prepared herself well. She

---

5. Hilda Graef, *The Scholar and the Cross: The Life and Work of Edith Stein* (Westminster, Md.: Newman Press, 1955), 52.

6. Ibid., 32.

was received into the Church on January 1, 1922. As de Fabregues puts it in his little biography: "Edith found her source in the intellect and came home to her Creator: the love dwelling in her soul responded to the searchings of her mind."[7]

Without Husserl and Thomas, Edith may not have been positioned to appreciate Teresa. Clearly, in her case, faith came as a gift perfecting nature. Husserl once said, "The life of man is only a progression towards God. I have tried to reach this progression towards God without theological proofs, methods or aids—in other words, I tried to reach God without God's help." Husserl added, "I have tried in one way or another to delete God from my scientific thought so that I might outline a way to Him for those who lack the security of faith in the Church which we have."[8] Husserl is also reported to have said that on his death he ought to be canonized since he has led so many people to the acceptance of Christianity. His philosophy, he thought, "converges towards Thomism and prolongs Thomism."

From the earliest days following her baptism, Edith desired the cloistered and contemplative life of which Teresa provided the model, but her spiritual mentors advised her to stay in the world where she would be more likely to influence others. She taught for eight years at the secondary level at St. Magdalene's, the Dominican nuns' training school at Speyer, and eventually she sought a university post, having completed her *habilitationschrift, Potency and Act.* Failing to secure a position at Freiburg, she accepted an appointment at Münster in the Institute for Educational Theory, an appointment that she held for less than a year owing to the Nazi ascendancy and their exclusion of Jews from university positions.

Although her teaching career at Speyer and Münster was brief, she was respected by pupils at both the secondary and the teachers college level. In her classroom she personified that virtue which she regarded as paramount for the Catholic teacher. Speaking of the Catholic teacher she wrote, "The most important thing is that the

---

7. *Edith Stein* (Staten Island, N.Y.: Alba House, 1965), 53.
8. As quoted by Jean de Fabrègues, in *Edith Stein*, 44.

teachers should really have Christ's spirit in themselves and really embody it in their lives."[9]

Although Husserl failed to support her for a chair at Freiburg, he used to call her his "best pupil." After her entry into the Cologne Carmelite convent, he said, "I do not believe that the Church has any neo-Scholastic of Edith Stein's quality."[10]

Every true Scholastic will become a mystic, and every true mystic a Scholastic. It is remarkable—Edith stands on a summit, so to speak, and sees the furthest and broadest horizons with amazing clarity and detachment, and yet there is another side, for at the same time she sees into herself with equal penetration. Everything in her is utterly genuine, otherwise, I should say that this step was romanticism. But—deep down in Jews is radicalism and love faithful unto martyrdom.[11]

Through her writing she gained a reputation that led to lecture invitations from Vienna to Paris. Known as a Catholic feminist, she lectured on behalf of the League of Catholic Women and the Association of Catholic Women Teachers on women's roles as professionals, responsible coworkers in the Church, homemakers, teachers, and mothers. She was distressed by the increasing destruction of family life and the glorification of sex. As Hilda Graef remarks, "She saw that the Catholic teaching on marriage as an indissoluble union was the only solid bulwark against the destructive tendencies of modern thought and education."[12] But as Graef notes in the introduction to her selection of the *Writings of Edith Stein* (1956), Stein thought that such teaching had to be explicated in language cognizant to the contemporary context. Graef continues: "She also demanded a more thorough training for women in their political and civic duties since she knew that part of the success of national socialism was due to the emotional attraction Hitler and his methods had for women, who constituted an appreciable part of the electorate who voted for him."[13]

9. Sister Teresia, *Edith Stein*, 70.
10. As quoted by Sister Teresia, *Edith Stein*, 155.
11. Ibid.
12. *Writings of Edith Stein*, trans. Hilda Graef (London: Peter Owen, 1956), 10.
13. Ibid.

Stein was clearly what we would call "a popular lecturer" on women's issues, but she never ceased to move in impressive philosophical circles. Perhaps her closest friends in the philosophical community were Hedwig Conrad-Martius, Alexander Koyré, and Max Scheler. Scheler, of course, had the most influence on her, and she might have had the amoral Scheler in mind when she wrote: "There is a lot of difference between being selected as an instrument and being in a state of grace."[14]

Between 1922 and 1929 she published a series of essays in Husserl's *Jahrbuch* on topics such as "the structure of the human person," "union of body and soul," "the nature of community," "the nature of the state," and "the relation of the individual to the state." In 1929, for a festschrift honoring Husserl on his seventieth birthday, she produced a comparative study of the philosophy of Saint Thomas and Husserl's phenomenology, showing that on many issues there is a remarkable agreement between Husserl and Thomas. For both, philosophy is an exact science, neither doubts the power of reason, and both look upon philosophy as a conscious effort to appropriate and transmit to others the *philosophia perennis*. Stein observes that while Husserl never contests the validity of the act of faith, he does not recognize the duty of reason to faith or the superiority of knowledge derived from faith to that provided by reason. "A Christian philosophy," she wrote, "will consider its principal task to prepare the way for faith."[15] The most serious difference between Husserl and Thomas, she thought, arises from Husserl's starting point. He begins with the epistemological question, putting the real world into brackets until he has completed his critique of knowledge. Stein thinks that with his doctrine of transcendentally purified consciousness, Husserl establishes a sphere of complete immanence wherein knowledge and its object are absolutely one. He thereby excludes all doubt. Husserl in effect asks: How is a world which I can immanently investigate constructed for a consciousness? From the pure data of consciousness

14. Sister Teresia, *Edith Stein*, 77.
15. As quoted by Hilda Graef, in *The Scholar*, 148.

the subject constitutes the intentional world through its own intellectual activity.

For Thomas, metaphysics is prior to any theory of knowledge; it is the normative science to which logic, epistemology, and ethics are subordinate. Although Husserl's transcendental phenomenology treats the subject as the starting point of philosophy and considers epistemology to be the basic science, Husserl and Aquinas would agree on three important issues: (1) both agree that all knowledge begins with sense perception; (2) both believe that human knowledge is characterized by an intellectual elaboration of sense data, which is the work of the intellect composing and dividing; and (3) both admit the active and passive character of intellection and deny that thought is simply a product of the intellect.

In 1931, on a trip to Vienna, Edith stayed with Rudolph Allers who later, as a member of the faculty of philosophy of The Catholic University of America, translated her article on Dionysius the Areopagite for Marvin Farber, then editor of the *Journal of Philosophy and Phenomenological Research*. Apparently Farber thought it was too "theological" or too "Catholic" for his journal. Allers then published it in volume 9 of *The Thomist* under the title "Ways to Know God." It was the only article she ever submitted for publication in an English-language journal.[16] Although she submitted it in the fall of 1941, she did not live to see it published.

But to back up a moment, in September 1932 we find Edith at a conference of the Thomistic Society in Juvisy, France, along with Jacques Maritain, Alexander Koyré, Etienne Gilson, and Nicholas Berdyayev. She exchanged correspondence with the Maritains and was the recipient of an inscribed gift copy of the first French edition of Maritain's *Degrees of Knowledge*.

Denied the possibility of a teaching position in Germany, she was free to pursue her contemplative vocation. She entered Mary Queen of Peace Carmel in Cologne on October 14, 1933. "Modest," "humble," "mischievously witty," "cheerful," and "friendly" are words used by

16. See "Translator's Afterword," in Edith Stein, *Jewish Family*, 511.

her coreligious to describe her.[17] Encouraged by her religious superiors at Cologne, and later at Echt, she continued to write. Her *habilitationshrift* was rewritten to become *Finite and Eternal Being*. No German publisher would dare bring it out under her name; it was finally published posthumously in 1950. This was followed by the article "Ways to Know God: Dionysius the Areopagite" and the book *Science of the Cross*. The latter was a study of the life, theology, and poetry of Saint John of the Cross. She was working on this book the day the Gestapo arrested her, August 2, 1942. She and her sister were two of more than seven hundred non-Aryan Christians who were arrested in reprisal for a pastoral letter the Dutch bishops had promulgated in all the churches on Sunday, July 26, condemning the Nazi treatment of the Jews. Only eight days had elapsed between the promulgation of the letter and her arrest. Within another seven she was dead. The death date normally given is August 9, 1942.[18] Interestingly, Wojtyla, who wrote a dissertation in philosophy on Max Scheler, also wrote a dissertation in theology on John of the Cross.

This sketch would be incomplete without some mention of Stein's habitual self-denial, her long hours at prayer before the Eucharist. The contemplative life is fraught with a multiplicity of psychological and spiritual dangers. In the religious life one can easily become carried into perilous regions of the soul through excessive or uncontrolled zeal. Stein was to maintain her sanity in spite of the mortification that she performed as a matter of course. Abbot Raphael Walzer, in comments prepared for a volume to commemorate the tenth anniversary of her death, echoed Husserl's earlier assessment when he wrote: "Her interior life was so simple and free from problems that from my conversations with her, nothing remains in my memory but the picture of a soul of perfect clarity and maturity."[19]

The point I wish to stress about Edith Stein and the reason for introducing these remarks with a reference to Miguel de Unamuno is to

17. Sister Teresia, *Edith Stein*, 141ff.
18. See "Chronology 1916–1942," in Edith Stein, *Jewish Family*, 430ff.
19. Sister Teresia, *Edith Stein*, 50.

suggest that Stein was intellectually prepared to grasp the faith she was eventually accorded. It is true that not everyone who embraces the Catholic faith has to go through a series of philosophical steps in order to be open to the gift of faith. Most receive the faith by virtue of family inheritance, but even the born Catholic is admonished to examine, in Socratic fashion, the received in order that it may be embraced rationally. The convert by definition is one who has experienced a change of outlook. The type of philosophy one espouses, implicitly or explicitly, either opens one to the faith or closes it down as an intellectual option. Furthermore, the type of philosophy one espouses determines the kind of Christianity one embraces. Classical Greek and Roman intelligence gave rise to and will forever lead to the ecclesiastical institution shaped by the Fathers and Doctors of the early and medieval church. As Edith Stein clearly saw, if one starts with modern philosophical nominalism or epistemology, one will not end up in the belief system that shaped Aquinas and which he subsequently developed. If Stein had not found her way to the objective phenomenological method of Husserl, her intellectual and spiritual biography would have been quite different. If Husserl had not been exposed to the Aristotelianism and Thomism of Brentano and Bolzano, he, too, may have philosophized differently. Conversely, although faith provides one with a basic outlook, if that faith is not accountable to a logically prior philosophical order, it may lose its intellectual integrity and dissolve into an unanchored fideism or biblical fundamentalism.

III

I began with Unamuno. If one returns to the book that gained him worldwide attention, *Del sentimiento trágica de la vida*, aptly translated into English as *The Tragic Sense of Life*,[20] one finds an author solely concerned with his own life, a life full of contradictions, torn between "the truth thought" and "the truth felt." His reason can

---

20. *Tragic Sense of Life*, trans. J. E. Crawford Flitch (New York: Macmillan, 1921), 261.

rise no higher than skepticism, his faith appears antirational and therefore incommunicable.

Contrast Unamuno's self-absorption with the detachment and self-ignorance of Edith Stein. Even when writing of her own inner experience she employed the impersonal "one." Her philosophical realism gives her work a "being"-centered objectivity. Nature, manifested as phenomena, controls her thought and dictates her action. When interpreting her contemplative experience as a phenomenologist, she distinguished between the phenomena of accepting the doctrines of the Church by faith and the phenomena of meditating on them in discursive prayer. Stein could never say, as did Unamuno, "Our ethical and philosophical doctrines in general are usually merely the justification *a posteriori* of our conduct, of our actions. Our doctrines are usually the means we seek in order to explain and justify to others and to ourselves our own mode of action."[21]

If Unamuno were to be taken seriously, one would have to say that philosophy is mere rhetoric. Clearly, no one in the "being"-centered tradition of Aristotle or Thomas would look upon philosophy as the rationalization of one's behavior. Stein's search for truth, her discovery of Catholicism, and her subsequent life are the inverse of the subjectivism and pessimism of Unamuno and his mentors, Nietzsche and Schopenhauer.

Clearly, one's philosophy does make a difference.

21. Ibid.

FOURTEEN

MARITAIN AT THE CLIFF'S EDGE

From Antimoderne *to* Le Paysan

I

Jacques Maritain was an "engaged" intellectual from the very beginning of his academic career. Never one to waffle or to avoid conflict, Maritain joined issue with some of the leading philosophers of
his generation. He proved to be an intractable critic of modernity.
Maritain was not alone in viewing the dominant philosophy of his
day as a danger to Christian belief and practice. Informed Protestants
and Catholics on both sides of the Atlantic evaluated nineteenth-
century intellectual currents in much the same way. To see this, one
has only to contrast the course of American idealism in the last quarter of the nineteenth century with the simultaneous appearance of
the Thomistic revival on the European continent.

In the second year of his pontificate, Leo XIII, on August 4, 1879,
promulgated the encyclical *Aeterni Patris*, endorsing a fledgling Thomistic movement that was eventually to enlist some of the best minds
of the following generation. That encyclical was followed by the
founding of philosophical institutes at Louvain, Belgium, and Washington, D.C., for the purpose of making available the thought of
Saint Thomas as an antidote to the then-dominant positivisms and
materialism. The Institut Superieur de Philosophie, under the direction of Desiré J. Mercier, came into being in 1891; the School of Philosophy at The Catholic University of America, under the direction of
Edward A. Pace, in 1895. The Institute Catholique de Paris was already

twelve years old when Leo became pope and in due course was to play an important role in the Thomistic revival; Jacques Maritain was to be offered a professorship there in 1914.

Leo recommended to the Catholic world the study of Saint Thomas because of the perceived value of his philosophy in meeting "the critical state of the times in which we live." Leo saw that the regnant philosophies of his day not only undercut the faith but were beginning to have disastrous effects on personal and communal life. Succinctly he says in *Aeterni Patris*, "Erroneous theories respecting our duty to God and our responsibilities as men, originally propounded in philosophical schools, have gradually permeated all ranks of society and secured acceptance among the majority of men."[1]

Leo recognized that some philosophies opened out to the faith, just as some philosophies closed it off as an intellectual option. Immanuel Kant may be the perfect philosopher for a fideistic form of Protestantism, but he can never become an adequate guide for the Catholic mind. With his dictum "I have therefore found it necessary to deny knowledge in order to make room for faith,"[2] he reflects the tradition of Luther and Calvin, whose doctrine of original sin holds that with the Fall intellect became so darkened that it cannot unaided conclude to the existence of God. Catholic thought, by contrast, is essentially and historically a system of intellectualism, of objectivism. The basic principle of Catholic thought asserts the reliability of intelligence, that is, that we are equipped with intellects that are able to know objective reality. Upon the reliability of our knowledge depends our practical decisions, our conduct. We can only *do* what is right on the condition that we *know* what is right. We can only live Catholic lives on the condition that we know what Catholic doctrine is.

By any measure, the nineteenth century was no less an intellectually tumultuous one for Europe than the twentieth. Dominated in

---

1. Maritain reproduces this encyclical in his *Le doctur angelique* (1930); translated by J. F. Scanlon as *St. Thomas Aquinas: Angel of the Schools* (London: Sheed & Ward, 1948), 134–54.

2. *Critique of Pure Reason*, Preface to Second Edition, Bxxx.

the intellectual order by the Enlightenment, in both its Anglo-French and German forms, Europe underwent a systematic attempt on the part of the intelligentsia to replace the inherited, largely classical and Christian learning with a purely secular ethos. The Napoleonic Wars in their aftermath added materially to this destabilization, eradicating many institutional structures, economic and social, as well as religious.

Startling advances in the physical sciences reinforced the Enlightenment's confidence in natural reason. In retrospect we can see that the ideas that formed the secular outlook of the nineteenth century were the product of two major intellectual revolutions. The first is associated with the biological investigations of the period and with the names of Spencer, Darwin, Wallace, Huxley, and Haeckel. Their work employed the vocabulary of "evolution," "change," "growth," and "development" and led to the worship of progress. The effect of the new biological studies was to place man and his activity wholly in the setting of a natural environment, giving them a natural origin and a natural history. Man was transformed from a being with a spiritual component and a transcendent end, elevated above the rest of nature, into a purely material organism forced to interact within the natural environment like any other living species.

The second revolution resulted from advances in physics that were taken to be a reinforcement of the fundamental assumptions of a mechanistic interpretation of nature. Convinced that all natural phenomena can be explained by structural and efficient causes, the disciples of Locke and Hume discarded any explanation that invoked the concept of "purpose" or of "final cause." This convergence of the concepts of physics and biology made possible the resurgence of purely materialistic conceptions of man and nature with no need for the hypothesis of a creative God or of a spiritual soul. The foremost symbol of the new outlook became Darwin's *On the Origin of Species* (1859). For the intellectual class, it codified a view that had been germinating since the preceding century. Darwin confidently marshalled evidence and systematically formulated in a scientific vocabulary ideas already known, but the spontaneous acceptance of his doctrine of evolutionary progress was possible only because the philosophical groundwork had been laid by the Enlightenment fathers.

Leo XIII was not alone in his assessment of the situation. On both sides of the Atlantic various philosophical idealisms were created in a defensive effort to maintain the credibility of religious witness. Challenged by purely naturalistic interpretations of faith, many found the rational support they needed as believers in a post-Kantian idealism. The *Journal of Speculative Philosophy*, the first journal of philosophy in the English language, was founded at St. Louis, Missouri, in 1867, the same year that the Institute Catholique de Paris was created, for the dual purpose of making available the best of German philosophy and of providing Americans with a philosophical forum. In the first issue of the journal, William Torrey Harris gave three reasons for the pursuit of speculative philosophy. In his judgment, speculative philosophy provides, first, a philosophy of religion much needed at a time when traditional religious teaching and ecclesiastical authority are losing their influence. Second, it provides a social philosophy compatible with a communal outlook as opposed to a socially devastating individualism. Third, while taking cognizance of the startling advances in the natural sciences, it provides an alternative to empiricism as a philosophy of knowledge. Speculative philosophy for Harris is the tradition that begins with Plato, a tradition that finds its full expression in the system of Hegel.

Of American idealists, Josiah Royce (1855–1916) became the most prominent. It is difficult to determine when Josiah Royce first read *Aeterni Patris*, but twenty-four years after it was published he wrote a laudatory essay entitled, "Pope Leo's Philosophical Movement and Its Relation to Modern Thought."[3] At the height of a distinguished career at Harvard University, Royce was invited to give the Gifford Lectures for 1900–1901. Published as *The World and the Individual*, they attempted to provide a rational basis for religion and morality. In

3. *Boston Evening Transcript*, 29 July 1903; reprinted in *Fugitive Essays* (Cambridge, Mass: Harvard University Press, 1925), 408–29.

those lectures Royce defended the possibility of truth against the skeptic and the reality of the divine against the agnostic. Royce had little respect for blind faith. The problem created by Kant's destruction of metaphysics he regarded as fundamental. In 1881, he wrote, "[W]e all live, philosophically speaking, in a Kantian atmosphere."[4] Eschewing the outright voluntarism of Schopenhauer, he sought a metaphysics that would permit him to embrace his Christian heritage rationally. Whereas his colleague William James was convinced that every demonstrative rational approach to God must fail, Royce was convinced that speculative reason gives one access to God. The code words of the day, "evolution," "progress," "illusion," "higher criticism," "communism," and "socialism," he thought evoked a mental outlook that reduces Christianity to metaphor and Christian organizations to welfare dispensaries.

Royce saw that the problem was not simply a philosophical one. The philosophers tutored the architects of the new biblical criticism, the *Redaktionsgeschichte* movement. David Friedrich Strauss, in his *Das Leben Jesu*, under the influence of Hegel, examined the Gospels and the life of Jesus from the standpoint of the higher criticism and concluded that Christ was not God but a supremely good man whose moral imperative deserved to be followed. This Royce could not accept; there was no philosophically compelling reason to embrace a purely naturalistic interpretation of the Scriptures. Like Leo, he recognized that philosophy must be fought by philosophy.

II

Jacques Maritain was born a generation after Royce and just three years after the publication of *Aeterni Patris*. By the time Maritain discovered Saint Thomas, the Thomistic movement was well under way. It was a movement that not only nourished his searching intellect, but one that he substantially enriched. He came to Thomas, he would

4. For an overview of Royce's thought, see Bruce Kuklick, *Josiah Royce: An Intellectual Biography* (New York: Bobbs-Merrill, 1972).

say, already a Thomist without knowing it. Maritain's influence eventually extended worldwide, notably to Italy, to Latin America (especially Argentina), and to North America.

The convert early on placed his intellect at the service of the Church. He knew firsthand the contemporary intellectual milieu and shared Leo's assessment of the dominant philosophies, clearly at odds with the Catholic faith. "If I am anti-modern, it is certainly not out of personal inclination, but because the spirit of all modern things that have proceeded from the anti-Christian revolution compels me to be so, because it itself makes opposition to the human inheritance its own distinctive characteristic, because it hates and despises the past and worships itself."[5]

Maritain's critique of Luther, Descartes, and Rousseau, and his early critique of his mentor, Henri Bergson, display an intellect fully aware of the impact of ideas and philosophical systems on the practical order. Much of that early work would not today withstand professional scrutiny, largely because of its apologetic character, but also because it was often marred by a vagueness and imprecision that his critics easily exploited. Furthermore, Maritain did not in practice always keep the distinction between philosophy and theology clear. It made him later an easy target for American philosophers schooled in the prevailing pragmatic naturalism, such as Sidney Hook and Ernest Nagel. It also hurt his chance for an appointment at the University of Chicago. Robert M. Hutchins, as president of that university, three times tried to get Maritain appointed to its faculty of philosophy. The department blocked the appointment each time, even when Hutchins offered to pay Maritain's salary from nondepartmental funds because, in the words of one member of the department, "Maritain is a propagandist." Hutchins shot back "You are all propagandists." On another occasion he sent an emissary, probably John Nef, to the chairman of the department, a well-known positivist. The response to Hutchins was, "Maritain is not a good philosopher." The emissary then asked, "Do you have any good philosophers on

5. Maritain, *St. Thomas*, ix–x.

your faculty?" The chairman answered, "No, but we know what a good philosopher is."[6]

As a critic of modernity Maritain was at times violent and cutting. Raïssa was to say of his style, "As for the men whose ideas he criticized, he certainly respected them personally, but they were for him scarcely more than vehicles for abstract doctrines."[7] Etienne Gilson, when asked by a journalist to comment on the difference between his method and that of Maritain, characterized Maritain's as one that sets bare ideas in juxtaposition, submerging the individuality of the philosophers who espoused them. Speaking of his own technique, Gilson said, "It is more important to try to understand ideas through men . . . in order to judge in a way that unites. . . . Pure ideas, taken in their abstract rigor are generally irreconcilable."[8] But Maritain was not put off. He responded: "It is not psychology, but the critique of philosophers which brings truth to light." Where truth is concerned there can be no compromise. One ought to be tenderhearted and tough-minded, not hard-hearted and softheaded. Yet Maritain could say, "I am content to owe something to Voltaire in what concerns civil tolerance, and to Luther in what concerns nonconformism, and to honor them in this." In *Theonas* he acknowledges a respect for Comte insofar as he seeks the realization of human order, for Kant for the restoration of the activity of the knowing subject, and for Bergson for the recognition of the spiritual.[9]

It is commonly acknowledged that Maritain's best work in social and political philosophy was accomplished during his years in America. What gives that work power, however, is its grounding in a solid metaphysics of being and in a realistic epistemology. Maritain the metaphysician is at his best in his *A Preface to Metaphysics* and in his

6. Cf. Milton Mayer, *Robert Maynard Hutchins: A Memoir* (Berkeley and Los Angeles: University of California Press, 1993), 118.

7. Raïssa Maritain, *Memoirs*, 353, as quoted by D. Gallagher and I. Gallagher, in *The Achievement of Jacques and Raïssa Maritain* (Garden City, N.Y.: Doubleday, 1962), 12.

8. Laurence K. Shook, *Etienne Gilson* (Toronto: Pontifical Institute of Medieval Studies, 1984), 194.

9. *Theonas*, trans. F. J. Sheed (New York: Sheed & Ward, 1933), 172.

Existence and the Existent. As a theorist of knowledge he produced *The Degrees of Knowledge, Philosophy of Nature,* and *Creative Intuition in Art and Poetry.* With the exception of the last mentioned, those works formed the background to his political philosophy, a political philosophy that had considerable influence on important thinkers such as Mortimer J. Adler, John Courtney Murray, and Yves R. Simon, and on more than one generation of Thomists who staffed the then flourishing Catholic colleges and universities in the United States. Many students were first exposed to philosophy through his clearly written *Introduction to Philosophy.*

III

It is Maritain's recognition of the practical effects of the materialisms and empircisms of his day and his critique of the Enlightenment spirit that is the focus of this enquiry. One of his earliest works sets the tone for much that is to come. The myth of "necessary progress" as found in philosophers like Condorcet and Comte is one of his major targets in *Theonas,* a dialogue first published in 1921. He quotes Condorcet: "There will then come a moment upon this earth when the sun will shine on none but free men who recognize no other master than their reason; when tyrants and slaves, priests and their stupid hypocritical instruments, will exist no more save in history and on the stage."[10] He also quotes Auguste Comte: "To reestablish the Catholic order it would be necessary to suppress the philosophy of the eighteenth century, and as this philosophy proceeds from the Reformation, and Luther's Reformation in its turn was but the result of the experimental sciences introduced into Europe by the Arabs, it would be necessary to suppress the sciences."[11] Maritain, through the character Philonous, responds to Comte as follows: "That surely is a perfect text, I know it by heart: and it illustrates as clearly as the historico-economic synthesis of Karl Marx—what havoc the myth of progress can work in the mind of an intelligent man."[12]

10. Ibid., 117.   11. Ibid., 126.
12. Ibid., 126–27.

As Maritain characterizes it, "the law of progress" demands the ceaseless changing of foundations and principles inherited from the past; but if foundations can change, that which rests on them must also change. The movement of humanity toward the better, according to this attitude, demands the regular destruction of all previous gains. The progressivists, says Maritain, fail to recognize that there are types of change. Some can be constructive, as Thomas's building upon Augustine. The truths of Ptolemaic astronomy survive in the Copernican revolution. The production of a plant is bound up with the corruption of the seed. "There is no destruction," he argues, "that does not produce something, no production that does not destroy some existent thing. The whole question is to know whether it is the production or the destruction which is the principal event."[13] Judgment is required. The conservative takes newness to be a sign of corruption; the mystics of revolution take all newness for a newness of achievement. Placed in perspective, the myths of "humanity," "the city of the future," "revolution," and "necessary progress" are but secular substitutions for Christian ideas such as the "church," the "heavenly Jerusalem," "regeneration," and "Providence." "When men cease to believe in the supernatural," Maritain says, "the Gospel is reduced to the plane of nature."[14]

Although Maritain's early targets are Bergson and the three reformers, his real enemy is Immanuel Kant. In Maritain's judgment, Kant's critical philosophy is born of the convergence of the three intellectual currents represented by: (1) Luther's revolt in theology (2) Descartes's revolt in philosophy, and (3) Rousseau's revolt in ethics. Kant represents a lack of confidence in the intellect's ability to metaphysically grasp 'being'. Bergson similarly underestimates the intellect. Maritain is willing to commend Bergson for attacking the antimetaphysical prejudices of nineteenth-century positivism, but in Maritain's judgment Bergson's notion of "intuition" and his theory of conceptual knowledge lead, not unlike Descartes, to a subjectivism and irrationalism. In retrospect, we can see that Maritain may have

13. Ibid., 137. 14. Ibid., 139–40.

more in common with Bergson than not; nevertheless, he saw the difficulty of maintaining an objectivist metaphysics and even natural science based on Bergson's somewhat anti-intellectualist epistemology. In Maritain's judgment, both Bergson and Kant give too large a role to the activity of the experiencing subject in constituting the known. Maritain's conviction that the realism of Aristotle and Aquinas is perfectly in accord with common sense and with modern science finds full expression in his mature work *The Degrees of Knowledge* (1932).[15]

Maritain's notion of philosophy is important. "Modern philosophies," he writes, "grow out of what has gone before, but rather by way of contradiction; the Scholastics by way of agreement and further development." The result is that philosophy in our day is like a series of episodes simply stuck end to end, not like a tree where each branch is organically related to each and all to the roots.[16] "The labor of the mind, by its very nature demands a collaboration running through the years." There is such a thing as a *philosophia perennis*; although its source is in antiquity, it is forever open-ended.

IV

In the closing years of his life Maritain returned to themes that he first approached as a young convert to the Catholic faith, grateful for the insight provided by his newly acquired faith. In the last decade of his life, the old philosopher, equipped with both the faith and years of experience, reflected at length on the condition of his beloved Catholic Church. Between 1966 and 1973 he produced three books. One may view these simply as works of apologetics, but one may also find in them profound philosophical insight. The most widely noted was his *Le Paysan de la Garonne*, published in 1966 shortly after the close of the Second Vatican Council, when Maritain was eighty-four years of age. *On the Grace and Humanity of Christ* appeared in 1969; *On the Church of Christ* followed four years later.

15. *Distinguer pour univ. ou les degrés du savior* (1932), translated by B. Wall and M. Adamson as *The Degrees of Knowledge* (London: G. Bles/ Century Press, 1937).

16. *Theonas*, 5.

Acknowledging that he was writing in a "troubled historical mo-ment," Maritain presents *On the Church of Christ* as the reflection of a philosopher on the faith accorded him through the instrument of the Church. The book, he proclaims, is not a work of apologetics: "It presupposes the Catholic faith and addresses itself above all to Cath-olics (and) to our nonseparated brothers who recite the Credo each Sunday."[17] It addresses itself to others to the extent that they "desire to know what Catholics believe even if the latter seem sometimes to have forgotten it."[18]

The last is not an idle remark. In Maritain's judgment, the Second Vatican Council unleashed a subversive movement in the Church that constitutes, perhaps, an even greater threat to her integrity than the external modernist attack of the nineteenth century. "The mod-ernism of Pius X's time," he writes, was "only a modest hay fever" compared to the sickness that besets the intellectuals today.[19] In *Le Paysan*, he speaks of an "immanent apostasy." The new theologians through an exhausting work of "hermeneutic evacuation" have emp-tied our faith of every specific object and reduced it to a "simple sub-limating aspiration." "The frenzied modernism of today is incurably ambivalent. Its natural bent, although it would deny it, is to ruin the Christian faith."[20] Ironically, Maritain says, the leaders of our neo-modernism declare themselves Christian, even though they have sep-arated themselves from its basic tenets. In a way, their attitude is a backhanded compliment to Christianity itself, insofar as they still cherish their identification with the Church.

Maritain asks: "If divine transcendence is only the mythical projec-tion of a certain collective fear experienced by man at a given moment in history," then why should an observer faithful to the tradition "be astonished that so many modernists believe they have a mission to

17. *De l'eglise du Christ* (1973), translated by J. W. Evans as *On the Church of Christ* (Notre Dame, Ind.: University of Notre Dame Press, 1973), vi.

18. Ibid.

19. *Le paysan de la Garonne* (1966), translated by M. Cuddihy and E. Hughes as *The Peasant of the Garonne* (New York: Holt, Rinehart and Winston, 1968), 14.

20. Ibid., 17.

save a dying Christianity, their dying Christianity for the modern world"?[21] Simply put, modernism and Christianity are incompatible.

A Greek confidence in the human intellect and the intelligibility of nature is the cornerstone of Maritain's philosophy of being. It led him, on first acquaintance, to an appreciation of the realism of Saint Thomas whom he came to venerate both as a person and as a philosopher/theologian. Even before the end of the Second Vatican Council, Maritain sadly detects a drift away from Saint Thomas on the part of Catholic theologians. The symptoms are many. He finds that all too often references to Saint Thomas and the Scholastics are made in a disparaging tone. The call to dehellenize Christianity, he is convinced, is usually a repudiation of philosophical realism and the first step toward a subjectivism that reduces the revealed word of God to mere symbols for truths accessible to human reason. He finds this regrettable not only because it repudiates a great teacher but because of its implications for theology as a discipline. Theology, heretofore, was thought of as "rational knowledge." The new approach, by contrast, when it does not reduce the faith to *praxis*, seems to adopt a fideistic starting point. Christ is the way, if one is inclined to adopt Him as a starting point. In an aside, Maritain notes that "some of our well bred contemporaries are repelled by the vocabulary of Aquinas." Yet it is hard to believe that men who understand Hegel, Heidegger, and Jean-Paul Sartre should be terrorized by Scholastic terminology. They should know perfectly well that every science has its technical vocabulary.[22] Their difficulty lies much deeper, in the skepticisms they have unwittingly embraced, skepticisms that deny the intellect's ability to reach 'being' in knowledge and speech. The only way we can logically and clearly express many of the truths of the faith is by appropriating the language of ontology. If we cannot know reality in itself but only as it appears to us, what are we to make of the teachings of Chalcedon, that is, that Jesus Christ is one person with two natures, one divine and one human? What are we to make of the doctrine of the

21. Ibid., 19.
22. Ibid., 155.

Eucharist, that Christ is physically present under the appearance of bread and wine?

Speaking of method, the teaching of Aquinas "is not the doctrine of one man, but the whole labor of the Fathers of the Church, the seekers of Greece, . . . the inspired of Israel,"[23] and the scholars of the medieval Arabic world. Far from reaching a dead end, the Thomistic corpus "is an intelligible organism meant to keep on growing always, and to extend across the centuries its insatiable thirst for new prey. It is a doctrine open and without frontiers; open to every reality wherever it is and every truth from wherever it comes, especially the new truth which the evolution of culture or science will enable it to bring out."[24] It is, too, a doctrine open to the various problematics it may see fit to employ, whether created from within or adopted from without. Because it is an open doctrine, it is indefinitely progressive. Those who adopt the philosophy of Saint Thomas recognize that their master does not require subservience: "The philosopher swears fidelity to no person, nor any school—not even if he be a Thomist—to the letter of St. Thomas and every article of his teaching."[25]

Josiah Royce saw this more than a half-century earlier. Writing as an outsider, he was convinced that the neo-Scholastic movement endorsed by Leo XIII was an important one, in Royce's words, "for the general intellectual progress of our time." The use of Saint Thomas, he says, entails growth, development, and change; he even uses the word "progress." "Pope Leo, after all, 'let loose a thinker' amongst his people—a thinker to be sure, of unquestioned orthodoxy, but after all a genuine thinker whom the textbooks had long tried, as it were, to keep lifeless, and who, when once revived, proves to be full of the suggestion of new problems, and of an effort towards new solutions."[26] But Royce was also fearful that a resurgent Thomism might give way to the Kantian legions and their demand that the epistemological issue be settled first. In Maritain he would have found a kindred spirit.

---

23. Ibid., 153.   24. Ibid.
25. Ibid., 161.
26. Josiah Royce, *The World and the Individual* (New York: Macmillan, 1900), 422–23.

The key to Maritain's conception of philosophy, his love for Saint Thomas, and his chagrin at contemporary drifts in theology is grounded, as I said, in his doctrine on being. "To maintain . . . that the object of our intellect is not the being of things but the *idea* of being which it forms in itself, or more generally that we apprehend immediately only our ideas, is to deliver oneself bound hand and foot to skepticism."[27] Maritain's controlling principle can be stated simply: 'being' governs enquiry. There are structures apart from the mind that can be objectively grasped. Or put another way, 'being' is intelligible. And not only 'being,' but 'being' in act is intelligible. The senses bring us into contact with a material, changing world but in the flux of events there are identifiable structures that control enquiry. Although the senses are limited to the material singular, there is more in the senses' report than the senses themselves are formally able to appreciate. The intellect's ability to abstract enables it to grasp the universal, the intelligible nature, the "whatness" of the thing. Those things that are not self-intelligible need to be explained by means of things other than themselves.[28] Thus, acknowledging the principles of substance and causality, Maritain avoids the phenomenalism of Locke and the empiricism of Hume. So equipped, he is able to reason to an immaterial order and to the existence of God, *ipsum esse subsistens*. Maritain's defense of the first principles of thought and 'being' in his little book *A Preface to Metaphysics* is difficult to surpass.

Philosophies that fail to achieve a doctrine of being will inevitably be subjective in tone. Methodologically, they will be cut off from the transcendent source of being itself. Oddly, philosophy seems to entail a theology whether it reaches God or not. "When Feuerbach declared that God was the creation and alienation of man; when Nietzsche

---

27.· *Eléménts de philosophy*, translated by E. I. Watkin as *Elements of Philosophy* (New York: Sheed & Ward, 1930), 186.

28. *Court traité de l'existence et de l'existant* (1947), translated by L. Galantiere and G. B. Phelan as *Existence and the Existent* (New York: Pantheon Books, 1948), chap. 1, pp. 10–46; *Sept lecons sur l'être* (1934), translated as *A Preface to Metaphysics* (New York: Sheed & Ward, 1948), Lectures 2–4, pp. 43–89.

proclaimed the death of God, they were the theologians of our contemporary atheistic philosophies."[29] They define themselves and their projects against a tradition they hope to supersede, but one in which their own roots are planted. "Why are these philosophies so charged with bitterness," Maritain asks, "unless it is because they feel themselves chained in spite of themselves to a transcendence and to a past they constantly have to kill."[30] Theirs is, in fact, a religious protest in the guise of philosophy.

V

If any conclusion is to be drawn from this, one must acknowledge that the chairman of the Philosophy Department at the University of Chicago may have had it right when he said "Maritain is an apologist." He was one all of his professional life. But Maritain was philosophizing within a Thomistic framework where philosophy in the service of theology loses nothing of its integrity. In fact, as Maritain consistently affirmed, the philosopher himself may gain insight by his association with a theological perspective that thrusts new problems on him and demands greater precision. Maritain maintains that philosophy in the abstract is pure philosophy and can never be "Christian," but concretely it is always pursued within a social setting which, in providing a milieu for reflection, gives it color, if not direction. In *Existence and the Existent* he writes: "We do not philosophize in the posture of dramatic singularity; we do not save our souls in the posture of theoretic universality and detachment from self for the purpose of knowing."[31] William James and John Dewey could have said as much.

Maritain the young apprentice and Maritain the aging philosopher are not only men of the faith but are both graced with that prelude to philosophy that we call "common sense." Both are philosophical realists, and both respect the claims of revealed truth. Maritain the lecturer at some of North America's most prestigious universities,

---

29. *Existence and the Existent*, 137.   30. Ibid.
31. Ibid., 135.

Maritain the signatory of the Declaration of Human Rights, and Maritain the ambassador to the Holy See—all remained in their diverse careers the disciple of Leon Bloy, Henri Bergson, and Thomas Aquinas. The aging Maritain may have written a seemingly nostalgic *Antimoderne*, he may have called himself "Le Paysan," but no historian will ever deny his "engagement" with the leading ideas of his day. Leon Bloy, Maritain's spiritual mentor, called himself the "Pilgrim of the Absolute"; Maritain, the inveterate foe of anti-intellectualism, could be called the "Pilgrim of the Transcendent."

FIFTEEN

JOHN PAUL II, DEFENDER OF
FAITH AND REASON

I

Although *Fides et Ratio* is the thirteenth encyclical written by John Paul II, and published some twenty years into his pontificate, it is not the first time he has had occasion to consider the relationship between faith and reason. As a philosopher and teacher of philosophy, Karol Wojtyla could not avoid it. To open the *Summa Theologiae* is to confront the subject in Question 1, Article 1, wherein Saint Thomas defends the necessity of revelation in spite of philosophy's ability to demonstrate the existence of God and "other like truths about God." For Thomas, faith presupposes natural knowledge.

The relationship between faith and reason is a subject of interest not only to the Holy Father as teacher of the universal Church but also to contemporary minds of various intellectual persuasions. *Ratio und Fides*, for example, is the title of a work by the German Bernard Lomse (1958). *Faith and Reason* is a collection of essays by the noted British philosopher R. G. Collingwood (1968). The same title is used by Richard Swinburne, another English scholar, whose book *Faith and Reason* (1981) discusses the nature of religious belief and its relation to reason. These are only a few of the many authors who have examined the relationship, but none has done so with greater authority than John Paul II. Although it makes no reference to contemporary discussions, *Fides et Ratio* was not written in an intellectual vacuum. It was produced in full awareness of the dominant trends in philosophy, which in their implication not only cut one off from faith but even render suspect the rational character of the natural sciences.

In contemporary literature the terms "faith" and "belief" are often used interchangeably, and "faith" is sometimes taken as a synonym for "hope." Given the diversity of usage, a lexicographer would have difficulty in fixing a meaning. In the history of Western philosophical thought the term "belief" has been used to designate diverse mental states and attitudes. To consider just a few, Plato distinguished between the realm of opinion and the realm of knowledge, and in the realm of opinion he further distinguished between conjecture and belief (*pistis*). "Belief" in this Platonic sense denotes the comparatively firm assent that the plain man gives to whatever he directly sees or hears or feels.

Aquinas also distinguished between belief and knowledge, but, for Aquinas, belief (*fides*) cannot refer to something that one sees or to what can be proved; belief is the acceptance of an assertion as true on the testimony of someone else. John Locke employs this concept when he defines belief as "the assent to any proposition not . . . made out of the deductions of reason, but upon the credit of the proposer, as coming from God in some extraordinary way of communication. This way of discovering truths to men we call revelation" (*Political Essays*). Hume defined belief as practical certainty about matters that cannot be justified theoretically. Kant looked upon belief as the subjectively adequate but objectively inadequate acceptance of something as true. In contemporary psychological literature, belief is often identified with emotional conviction. Pragmatic conceptions emphasize the operative character of conviction. Some authors maintain that belief is relative to what the agent has at stake.

Even with the history of Western thought before us, certain key words remain ambiguous. Words like "belief," "faith," "knowledge," and "truth" vary in meaning from context to context and from author to author. Yet all of the authors cited above have produced insights into the cognitive process, or, if you will, into the dynamics of rational assent. At different periods of history, interests are specific.

Medieval discussions of belief focused upon religious belief and its relationship to empirically derived knowledge. Some of the most profound contemporary discussions of belief analyze the concept within the context of the physical sciences. The relatively recent works of a number of English-speaking philosophers carry such titles as *Knowledge and Belief, Belief and Probability*, and *Belief, Existence, and Meaning*; all these are written from a purely secular perspective and have a bearing not only on our understanding of science but also on our understanding of religious faith.

I I

One wrinkle in discussions of belief is the fact that some philosophers assume that the object of belief is propositional. They argue that one's internal commitment to the truth of a given proposition depends upon the external circumstances governing one's needs for action and one's stakes in these circumstances. There is merit in this analysis, but it is not the whole story. After all, we do know, believe, or assent to many truths that have no bearing on our practical life. Furthermore, the giving of assent to propositions cannot be primary. The proposition, verbal or written, is simply the assertion of a judgment taken to be true.

If we start with the notion that each of us has a set of beliefs that can be expressed in propositional form, we must affirm that our beliefs depend in some way upon our awareness. What is believed are judgments that we have previously accepted and that are usually asserted by means of propositions. Assertion, it should be noted, is closely tied to language but not exclusively so. Usually we speak or write to make an assertion. Of course, not everything spoken or written is an assertion. Certain conditions must be met. The speaker must know what it is that he asserts. Usually by his assertion he intends to reveal his conviction in the proposition asserted. Certain nonstandard cases come to mind, for example, where a man does not believe what he asserts or where he asserts a proposition other than what he intended. These nonstandard cases may be a problem, but they are not important for the present discussion. It should also be noted that there are conventions that enable assertions to be made without actual speech or writing. Hilaire Belloc noted that we daily communicate much more by our grunts and groans than we do through polished speech. Even so, this does not loosen the bonds between assertion and language, for what is asserted is always capable of being expressed in language.

Any analysis must eventually establish the relationship between belief and judgment. From a Thomistic point of view, judgment is very much like private assertion. One may make a judgment without asserting it, and later assert what one has judged. Judgments need not be manifested in the public conduct of the judger. For one thing, opportunities for such manifestation do not always arise. For another, the agent may be reluctant for prudential reasons to let his judgments be known. From the outside, it is often difficult to establish criteria for deciding when a person has or has not made a judgment. We all know what it is like to make a judgment, but the phenomenology of judgment is itself elusive. Judgment, it seems, has only partial and inconstant connections with an agent's conduct. The operative character of a man's belief in a given situation depends on his desires and the many other beliefs that he holds.

The enduring characteristic or nature of belief may be contrasted with the relative transitory character of judgment. Judgments made here and now may remain as lifelong beliefs or as components of a belief system. A person's beliefs remain while he sleeps or is otherwise unaware of them; indeed, many of one's beliefs, some of which are held with great security and endurance, are rarely, perhaps never, brought to consciousness. Consequently, an individual as a moral agent may have many beliefs that are never overtly manifested or consciously recognized. If a particular occasion had not arisen, the belief may never have become apparent to the person or to others.

If belief is not necessarily manifested directly by a person's conduct, it must nevertheless be admitted that by its endurance, dispositionality, and causal relation with the person's awareness that belief does seem to be more closely related to action, and in a different way, than does judgment. A person's beliefs may be more public and objective than his judgments. And because a person can be surprised by his beliefs, he may be mistaken about them—that is, he may judge falsely that he does or does not believe something. In short, a person may have incorrect beliefs about what he believes. Interestingly, we are much readier to contest an agent's assertions about his beliefs than we are to contest what he says about his judgments.

III

I offer one final note regarding belief, judgments, and truth. Belief and truth may coincide, but a person may believe certain things to be true that ultimately turn out to be false. Those philosophers may be right when they acknowledge the dispositional character of belief although belief may not be identical with preparedness to act. Much of what we hold to be true is of a speculative nature, consisting of the science that we have inherited. Disposition, as a psychological state, characterizes the subjective side of the cognitive process and is not to be ignored. Recognizing the dispositional character of belief, we are more likely to avoid the danger of hasty judgment. But it must be emphasized that it is in the judgment act of intellect that we achieve truth. In the judgment act of affirmation or denial we assert that reality is in fact as we have grasped it. Propositions are merely the vehicles by which acts of judgment are expressed first internally, then externally. Our statements may become objects of belief for others, but they are not primary objects of knowledge for us or even for others. In this analysis, John Paul II would concur. If I explain to a student that the electron configuration of the copper atom is such and such, I am making a statement that I hold to be true. I hold it to be true on faith because I have not performed the chemical analysis that revealed the element's structure, nor have I made the observations that lead to the structural explanation. A disposition to assent is not the assent itself. A student is disposed to accept the word of his teacher. A teacher is careful to substantiate his assertions, though in many cases substantiation may elude him. Substantiation amounts to demonstration. Demonstrative knowledge we normally call "scientific knowledge." Some, but not all, of our beliefs are based on demonstration.

When certitude, which depends on demonstration, is not available, we get opinion. The strength of our opinion will determine action or inaction. The conviction that intervention by the Federal Reserve will create monetary stability may lead a president to take action. Where there is no certainty that a given action will produce the desired result, an intemperate move may nevertheless lead to action. But does action really demonstrate the strength of the opinion held? Rashness remains possible. This analysis may help to explain the permanence of scientific knowledge, on the one hand, and the rashness or disparity between belief and action on the other.

IV

We return now to the key issue addressed by *Fides et Ratio*. Although discussions of the above sort are not explicitly invoked, John Paul II is aware of the many insights and distinctions provided by contemporary literature. Aware, too, of the distrust of reason found in much contemporary philosophy, he is at once a defender of reason per se and of the reasonableness of belief.

To accept the Catholic faith is not to take a leap into the dark. Reason lays the foundation for belief, insofar as philosophy can demonstrate the existence of God and disclose something of His nature. As a result of rational inquiry, it is reasonable to believe that a benevolent God, out of love for mankind, has revealed truth about Himself that unaided reason could not attain. John Paul II speaks of the *intellectus fidei* and its innate unity and intelligibility, a body of knowledge, logically coherent in itself, consistent with experience, and perfective of natural understanding. Such knowledge comes to us as a logical and conceptual structure of propositions through the teaching Church. Of necessity the Church's teaching is framed in language that draws upon a host of definitions and distinctions provided by natural reason, that is to say, by philosophy. While philosophy assists in articulating and clarifying the truths of the faith, John Paul II is convinced that philosophy is valuable only insofar as it remains true to its own methods. Philosophy is not apologetics. He is convinced that if it retains its professional integrity, it will remain open, at least implicitly, to the supernatural. "The content of Revelation can never debase the discoveries and legitimate autonomy of reason." Yet to the believer, "Revealed truth offers the fullness of light and will therefore illumine the path of philosophical enquiry." Reason must never lose its capacity to question but is not itself above being questioned.

These reflections have implications for Catholic education at all levels, especially for the training of future priests and for the curricula of Catholic colleges and universities. John Paul II is aware that some remedial work needs to be done where second-order disciplines have been substituted for logic, metaphysics, and philosophical anthropology. To fully master the Catholic intellectual tradition, one needs to be steeped in the history of Western philosophy, but such mastery does not cut one off from insights to be garnered from other traditions. The Holy Father specifically mentions India as a locus of a major cultural and intellectual tradition.

While his appeal to philosophers not of the Catholic faith to recover the great classical tradition flowing from ancient Athens and Rome, a tradition commented on and amplified in every generation since, is an appeal that may go unheeded, it is rightly proffered. In a previous generation it would have been endorsed by Werner Jaeger, Etienne Gilson, and Jacques Maritain, among countless others. Only someone standing on the shoulders of his giant predecessors can say with assurance to his now-directed contemporaries, "Look what you are missing."

SIXTEEN

THE INTERIOR LIFE

I

To speak of Catholic education is to acknowledge, for one thing, a specific *telos* to education and, for another, a distinctive tradition. The recognition of that *telos* is, of course, shared by other believers. It consists in the awareness that the grave is not the end of man, that man is called to a life in union with the divine, a life, whatever else it might be, consisting primarily in a knowledge and love of God. Acknowledgment of this transcendent end colors the whole of education. At no stage is ultimate fulfillment confused with terrestrial happiness.

The distinctive feature of Catholic education is the Catholic tradition itself, a very complex tradition spanning two thousand years of history. One need only enter the Basilica of St. Ambrose in Milan to have the historical asserted. There, under the high altar, lie the remains of Ambrose, who died in 397, accompanied by the remains of Saints Gervase and Protase, both first-century martyrs.

Physical continuity is a visible reminder of intellectual inheritance. Ambrose taught Augustine and Augustine taught the West. The Fathers, no less than the Greeks and Romans upon whom they drew, were concerned with education. From Augustine's *De Magistro* to Newman's *Idea of a University*, one can find dozens of books, some of them Christian and literary classics, that speak to the aims of education. In common they recognize that the end of life is contemplation and that the road to the Beatific Vision requires a kind of interiority even in the midst of the crassest temporal pursuits. What follows are reflections on what I take to be the features and conditions of this interior life.

By the "interior life," I mean the life of the intellect in general but even more the life of the intellect under certain conditions: the intellect drawing upon its experience of the present, on experience understood and interpreted within the context of an appropriated past, but future-oriented in a movement whose ultimate end is nothing less than self-fulfillment. Christ himself is the model. In teaching he appealed to common sense and built upon the inherited. Christ came to proclaim a new law but in doing so he was respectful of the best of ancient codes. He drew upon his listeners' grasp of nature's laws, and on that foundation taught those things that unaided intellect alone could not fathom. His disciples found him credible. When Saint John Chrysostom sought an empirical proof for the existence of God, he found it in the splendor of the Church. The evidence that he found compelling came from the fact that the Church in its teaching appealed to noble and low, rich and poor, learned and illiterate, and had by that teaching in a brief span succeeded in transforming the lives of individuals and nations for the better. An institution that produced such good effects, thought Chrysostom, could only have a divine origin.

Three things I wish to underscore: the requirement of critical intelligence, the need for learning, and the need for the Church. Unaided intelligence will not suffice. Isolated from tradition and from community, it will become as sterile as Hume's believer, sequestered in a private meditation for a moment in the confines of his study. Just as a knowledge of the practical arts is required for success in most of life's activities, so too in matters of religious activity learning is required. It would be foolish to proceed as if God and the way to God were unknown. Religion is a communal activity. The acknowledgment of God's existence, the acknowledgment of man's debt to Him, and an awareness of the propriety of paying that debt are communal affairs. Awareness of the need to worship is found wherever men are found. Piety is thus a natural virtue. "Spirituality" is but a term for the lifting of intellect and will to things divine. It is a habit of referral, grounded in contemplation, a habit of understanding things in the light of their finality.

The love of God requires some knowledge of God. No one can love an unknown God. God has to be present in some manner before His goodness can command the volitional act. Awareness is the result of some act on our part, the result of our attentiveness to a witness, be it oral or written. The normal channel of awareness is parental teaching reinforced by formal education. Formal education can carry us to the heights of theological speculation, but the basic truths that ground appreciation are simple and are available to the whole of mankind. There are degrees of knowledge and there are degrees of appreciation. Natural knowledge is complemented by revelation, and he who hears and is privileged to possess the best of human knowledge can advance without limit. Development is open-ended. Like science, the augmentation of a knowledge of things divine profits from concerted effort. Rational disputation is social. John of the Cross and Teresa of Avila were learned people. They made use of both native intelligence and education to ferret out the secrets of the divine.

II

The interior life is not to be confused with a life of introspection. The latter is fraught with danger. Self-questioning, which leads to a constant scrutiny of motives, to a perpetual assessment of goals, can distract one from the proper task. Introspection can generate unhappiness and dissatisfaction. One may object that there can be no progress unless one is dissatisfied with one's self. Did not Socrates proclaim as much? With the interior life, as with all things, there is a knowable objective order to which one must conform if one is to be successful. One need not begin as if human nature first came into being with one's self.

The interior life is the life of the mind in the context of divine revelation buttressed by centuries of ecclesiastical teaching. That life of the mind is object-directed even in the depths of its interiority. It seeks, as Socrates taught, a tripartite wisdom: a knowledge of one's self in the light of self, a knowledge of one's self in the light of nature, and a knowledge of one's self in the light of God. It proceeds with confidence that there is objective knowledge about human nature, about the material order, and about God. To know who one is is first to identify with mankind, while recognizing the vagaries of inheritance, chance, custom, and geographic setting. One's possibilities and limitations can only be assessed in context. That context includes nature. Avila is not the Grand Meteora. Other things must be borne in mind: intelligence is not evenly distributed; nor are health, nervous constitutions, or other physical traits that influence behavior.

Man, while rational, is an animal. The great rule-givers in the history of Western monasticism recognized that truth and provided accordingly. Only so much can be tolerated by the human body without psychic damage. What is possible and what is not possible is, after centuries of experience and reflection, knowable. If one is not to go it alone, one has to appropriate this knowledge through study. Given man's discursive mode of intelligence, study is necessarily protracted. If knowledge of nature is difficult, how much more so is a knowledge of God! With respect to nature, human nature, and God there are sciences with principles, methodologies, and laws that demand recognition. These principles and laws, once acknowledged, begin to control. Where an overzealousness might prevail they mitigate excessive bodily deprivation; they prevent flights of fancy in divine meditation. While we may be amused by tales of Don Giovanni arguing with the Crucified Christ about his problems with the communist mayor, we would not take the fictional priest as an example to be followed in ordering our interior life.

The contemplative mind is a discursive mind. It combines and divides and proceeds from one judgment to another. It feeds off experience—its own and what it knows of the experience of others. When it takes God as its object, it focuses most often upon the person of Christ. The life of Christ is available to all, from the child who may be taken with the infant Jesus in the manger, or with the boy Christ, to the sage who has the benefit of centuries of meditation upon the divine Incarnation. To think about things divine, we need our images.

The public life of Christ supplies an object, a focus of the imagination as well as a fount of learning. His teaching and his person comingle into an awesome whole. But Christ has to be understood within the context of a triune God, a creating, begetting, bequeathing God who not only gave us His Son but a Church infused with His Spirit. Unaided imagination without the teaching of the Church cannot fully grasp the significance of the man from Galilee. That teaching itself is not ready-made but requires the efforts of the wisest of men, adjudicated by the successors of the Apostles. Without the authoritative influence of the Church the-all-too fallible intellect can go astray.

Perhaps no one was more aware of this than the great Origen, who wrote: "I want to be a man of the Church. I do not want to be called by the name of some founder of a heresy, but by the name of Christ, and to bear that name which is blessed on the earth, it is my desire, in deed as in spirit, both to be and to be called a Christian." Origen, who was certainly one of the greatest theologians of his day, a man who inspired Jerome and Ambrose, also had a realistic appreciation of the limited role of the theologian in the Church:

If I [he says] who seem to be your right hand and am called a presbyter and seem to preach the word of God, if I do something against the discipline of the Church and the rule of the Gospel so that I become a scandal to you, the Church, then may the whole of the Church, in unanimous resolve, cut me, its right hand, off, and throw me away.

What makes a theology useful to the believer is that it is grounded in a shared insight. Theologies can be plural. The Church, though it has recommended some, does not adjudicate between theologies, but it does adjudicate between the propositions that they engender. It can say, in effect, "Such teaching is consistent with the tradition," or conversely, "Such teaching is deficient, examine your premises, and your arguments." The starting point of theology is propositions given on the side of faith. But what one makes of those propositions is determined by the philosophical intelligence one brings to their explication. Theologies differ because philosophies differ. There can be a plurality of roads to the same affirmation, but usually not. If one believes that philosophy is a science, one must believe that theology is a science. From agreed-upon data, whether garnered by faith or reason, the conclusions flow. As long as discourse is straight, and all parties are talking about the same thing, arguments can be checked for accuracy.

The discursive intelligence of the theologian, sometimes the poet/ theologian, grounded as it is in Sacred Scripture and in its knowledge of nature, can lead the contemplative mind along fruitful paths and to the heights of human insight. God's grace and special intervention may produce that infrequent special witness we call the "mystic." Some spiritual writers say all are called to the mystical life, but none say to the same degree. We appreciate to the extent that our natural light and learning permit. The child with all his might can love the Crucified Christ and the intensity of his love may never be surpassed in later life, but the object of that love will grow with the understanding that comes with effort and with maturity. To remain childlike in matters of faith is to retain the intensity of love while expanding its object. The Hound of Heaven pursues endlessly throughout temporal life. The chase ends only when the pursued has been admitted to the Beatific Vision.

It is sometimes said that the God of the philosophers is not the God of Abraham, Isaac, and Jacob, but this remark fails to acknowledge a vast difference between philosophies. Certainly the God of the philosopher Aquinas is compatible with the God of Revelation. The same could be said for the philosophical God embraced by the Fathers and of that subscribed to by nearly all of the medieval Doctors. One may not recognize the God of Alfred North Whitehead or of Charles Hartshorne in the pages of the Hebrew Bible. It is evident that not all philosophy will be of assistance to the believer as he seeks to know better the object of his quest. God has revealed Himself in the Sacred Scriptures, but He remains an elusive God nevertheless. The Scriptures are full of contradictions and ambiguities that beg for the clarifying light of reason.

There is an interesting reciprocity here. What we make of reason or intellect is settled on the philosophical side. And whether we confidently accept the conclusions of philosophy or look upon them as illusory determines, first of all, whether we are open to Christianity

and then to the kind of Christianity we embrace. The difference
between Catholicism and much of Protestantism is determined by
what is made of classical learning. A Von Harnack and his contemporary counterparts such as Leslie Dewart and Paul van Buren will
decry the Hellenization of Christianity. Luther and Calvin both embraced a doctrine of the Fall that lessened their confidence in natural
intelligence. Both thought a natural theology impossible and were
untroubled because they thought it unnecessary. For Luther and Calvin, faith is completely gratuitous; there is no rational preamble. In
the words of Kierkegaard, "Faith is a leap into the dark."

Catholic spirituality centers on the Eucharist, but it doesn't begin
there. What one thinks when one is on one's knees before the Eucharist depends on what one brings to the occasion. That one is upon
one's knees before the tabernacle is the result of the assent given to a
series of propositions that the believer holds to be true, namely, that
God is, that God is the creator of the universe, that man fell and was
redeemed by the sacrificial act of the God-man, Christ, that Christ
founded a church and gave to it a priesthood with awesome power,
including the power to consecrate. That bread becomes the body and
blood of Christ requires the coaction of man and God. That all of
this makes sense to the believer is due to a certain education, if you
will. That these doctrines can be held by a rational person is due to
the fact that they are consistent with experience and reason. The
claim that Christ came in the fullness of time is not without justification. The intellect of the then civilized world had been prepared by
centuries of Greek and Roman learning.

Reflecting on early Christian conceptions of learning, we find it
interesting to note that Saint Benedict in composing his *Rule* had little to say about spiritual life, but it is clear that his *Rule* is designed to
make that life possible. Benedict's asceticism is tempered compared
with that of the desert Fathers or with that of the Celts. It is an asceticism within the reach of a much greater number, largely because
Benedict recognized the role that community plays in shaping the individual. A high priority is assigned to communal reading; table reading is, in fact, mandatory. Its end is the promotion of the interior life.

Each monastery is to have a library and an archive; chronicles are to be kept. Within Benedict's own lifetime monasteries became centers of learning and were soon famous for their *scriptoria* where the classics of antiquity were copied for posterity. The librarian is specifically enjoined by the *Rule* to acquire new works.

This attitude toward learning had important and lasting effects. The great monasteries became the cultural centers of Europe. Independent schools emerged in the abbeys, each seeking to outdo the others by increasing its library, by attracting professors of renown, and by drawing students to its intellectual tournaments. These schools promoted the study of the sciences and were to create a legion of remarkable theologians, philosophers, lawyers, and scientists. We need but cite the schools of Cluny, Citeaux, Bec, Aurillac, St. Martin, and St. Omer. A roll call of the leading scholars of the age, from Gregory through Bede, Lanfranc, and Anselm, would name the abbots of many of those monasteries. The twelfth-century Benedictine Bernard of Clairvaux became an author almost against his will when monks clamored for the text of his homilies. His books and monographs grew out of lectures recorded by fellow monks who circulated them sometimes without his knowledge and often without his editorial scrutiny. A Brother Godfrey asks him to write about the virtue of humility, and the result is *De Gradibus Humilitatis*. Those books are part of our intellectual and spiritual heritage. With Sertillanges we can say, "Contact with genius is one of the choice graces that God grants to humble thinkers." But the availability of this heritage is not to be taken for granted. Alternative conceptions of the religious life militate against it.

The nineteenth-century Protestant theologian Albrecht Ritschl reminds us of important differences between the traditional Catholic mind and the spirit of the Protestant Reformers. Of Protestantism he says, "Essentially a religion of action, [it] is hostile to both monasticism and asceticism. Abandoning the contemplative ideal, it substitutes in its place the standard of practical moral duty." This difference in emphasis is frequently overlooked by contemporary Catholic thinkers who have themselves substituted social work and counseling for theological inquiry and contemplation. Who has not heard it said, "What men think about God is of little importance as long as they live up to their social and moral ideals." Contrast that if you will with the dictum of Saint Bonaventure: "If you wish to contemplate the invisible traits of God insofar as they belong to the unity of his essence, fix your gaze upon Being itself." For many, belief and theology are no longer the central features of the religious life. Almost without notice religion has degenerated into a man-centered enterprise of moral concern and healing.

It should never be forgotten that the primary aim in making life comfortable for others is to enable them, too, to lead the interior life. The greatest service that we can render others is to introduce them to the storehouse of Christian wisdom that gives life meaning. The pursuit of that wisdom is compatible with the acquisition of those skills that enable the subject through his labor to transform materials into economic resources. The impulse to beneficence has to be rightly directed. The active life is rudderless without the contemplative mind at its helm. We should never allow a false ecumenism to blur contradictory modes of approach. There are real differences between a Catholic outlook and a Protestant or secular perspective. As Sertillanges reminds us, "The choice of an intellectual father is always a serious thing." Respect for the contemplative life, whether it be pursued amid the distracting chaos of urban life or within a secluded cloister in the countryside, is a distinguishing mark of the Church. If indeed the contemplative way has been neglected in favor of an active life and one pursued largely for material goals, then the Bernards and Theresas among us ought to speak out. No matter life's fortunes, there is available to all that serenity that comes with contemplation and adoration before the Eucharist, and this ought to be said, and often.

Bibliography

Adler, Mortimer. *Philosophy, Law, and Jurisprudence.* Chicago: Encyclopaedia Britannica, 1961.

———. *Scholasticism and Politics.* New York: Macmillan, 1940.

Allers, Rudolph. *The Successful Error.* New York: Sheed &Ward, 1940.

Anderson, Gordon L., and Morton A. Kaplan, eds. *Morality and Religion in Liberal Democratic Societies.* St. Paul, Minn.: Paragon House, 1992.

Anonymous. *A Suggestion as to Causation.* Cambridge: Riverside Press, 1874.

Aquinas, Thomas. *De Veritate.* Translated by R. W. Schmidt. Chicago: Henry Regnery, 1954.

———. *Summa contra Gentiles.* Translated by Vernon J. Bourke. Garden City, N.Y.: Hanover House, 1956.

———. *Summa Theologiae.* Translated by the Fathers of the English Dominican Province. New York: Benzinger Brothers, 1947.

Aristotle. *Nicomachean Ethics.* Translated and edited with a commentary by G. Ransauer. New York: Garland, 1987.

Babbitt, Irving. *Democracy and Leadership.* New York: Houghton Mifflin, 1924.

Backus, Irena, ed. *The Reception of the Church Fathers in the West: From the Carolingians to the Maurists.* 2 vols. Leiden: E. J. Brill, 1997.

Berns, Walter. *The First Amendment and the Future of American Democracy.* New York: Basic Books, 1976.

Braybrooke, David. *Three Tests for Democracy: Personal Rights, Human Welfare, Collective.* New York: Random House, 1968.

Cicero. *On the Commonwealth.* Translated with an Introduction by C. H. Sabine and S. B. Smith. Indianapolis, Ind.: Bobbs-Merrill, 1950.

———. *On the Good Life:[Selected Writings of] Cicero.* Translated by Michael Grant. London: Penguin Books, 1971.

Collins, Hugh. *Marxism and Law.* Oxford, U.K.: Clarendon Press, 1982.

Cord, Robert L. *Separation of Church and State: Historical Fact and Current.* New York: Lambeth Press, 1982.

Dawson, Christopher. *Christianity and European Culture.* Edited by Gerald J. Russello. Washington: The Catholic University of America Press, 1998.

———. *The Historic Reality of Christian Culture.* New York: Harper & Row, 1960.

De Fabregues. *Edith Stein*. Staten Island, N.Y.: Alba House, 1965.

de Rougemont, Denis. *The Meaning of Europe*. Translated by Alan Braley. New York: Stein & Day, 1965.

Devlin, Lord Patrick. *The Enforcement of Morals*. London: Oxford University Press, 1968.

Dewey, John. *A Common Faith*. New Haven, Conn.: Yale University Press, 1934.

———. *Essays in Experimental Logic*. Chicago: University of Chicago Press, 1916.

———. *Experience and Nature*. Chicago: Open Court, 1925.

———. *Reconstruction in Philosophy*. New York: New American Library, 1939.

———. *Theory of Valuation*. Chicago: University of Chicago Press, 1939.

Dougherty, Jude P. *Recent American Naturalism*. Washington, D.C.: The Catholic University of America Press, 1960.

Douzinas, C., et al. *Postmodern Jurisprudence*. London: Routledge, 1991.

Durkheim, Emil. *The Division of Labour in Society*. New York: Free Press, 1964.

———. *Rules of Sociological Method*. Translated by S. Soloway and J. Mueller. Edited by E. Carlin. New York: Free Press, 1964.

Dworkin, Ronald. *Law's Empire*. London: Fontana, 1986.

———. *Taking Rights Seriously*. Cambridge, Mass.: Harvard University Press, 1977.

Feuerbach, Ludwig. *The Essence of Christianity*. Translated by George Eliot. Buffalo, N.Y.: Prometheus Books, 1989. (Originally published as *Das Wesen des Christentums*, 1841.)

Finnis, John. *Natural Law and Natural Rights*. Oxford, U.K.: Clarendon Press, 1980.

French, Peter A. *Collective and Corporate Responsibility*. New York: Columbia University Press, 1984.

Freud, Sigmund. *The Future of an Illusion: Basic Writings of Sigmund Freud*. Edited by A. H. Brill. New York: Modern Library, 1938.

Gallagher, D., and I. Gallagher, eds. *The Achievement of Jacques and Raïssa Maritain*. Garden City, N.Y.: Doubleday, 1962.

Gay, Peter. *A Godless Jew*. New Haven, Conn.: Yale University Press, 1987.

Gewirth, Alan. *Reason and Morality*. Chicago: University of Chicago Press, 1978.

Gilson, Etienne. *A Gilson Reader*. New York: Doubleday, 1957.

———. *The Spirit of Medieval Philosophy*. Translated by A. H. C. Downes. New York: Charles Scribner's Sons, 1940.

Goodman, L. E. *On Justice: An Essay in Jewish Philosophy*. New Haven, Conn.: Yale University Press, 1991.

Graef, Hilda. *The Scholar and the Cross: The Life and Work of Edith Stein*. Westminster, Md.: Newman Press, 1955.

Hart, H. L. A. *Causation in the Law*. 2d ed. Oxford, U.K.: Oxford University Press, 1985.

Herberg, Will. *Judaism and Modern Man*. New York: Atheneum, 1970.

———. *Protestant—Catholic—Jew*. Garden City, N.Y.: Doubleday, 1955.

Hollander, Paul. *The Many Faces of Socialism*. New Brunswick, N.J.: Transaction Books, 1987.

Honderich, T., *A Theory of Determinism: The Mind, Neuroscience, and Life Hopes*. Oxford, U.K.: Clarendon Press, 1988.

Hook, Sidney. *Education for Modern Man*. New York: Dial Press, 1946.

———. *Political Power and Personal Freedom*. New York: Criterion Books, 1959.

————. *Reason, Social Myths, and Democracy.* New York: John Day, 1940.

Huber, Peter W. *Liability: The Legal Revolution and Its Consequences.* New York: Basic Books, 1988.

Jaeger, Werner. *Paideia: The Ideals of Greek Culture.* Translated by Gilbert Highet. New York: Oxford University Press, 1939.

John Paul II. *Sollicitudo Rei Socialis.*

Justinian. *The Digest of Roman Law: Theft, Rapine, Damage, and Insult.* Translated by C. F. Kolbert. New York: Penguin Books, 1979.

Kairys, David, ed. *The Politics of Law.* New York: Pantheon Books, 1990.

Kant, Immanuel. *The Metaphysics of Morals.* Translated by Mary Gregor. Oxford, U.K.: Oxford University Press, 1991.

Kuklick, Bruce. *Josiah Royce: An Intellectual Biography.* New York: Bobbs-Merrill, 1972.

Lichter, S. R., L. Lichter, and S. Rothman. *Prime Time: How T.V. Portrays American Culture.* Washington, D.C.: Regnery, 1994.

Lippmann, Walter. *Essays in the Public Philosophy.* Boston: Little Brown and Co., 1955.

Livy. *History.* Vol. 1. Cambridge, Mass.: Loeb Classical Library, Harvard University Press, 1924.

Lowith, Karl. *From Hegel to Nietzsche: The Revolution in Nineteenth-Century Thought.* Translated by David E. Green. New York: Columbia University Press, 1964.

Lucas, J. R. *Responsibility.* Oxford, U.K.: Clarendon Press, 1993.

Luhmann, N. *A Sociological Theory of Law.* London: Routledge & Kegan Paul, 1985.

Lukes, Steven. *Marxism and Morality.* Oxford, U.K.: Clarendon Press, 1985.

Lyons, David. *Ethics and the Rule of Law.* Cambridge, U.K.: Cambridge University Press, 1984.

————, ed. *Rights.* Belmont, Calif.: Wadsworth, 1979.

Machan, T. R. *Human Rights and Human Liberties.* Chicago: University of Chicago Press, 1975.

MacIntyre, Alasdair. *After Virtue.* Notre Dame, Ind.: University of Notre Dame Press, 1981.

————, *Three Rival Versions of Moral Enquiry.* Notre Dame, Ind.: University of Notre Dame Press, 1990.

————. *Whose Justice, Which Rationality?* Notre Dame, Ind.: University of Notre Dame Press, 1988.

Maritain, Jacques. *Christianity and Democracy.* Translated by Doris C. Anson. London: Geoffrey Bles, 1946. (Originally published as *Christianisme et démocratie*, 1943.)

————. *The Degrees of Knowledge.* Translated by B. Wall and M. Adamson. London: G. Bles/Century Press, 1937. (Originally published as *Distinguer pour unir; ou, Les degrés du savoir*, 1932.)

————. *Democracy and Education.* New York: Macmillan, 1961.

————. *Elements of Philosophy.* Translated by E. I. Watkin. New York: Sheed & Ward, 1930. (Originally published as *Eléménts de philosophie*, 1921.)

————. *Existence and the Existent.* Translated by L. Galantiere and G. B. Phelan. New York: Pantheon Books, 1948. (Originally published as *Court traité de l'existence et de l'existant*, 1947.)

————. *Introduction to Philosophy.* Translated by E. I. Watkin. London: Sheed & Ward, 1930. (Originally published as *Introduction generale à la philosophie.*)

———. *Man and the State.* Chicago: University of Chicago Press, 1951.

———. *On the Church of Christ.* Translated by J. W. Evans. Notre Dame, Ind.: University of Notre Dame Press, 1973. (Originally published as *De l'eglise du Christ,* 1973.)

———. *The Peasant of the Garonne.* Translated by M. Cuddihy and E. Hughes. New York: Holt, Rinehart and Winston, 1968. (Originally published as *Le paysan de la Garonne,* 1966.)

———. *A Preface to Metaphysics.* New York: Sheed & Ward, 1948. (Originally published as *Sept lecons sur l'être,* 1934.)

———. *The Rights of Man.* Translated by Doris C. Anson. London: Geoffrey Bles, 1944. (Originally published as *Les droits de l'homme et la loi naturelle* 1942.)

———. *St. Thomas Aquinas: Angel of the Schools.* Translated by J. F. Scanlon. London: Sheed & Ward, 1948. (Originally published as *Le doctur angelique,* 1930.)

———. *Theonas.* Translated by F. J. Sheed. New York: Sheed & Ward, 1933. (Originally published as *Théonas,* 1932.)

Marty, Martin. *The One and the Many.* Cambridge, Mass.: Harvard University Press, 1997.

Marx, Karl. *Das Kapital: A Critique of Political Economy.* Chicago: C. H. Kerr, 1906.

Marx, Karl, and Friedrich Engels. *Collected Works.* New York: International Publishers, 1976.

Marx, Werner. *Is There a Measure on Earth? Foundations for a Nonmetaphysical Ethics.* Translated by T. J. Nenon and R. Nenon. Chicago: University of Chicago Press, 1987.

May, Larry. *The Morality of Groups: Collective Responsibility, Group-Based Harm, and Corporate Rights.* Notre Dame, Ind.: University of Notre Dame Press, 1987.

Mayer, Milton. *Robert Maynard Hutchins: A Memoir.* Berkeley and Los Angeles: University of California Press, 1993.

Melden, A. I. *Human Rights.* Belmont, Calif.: Wadsworth, 1970.

———. *Rights and Persons.* Berkeley and Los Angeles: University of California Press, 1977.

Murray, John Courtney. *We Hold These Truths.* New York: Sheed & Ward, 1960.

Nagel, Ernest. *Sovereign Reason.* Glencoe, Ill.: Free Press, 1954.

Niebuhr, Reinhold. *The Nature and Destiny of Man.* 2 vols. New York: Charles Scribner's Sons, 1941–1943.

Nietzsche, Friedrich. *Beyond Good and Evil.* Translated by Helen Zimmern. Buffalo, N.Y.: Prometheus Books, 1989.

———. *"The Birth of Tragedy" and "The Genealogy of Morals."* Translated by Francis Golffing. New York: Anchor Books, 1990.

O'Hagan, Timothy. *The End of Law.* Oxford, U.K.: Basil Blackwell, 1984.

Owens, Joseph. *The Doctrine of Being in the Aristotelian Metaphysics.* 3d ed., rev. Toronto: Pontifical Institute of Mediaeval Studies, 1978.

———. *Towards a Christian Philosophy.* Washington, D.C.: The Catholic University of America Press, 1990.

Randall, John H. *The Making of the Modern Mind.* New York: Houghton Mifflin, 1940.

Rawls, John. *A Theory of Justice.* Cambridge, Mass.: Harvard University Press, 1972.

Rorty, Richard. *Philosophy and the Mirror of Nature.* Princeton, N.J.: Princeton University Press, 1979.

Sher, George. *Beyond Neutrality: Perfectionism and Politics.* New York: Cambridge University Press, 1997.

Shook, Laurence K. *Etienne Gilson.* Toronto: Pontifical Institute of Medieval Studies, 1984.

Silber, John. *Straight Shooting.* New York: Harper & Row, 1989.

Simon, Yves R. *Philosophy of Democratic Government.* Chicago: University of Chicago Press, 1961.

Sokolowski, Robert. *The Formation of Husserl's Concept of Constitution.* The Hague: M. Nijhoff, 1964.

———. *Husserlian Meditations.* Evanston, Ill.: Northwestern University Press, 1974.

Stankiewicz, W. J. *Approaches to Democracy.* New York: St. Martin's Press, 1980.

Stein, Edith. *Life in a Jewish Family.* Translated by J. Koeppel. Edited by L. Gelber and R. Leuven. Washington, D.C.: ICS Publications, 1986.

———. *Writings of Edith Stein.* Selected and translated with an Introduction by Hilda Graef. London: Peter Owen, 1956.

Strauss, David. *The Life of Jesus, Critically Examined.* Translated by George Eliot. Reprint, Philadelphia: Fortress Press, 1973. (Originally published as *Das Leben Jesu, kritisch bearbeite,* 1835–1836.)

———. *The Old Faith and The New.* New York: Prometheus Books, 1997. (Originally published as *Der alte und neue Glaube,* 1872.)

Sypnowich, Christine. *The Concept of Socialist Law.* Oxford, U.K.: Clarendon Press, 1990.

Teresia de Spiritu Sancto, O.D.C. *Edith Stein.* London: Sheed & Ward, 1952.

Tierney, Brian. *Religion, Law, and the Growth of Constitutional Thought.* Cambridge, U.K.: Cambridge University Press, 1982.

Tuck, Richard. *Natural Rights Theories.* Cambridge, U.K.: Cambridge University Press, 1979.

Unamuno, Miguel de. *The Private World.* Translated by A. Kerrigan, A. Lacy, and M. Nozik. Princeton, N.J.: Princeton University Press, 1984.

Unamuno, Miguel de. *Tragic Sense of Life.* Translated by J. E. Crawford Flitch. New York: Macmillan, 1921.

Warton, Francis. *Treatise on the Law of Negligence.* Philadelphia: Kay and Brother, 1874.

Weigel, Gustav. *Faith and Understanding in America.* New York: Macmillan, 1959.

White, G. Edward. *Tort Law in America.* Oxford, U.K.: Oxford University Press, 1980.

Wippel, John. *Metaphysical Themes in Thomas Aquinas.* Washington, D.C.: The Catholic University of America Press, 1984.

Index

Western Creed, Western Identity: Essays in Legal and Social Philosophy
was composed in Minion by Generic Compositors in Stamford,
New York; printed on 60-pound Writer's Offset Natural and
bound by Thomson-Shore, Dexter, Michigan; and designed
and produced by Kachergis Book Design,
Pittsboro, North Carolina.

* * *